Ancient Mexican Art

Ferdinand Anton

Ancient Mexican Art

with 314 illustrations, 40 in color

G. P. Putnam's Sons · New York

Translated from the German
Alt-Mexiko und seine Kunst
by Betty and Peter Ross

Library of Congress Catalog Card Number 77-75,212

First American Edition 1969
Copyright © 1965 VEB E A Seemann Verlag Leipzig
This edition © 1969 by Thames and Hudson Ltd London
Printed in Germany (East) by Druckerei Magnus Poser, Jena, and Sachsendruck Plauen

Contents

Introduction

For nearly four hundred years the art of the American Indian peoples was disdained and misunderstood. Its artistic discovery owes its inception, on the one hand, to the knowledge that had been acquired of its exciting history, and on the other, to the eclipse of the values of Greek aesthetics, for nearly two thousand years the determinant of European artistic thought. This revaluation and fresh appraisal of Indian art has drawn together, as equal partners and as centres of artistic stimulation, the museum of art and the museum of ethnography, the latter of which had been regarded hitherto rather as a collection of curiosities.

The French ethnologist Paul Rivet estimated the total number of Indians in both Americas before the Conquest at forty to fifty millions. He was able to establish 123 distinct linguistic families, all of which were wholly unrelated to each other. It is not only in the field of language that the old cultures of the New World and their artistic heritage present many and varied aspects. One region of advanced civilization was the Central Andes (Peru and Bolivia); another was Mesoamerica,[1] the name given to an area encompassing south and central Mexico, Guatemala and British Honduras. In Mexico, a country that if superimposed on a map of Europe would extend from the northern tip of Scotland to the south coast of Sicily, archaeologists have unearthed evidence of 3,000 years of development in the history of art. Artists of many countries have paid homage to the visionary force and high ability of these unknown artists, who have left no names and of whom not even one 'self-portrait' is to be found.

The linguist will look in vain for a word that means 'art' in any one of the many Indian languages. Since early Indian artifacts served the after-life and the supernatural, their interpretation sets problems the solution of which is to be found mainly in an almost forgotten religion. The anonymous artist who created pottery burial offerings, the unknown sculptor who, with stone implements, carved stone images to his gods, the nameless architect who raised temples and sacred palaces, all were on a different plane of consciousness from those who today seek to explain this departed world. Nevertheless, it has, in most cases, been possible to enter into the complex spirit of these intricate forms that combine so many opposites. Myths and prayers, stories of the gods and legends of heroes, whether carved in stone, preserved in picture writing, or set down on paper in the colonial period, open the way to an insight into Indian thought.

There was nothing, only the silent water, the gentle sea, lonely and calm. Nothing was there. There was only stillness and the dark of the night. Only the creators and moulders

Tepeu Gucumatz, mother and father together, were in the water . . . They spoke gravely and reflectively. They discovered each other in the darkness of the night. They married their thoughts and words. And as they spoke, it became clear to them that when twilight came, man must appear . . . who will provide nourishment and support [for the gods].[2]

The gods needed four attempts to create man as their 'provider of nourishment and support', for they demanded much of their creatures. The polychrome pottery in the graves, the jade pendants at the necks of the priests, the obsidian masks for dead notables, the rock sculpture at the foot of the pyramids, the immense buildings with their frescoes, the hearts of sacrificed captives, everything, whether art or cult, had but one function: the preservation of the gods, the maintenance of the cosmic order.

In a land of volcanoes and hurricanes, immeasurably prodigal both in giving and taking, man achieved great things. Nature's unceasing challenge instilled in him a disquiet that later, under foreign masters and a new god, degenerated into fatalism. Driven by the fear that the sun god might succumb to his adversaries, the Indians built the largest pyramid in the world,[3] and, using the most primitive methods, fashioned imperishable works of art. Neither the canons of Greek architecture nor the mysticism of Gothic are to be found in Mexico. The Indians imposed their own laws on form, and created their own gods that had nothing in common with those in other parts of the world, even though the pyramids are, at first glance, reminiscent of the tombs in the Valley of the Kings in Egypt. Quetzalcoatl, too, the god who meets his fate by drinking one glass too many of strong pulque, might well have a relative in the Aegean. These are coincidences and of small significance. The never-ending struggle against the unfathomable powers of nature is the focal point of Mexican thought. Nothing is explained in terms of physical phenomena; all is seen metaphysically. Every morning the sun god, fortified by human sacrifice, enters upon his journey through the heavens of the day. Every evening he succumbs to the powers of the night, the rulers of the realm of the dead. These he conquers, to start again his day-long journey into night.

In this image lies the core of Indian philosophy: the postponement of fate, made possible only by continued sacrifice, and the futility of seeking to evade supernatural powers. The idea of exclusively good and evil gods, the concept of something wholly pure or wholly impure, was foreign to Mexican religion. Its exemplars are to be sought in the unpredictable behaviour of the forces of nature. Thus, the rain god Tlaloc can cause the harvest to prosper, but he can also destroy it. The wind god Ehecatl, who is depicted with a bird-like mask, may drive the rain-laden clouds over the land from the sea, but he also destroys the peasant's huts. Coatlicue, the earth goddess, is not only the universal mother, but likewise the deity that destroys everything again. Thirteen heavens towered unseen above the Aztecs, while nine hells lay below their feet. There were 'departmental' gods by the hundred, responsible for birth and death, for intoxication and flowers, for war and trade. Their memory is still by no means dead. Although the new religion of the 'white gods' undoubtedly bore fruit, it was unable to take deep root in Mexican soil. The same Indian who makes his pilgrimage to the Virgin of Guadalupe, on 12 December, will first ask the ancient gods to watch over his journey.

In early Mexican art, the concept that the licence to exist entailed an unrepayable debt was the motive power of tremendous human achievements. Early Indian ideas were cloaked in strange forms which strove to become reality – a transcendent reality, at once concealed and revealed. Religious conceptions engendered strange images from the world of man and beast. They frequently passed into the abstract in order to convey what could not otherwise be explained. Images were born and reborn in entirely new forms. They conjure up a dream world where man's primeval fear seeks its characteristic images. There is, too, a strangely abstract element of sadism in these symbolical creatures. The forms in which the figures of men, gods, goddesses, women, and animals are portrayed, are almost inexhaustible. Here, in the course of three centuries, many tribes and peoples have tended their fields, raised their children, and buried their dead. All have left behind them the face of their gods, and with it their own.

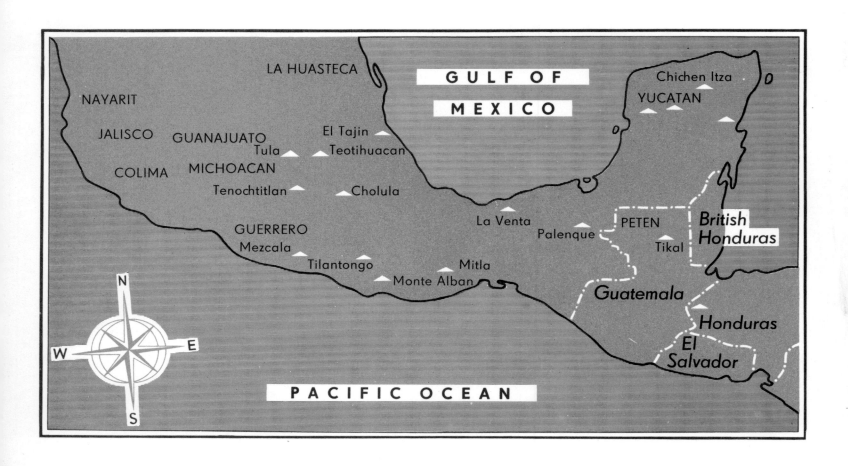

1 History and Geography

Then, once in the open sea, we steered at a venture towards the west, without knowledge of the depths or currents, or of the winds that prevail in those latitudes. So we were in great hazard of our lives when a storm struck us which lasted two days and two nights and had such force that we were nearly wrecked.

Thus the soldier, Bernal Díaz del Castillo, at the end of his full life, when, angered at the courtiers' false and impertinent scribblings, he resolved to set down 'the true history of the conquest of New Spain'.

In February 1517 three caravels carrying 150 men sailed from Cuba to take possession of more land in the Spanish half of the world. (A Borgia Pope had generously divided between the Spaniards and Portuguese the discovered and as yet undiscovered territories.) Through this expedition the Spaniards brought Mexico into the European consciousness. Nevertheless the first expedition, whose purpose was the establishment of a settlement either on the Yucatan peninsula or the Gulf coast of Mexico, miscarried in the face of Maya resistance. Having lost many lives, the commander, Córdoba, returned to Cuba with every man on board wounded. There he and many others, whose names are now forgotten, later died of their wounds. However, the fate of the adventurers was not enough to overshadow the glamour of the few spoils they brought back with them. Stories of magnificent cities and richly garbed princes seen beyond the ocean, caused men to forget the bloody setbacks encountered by Córdoba. After only fourteen months, a second expedition left Cuba, this time under the command of Juan de Grijalva, a cautious man who had never forgotten his predecessor's defeat, and who returned without hazarding an advance into the interior. Reports of the wealth of this land gave the Spaniards no peace. Here before them there clearly lay a different, richer world than that of the West Indies.

Hernando Cortés, who, like all Spaniards of the period, dreamed of the fabulous treasures of the New World, succeeded in outwitting his rivals and in winning the race for the conquest of this coveted land. On 22 April 1519 the small fleet he had fitted out reached land near what is today the city of Vera Cruz. To prevent the faint-hearted from beating a premature retreat, this intrepid entrepreneur at once ordered the burning of the vessels in which they had come. Before the small army, four hundred strong, lay a country ten times larger than their homeland; and for the first time since the discovery of America, Europeans were confronted by a thoroughly organized political system and an effective military power, that of the Aztec state. Had Cortés' troops met a reception similar to that provided by the Maya for the two previous expeditions, the course of history might, perhaps, have been more favourable for the inhabitants of these lands. The reason why the numerous and superbly trained troops of the Aztecs were not engaged at the right time is largely explained by an ancient religious tradition, according to which the Toltec deity Quetzalcoatl turned from his people in disillusionment, being driven away across the sea to where the sun rises by his divine antagonist Tezcatlipoca. Quetzalcoatl left behind him a promise that he would return and avenge himself in the year 1 Reed.[4] For centuries this legend had been deeply embedded in Indian thought. When Cortés, with his band of adventurers, arrived promptly in the year 1 Reed *(Ce Acatl)*, coming from where the sun rises as the priests had prophesied – white-skinned, bearded, with glittering armour, neighing horses, and noisy, fire-spitting tubes, the prediction, already heralded by a series of strange occurrences, seemed indeed to have come true. High Aztec notables approached the 'white gods' and implored them to leave the country once again, offering precious gifts as an added inducement. For the Spaniards, however, the golden objects provided confirmation that before them lay the land of their dreams. Far from causing them to return, the presents only reinforced their decision to press further into the heart of the country and march on Tenochtitlan, the Aztec capital. Cortés, an intelligent man, who had already outwitted his compatriots, now assumed the alternating roles of Cortés and Quetzalcoatl in a lengthy tragedy of mistaken identity, and by so doing ruthlessly expoited the blind trust of the inhabitants of Mexico. Intense fear of the gods inhibited even the strongest, who might, at the beginning, have turned successfully against the invaders.

The other circumstance conducive to the destruction of the flourishing culture of the Mexican Indians was the adroit exploitation of their disunity. Like a royal intriguer in a Shakespearean tragedy, the Spanish nobleman knew how to turn this unfortunate characteristic to his own advantage. The firearm, and the horse – an animal unknown to the Indians – were merely incidental props. In the main, Cortés made use of a band of Indian auxiliary troops, many thousands strong, composed of malcontents from the Gulf coast, an Aztec province, and from the sovereign state of Tlaxcala. These tribes, grown weary of their tributary obligations to the Aztecs, marched unhesitatingly alongside the 'new gods'. In the drama of the conquest of Mexico the prologue is still written with quill and ink, the play itself in blood. Although there were still heroes on both sides. the epilogue portrays nothing but the cruel raging of plagues brought in from abroad and, later, the unimaginable horrors of the Inquisition. A few on either side of the ocean, chief among them Bishop Bartolomé de las Casas, the 'Father of the Indians', raised their voices against the natives' fate, but their protests beat in vain against an impenetrable wall.

An idea of the fearsome havoc wrought among the inhabitants of the New World by their new masters may be had from figures in respect of the West Indies which are given here for comparison, since history does not record exact figures for Mexico in the first ten years after the Conquest.[5] The population of the island of Hispaniola, when the Spaniards arrived, was about 1,100,000; by 1510 it was 46,000, and four years later a miserable 1,000. The losses of the Mexican Indians were certainly far less catastrophic, since large groups withdrew into inaccessible areas, and the Indians in general could take the field in more compact tribal units. According to the highest estimate, the total Indian population of Mexico was reduced in the first 60 years of Spanish colonization to about one sixth of its former level.

It was the Dominican bishop mentioned above, Fray Bartolomé de las Casas, who passed the harshest judgement on the atrocities of his countrymen, men whose presence in the country render the exoneration of Charles V or his predecessor Ferdinand the Catholic almost impossible, 'for the Spanish rulers knew the rabble that went overseas, and nevertheless they let them go merely for the sake of miserable percentages'. (Today, a large town in the middle of exclusively Indian territory bears the bishop's name, whereas throughout Mexico not even an alleyway is named after Cortés.)

> God has suffered the counsellors of our kings to pillage and lay waste a great and rich land, to the huge disgrace of Christendom. For this devastation and this unprecedented diminution of mankind, they have no manner of excuse; for it did not happen in a day, nor yet in ten or twenty years, but in sixty years and more. . . . During this time reports of these conditions from many monks and trustworthy men were coming in daily, but without result. God then turned away, and the Kings of Spain, instead of being the richest and happiest of princes, are now the poorest of the poor. Although they have won from the West Indies more than two hundred million ducats in gold, silver, pearls, and precious stones, yet all has vanished as it were smoke. None of these treasures has helped them out of their great and endless wars and want.[6]

Such was the general situation in the sixteenth century, when European colonization of the New World first began. The colonization process would without doubt have turned out less successfully had not the indigenous inhabitants, in the course of thousands of years of development, exploited the land's natural resources by growing a variety of domesticated plants, thus maintaining a food-producing capacity which in turn came to be of benefit to the Old World.

In the course of eight to ten thousand years these nomadic hunters and gatherers traversed the entire continent, driven by the vital problem of the search for food and urged on by groups following behind. At that time, unimaginable obstacles faced those who sought to overcome this huge and inhospitable area. The first immigrants might be compared with man during the glacial period in Europe, who lived in caves or, in the more temperate zones, under trees, who went about naked, or clothed himself with the skins of the animals he killed. Their implements, which also served as weapons, were of stone shaped into a point, or bone splinters. Fire was known to them but not as yet, pottery. In all probability they brought the dog with them from Asia as a faithful companion – as an 'iron ration', too.

In course of time, the exigencies of big game hunting brought social changes. The bands joined together in clans, from which they were later to form tribes.

The highland Valley of Mexico, with its extensive woods and large lakes, was a paradise for game. The hunters waited for an opportunity of driving the tired or wounded beasts on to the marshy shores where they were helpless and could be despatched. These drives were the responsibility of the men, while the women busied themselves with the gathering of shellfish and wild vegetable food. Remains of game animals, American horse, mammoth, bison and giant sloth, have often been found in association with the flint and obsidian weapons of these early hunters.

In 1945, the geologist Helmut de Terra made a discovery that cast light on the history

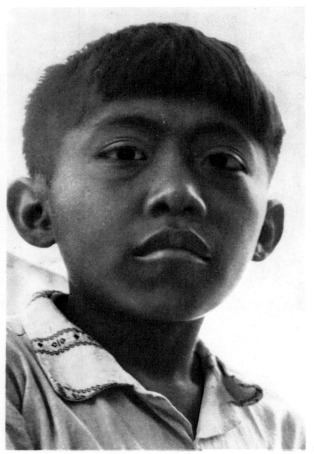

3

4

5

of the early immigrants. After a mammoth had been found at Tepexpan, not far from the present capital, the geologist examined the area surrounding the find with modern electrical equipment. The mine-detector registered three times. On the first occasion, much to the disappointment of the excavators, nothing was found but damp, closely packed earth. In the second place they met with success. Four feet below the surface lay the fossilized skeleton of a man, about fifty-five to sixty years old, who had fallen into the swamp while hunting and perished there. His position was in the same level as the mammoth he had waylaid. Some parts of this oldest American man have not been found; perhaps they were eaten by animals. Nevertheless, his skull and the main parts of his skeleton were enough to enable anthropologists to reconstruct 'Tepexpan Man'. In appearance, he differs little from the Indian of the highlands, and even in the streets of Mexico City no one would turn round to look at him. According to scientific tests employing the C-14 method, this hunting accident, so important to research on America, happened some 11,000 years ago.[7]

Since then, many peoples and tribes have settled on Mexican soil, sometimes concurrently, sometimes in succession. Today there are 90 authenticated languages which, according to Wigberto J. Moreno, can be classified under 19 linguistic families. A great many peoples and languages, too, have certainly escaped our knowledge.[8]

The radical discovery that brought to an end the early hunting and gathering cultures was the cultivation of the maize plant.[9] Maize, to which the Maya erected their fairest memorial in the shape of the young corn god, ended their insecure nomadic life and effected the second social change. Gradually there arose communal dwellings and village settlements. The nomad's thoughts, which previously had concerned only the procurement of food for himself and his family, his sex life and, later, death, underwent a change on his adoption of a sedentary existence. Survival no longer depended on the luck of the chase, but on the forces of nature which determined whether seed flourished or died, and which were inexplicable. Stimulated by the interaction of natural processes, by drought and rain, by phenomena such as thunder, lightning, sun and moon, and, not least, by the mysterious workings of the countless volcanoes, there evolved over many centuries a polytheistic religion in striking contrast to the animistic magic which characterizes hunters and gatherers.

Before considering the many and varied peoples, their history, and their art, we must briefly examine the geography of the land in which the first immigrants found themselves. Mexico lies in the sub-tropical zone, where the damp climate changes to one of dry heat. The north for the most part is desert, incapable of supporting more than a few people, and is thus unlikely to have altered very much during the last millenia; with the exception of Casas Grandes, no major cultural centre is known to have existed in northern Mexico. Not until it reaches the latitude of the present capital does the mountainous desert become the fertile basin of the Valley of Mexico, about 7,000 feet above sea level. Across this funnel-shaped plateau, known also as the Mesa Central, ran the ancient routes men had followed since their immigration from north to south. It was a halting place for the many peoples and tribes who have left their traces in this ancient cultural arena.

Tepexpan Man lay buried in the Valley of Mexico whose soil harboured, too, the 'pretty ladies' of Tlatilco, the highly artistic burial offerings of a much later pastoral community. Here stand the pyramid of Cuicuilco, the oldest in America, and the largest building in the world, the pyramid of Cholula. The buildings at Teotihuacan, 'the place where they became gods', can be seen from afar, and at Tula, the Toltec capital, the more than life-size atlanteans, which survived the destruction of the city in 1168, still guard some of their secrets as they stare out across the historic site. Over the ruins of Tenochtitlan, the Aztec capital, stands Mexico City with its millions of inhabitants. The conflicting evidence of millennia lies in the soil of the Mesa Central, some at different depths, some jumbled together, some side by side.

Further south, the highland valley of Oaxaca may have become a second home for those displaced by the tribes migrating south. The Zapotecs, followed somewhat later by the Mixtecs, settled there, possibly at the time of Christ's birth; both are there today, still speaking their ancient languages. Further south, beyond the isthmus of Tehuantepec, lies the home of the Maya tribes who, because of their essentially non-Mexican character, will only be briefly mentioned in this book.[10] The Pacific side is predominantly mountainous, barren, and, archaeologically speaking, virtually unexplored.

On the Atlantic side, the coastal area consists almost entirely of a strip of jungle, some 30 miles across, widening to nearly twice this distance in the south. Despite the unhealthy climate, here, sheltered by tropical vegetation, are the remains of ancient religious sites which are in no way inferior to those of the highlands. The dominant image of the Olmec or La Venta culture, the 'baby face', ranging from minute jade carvings to massive stone sculptures excavated from the marshy ground of the Gulf coast, presents the most puzzling aspect of the evolution of Mexican cultures. North of the Olmec sites, surrounded by jungle, are the pyramids of El Tajin. For many hundreds of years, this central coastal strip has been inhabited by the Totonacs, whose ancestors have left a most impressive art. Still further north up the Gulf coast the Huaxtec tribe have had their home for three thousand years. Both from a linguistic and an anthropological standpoint these people form part of the Maya family, and it is possible that they remained behind at the time of a southward population movement, taking no part in the great cultural development of Classic Maya culture.

The multiplicity of different aspects presented to us by pre-Columbian Mexican art is attributable not least to the great topographical variety of the country, which has always been an obstacle to cultural assimilation.

In this archaeologist's paradise, not only do we encounter peoples who, up to the arrival of Europeans, had not progressed beyond the most archaic stage, but also cultures whose buildings and artistic legacies fill us with wonder. And on the eve of the conquest, we finally encounter an alliance of city-states, subject to the overall domination of a single ruler and comparable in power, stature, and prosperity with those of Europe.

6

7

8

9

10

2 Archaic cultures: the Preclassic

The American archaeologist George C. Vaillant circumspectly used the term 'Middle culture' for the Preclassic period, in order to leave the description 'Early culture' available for older cultures that might be discovered in the future. Since Vaillant's death, discoveries have been made (in Chalco and the state of Tamaulipas, to name only the most important) that belong to the Lower Preclassic period. They have provided proof that American man first cultivated maize, gradually going on to basket-making and, only later, to the manufacture of pottery. When he first settled is still in doubt, but it must have been about six thousand years ago. The eloquent soil of Mexico itself provides the proof. In northern Mexico, the Canadian archaeologist MacNeish found a grave whose occupant lay on straw mats beside an offering of maize-cobs. Scientific examination put its age at six thousand years.

The American Indians were the world's most successful cultivators of domesticated plants. No less than half of the plants in cultivation today are Indian discoveries, among them maize or Indian corn, America's most important, and the world's second most important, foodstuff. The potato, too, Europe's chief food plant, as well as beans, cocoa, tobacco, tomatoes, gourds, quinine, vanilla, coca and many others, originate from the New World. It was maize that put an end to the restless hunting life of the primitive Americans, and secured a home for Indian man. Many thousands of years elapsed from the time of the first attempt at food cultivation to that of a relatively secure settled existence. Not until about 1,500 BC did the food problem seem sufficiently mastered to afford man leisure to turn to other things. Gradually he started to make baskets, to mould clay, and to fashion objects for use as well as for play. He began to broaden his outlook and to philosophize. At this stage the door opens on the history of early Mexican art. From now on archaeology, which has to do with the visible remains of generations long since departed, enters upon a wider field. After many millennia of early history which, as we have been able to observe, saw little change in tools and implements, there now followed a variety of opportunities for expression made possible by the use of ceramic techniques. Though at the beginning this new departure was often very deficient in technique and had a childlike lack of form, progress was rapid and cumulative. As a graphologist seeks to draw conclusions about a man's character from his handwriting, so the archaeologist, by examination of the decoration and workmanship of earthen plates and bowls, or of the way in which a small votive figurine is modelled in clay, attempts to establish the cultural level of those who made them. The extent to which men's thoughts revolved around the same theme is apparent from all the

Body stamp. Valley
of Mexico

artifacts of Preclassic culture. With small clay figurines, it is only the treatment of the eyes that distinguishes them from the products of a neighbouring valley. Thus, for example, the discoveries in the Malinalco area form a stylistic link between those in the Valley of Mexico and the San Jeronimo figurines from Guerrero on the Pacific coast. It is no coincidence that this place also lies in the geographical centre. The same is found in other parts of Mexico. In his search for missing, or still hidden, links in this long chain that makes the Preclassic a unified whole, and as such unique in the Mexican archaeological record, the archaeologist turns of necessity into an art historian, seeking, by means of a comparison of styles, to separate different influences and 'schools'. Only by such a stylistic comparison of the entire material will it be possible, one day, to isolate the place of origin and to determine the influence exerted by the various cultures. In the Valley of Mexico alone, sharp distinctions are evident within the Preclassic cultures.[11]

One of the oldest and most productive places of discovery is Tlatilco, the place 'where things lie hidden', to give a free rendering of the Nahuatl. It is situated on the outskirts of the present capital, and does justice to its name. Some twenty years ago brickworkers came upon what is perhaps the richest and most comprehensive burial ground of the Preclassic period. What emerged there out of ten feet of earth was to arouse the greatest enthusiasm among artists and collectors, including the modern Mexican painters Diego Rivera and Miguel Covarrubias. These excavations were started just in time, for the Mexican capital grows daily, and in a very short time, this burial ground, over which now live the poorest of the poor, will itself be buried beneath modern blocks of flats. The settlement shows no sign of temples or other cult buildings, and lies on the banks of the now dry lake. It was occupied for a fairly long period; according to a C-14 dating, from 1,455 BC $\pm$ 260 to 568 BC $\pm$ 250.

The picture Tlatilco presents is one of overpowering beauty, and because of its special charm, it will serve here to represent other Preclassic excavations. The first peasants of whom we learn through the excavations still went about naked and lived in mud and wattle huts. Living together in small autonomous communities they cultivated corn and chili peppers, and fattened small dogs which they ate on feast days. They hunted deer and waterfowl,

Distribution of Preclassic female clay figurine types

and had already begun to fish with nets. Their belongings were few: tools of bone and stone, a few straw mats, rope and, astoundingly, beds on four legs, an invention most of their successors allowed to fall into disuse. All this is evident from the traditional pottery and other burial offerings. There is still no indication of an organized priestly caste, although small figurines and masks perhaps furnish proof of the existence of shamans.

The finest pottery was made for presentation to the dead when embarking on their journey into the other world. During burial, figurines were in most cases ritually 'killed' by being broken. From all this extensive legacy, we are tempted to deduce the manner of its development. Once understood, the techniques of manufacturing small figurines and pottery vessels gave free rein to artistic development. Whereas in Chavin, far away in Peru, during the same period, the dead were provided, under the supervision of the priestly caste, only with works of high quality, contemporary wares in use in Mexico were of average and even below-average quality.

Ceramic vessels from Tlatilco occur in a variety of forms which was never recaptured in the succeeding theocratic cultures, in which the few characteristic forms were to be prescribed and distributed by the priestly class. The Preclassic era, before men became strictly circumscribed by a distinct religion, was a time of experiment. The pattern was continually changing as attempts were made to create something new. Vases, cups, and platters were, for the most part, embellished with painted or incised decoration. Negative painting, too, a kind of batik process, was already being practised in Tlatilco.[12] Even though we may admire the assured sense of form of the simple pottery, this admiration becomes immeasurably greater on meeting the clay figures which the archaeologists have *pl. 1* nicknamed 'pretty ladies'. Originally the term 'pretty ladies' had a sarcastic connotation, when applied to the somewhat ungainly figurines from El Arbolillo and Zacatenco. Tlatilco gives the lie to this facetiousness.

Vaillant was of the opinion that these charming beings are corn goddesses. I am not so sure, for over hundreds of years they increasingly came to resemble small, bacchante-like dancers, with all manner of feminine vanities, cosmetic embellishments, and fashionable novelties. All this would have been contrary to the general Mexican conception of maize,

23

Body stamp. Valley of Mexico

the greatest of benefits. In my opinion, these little Eves manifest the sensual zest for life of what must have been a carefree culture. This would seem to be confirmed by the apparent absence of a developed religion, as well as by a slight and apparently unopposed infiltration by other cultural elements at the end of the Preclassic period. Far harder to interpret are the two-headed figures, or those whose face is portrayed with three eyes, two noses, and two mouths. Perhaps the former was suggested by the birth of Siamese twins, while the latter may have been an attempt at the plastic interpretation of a dancer's head movements. A similar desire may be found in Indian art to express the dancing Shiva's gracious and meaningful arm and hand movements. In our own day, Picasso has often painted in a related manner – long before the discovery of Tlatilco – and only he could tell us anything about his processes of thought. In Tlatilco, then, was it magic, or was it playfulness? There is no hard and fast answer; we can only be certain that these beings disappeared at the fall of Tlatilco, leaving no heritage, unless it be in some of Picasso's paintings between 1937 and 1938.

pls 3–4

Let us now consider the 'pretty ladies', and their real-life models, more closely. Even at the outset of a thousand years of development, these women who lived naked under Mexico's sun loved to adorn themselves and to paint face and body with red or yellow earth. This was probably applied with cylindrical or flat stamps which have frequently been found in the graves. Their hair, too, was dyed red or yellow, no doubt in order to please the male sex – or is there some other explanation? The chief ornament which later men, too, were to use as an indication of their wealth and rank, was the earplug, sometimes of painted clay, sometimes of polished, coloured stone for those of high status. Besides this almost obligatory item of adornment, necklaces were also worn. And any who wished to look specially beautiful must be prepared to suffer. Almost unimaginably, some human remains show incisors with green jade inlays; only stone implements were available for such feats of cosmetic dentistry. Still unclothed except for decorative sandals, almost all the 'pretty ladies' had magnificent and varied hairstyles. By the way they fashioned the hair, it is evident that the artists tried to portray individual personalities. In San Antonio, another burial ground near the capital, chronologically about contemporary with Tlatilco, the hairstyles are so exaggerated that they might be taken for caricatures. Indeed, they are reminiscent of the towering wigs of the French rococo.

pls 5–6

pl. 12

In the thousand years or more embracing the Transitional and Upper Preclassic culture, woman's physical characteristics changed, as did the ideal of beauty. At the outset, the small Eves, with their opulent breasts and widely curving hips, could be close relatives of the Venus of Willendorf. They are reminiscent of the mother of mankind, of a fertility goddess. In course of time they became ever more graceful, narrow-hipped, and coquettish. Opulent breasts dwindled. The posture became more like that of a dancer, the simple girl with long pigtails giving way to one more sophisticated, her hair in a deep fringe over the forehead. Hence Tlatilco provides something for almost every taste. Curiously, men seldom appear in these representations. Had bones and stone implements not been found in association with male skeletons, we would almost have been led to believe that it was an Amazon state. Or are the first of the many 'pretty ladies' indeed proof of an early, matriarchal, agrarian culture? Despite all the sweetness, coquettishness, and sensuality of the small earthen women, there is an absence of sexual or obscene representations. Among thousands of discoveries, I know of only one sexual symbol: a small clay figurine, half phallus, half female figure.

pls 7–8

pl. 2

Not only freely modelled figures but other forms of pottery demonstrate the strong growth of artistic powers of expression. The bowl of a vase will often be fashioned into a figure of high artistic quality. In the Preclassic, the ceremonial vessels used in the cult of the dead depict birds, dogs, or people, and were evolved from conventional forms of vessel. Often the artist goes a step further, modelling so freely that only the spout serves to remind us that the sculpture is, indeed, a vessel. Three portrayals of an acrobat found at Tlatilco show a conscious use of every opportunity to represent the human body in all its beauty.

pl. 16

About 500 BC there was a change in the carefree faces of the life-loving dancing girls. Other ideas and other forms of society were forcing their way into the Valley from outside. The bearers of these changes, the so-called 'Olmecs',[13] left their image, the 'baby-face', in many graves in Tlatilco and its neighbourhood. The encounter with this superior people was, apparently, of short duration but nevertheless of great importance. As a meeting between a younger man and his senior may often have long-lasting and decisive effects, so it appears that the Olmecs helped a number of Preclassic cultures towards spiritual maturity. In this connection the Mexican painter and archaeologist Miguel Covarrubias speaks of the 'mother culture of the Olmecs'. To what extent the various cult sites in the Valley owe their origin to the direct or indirect influence of the Olmecs is for future archaeologists to try and find out. Another of their tasks will be to answer the question why Olmec influence in the Valley of Mexico did not succeed in making a deeper and more lasting impression. There are various indications that efforts were already being made in a number of places to form an intellectual élite and an organized religion. That would be the most plausible explanation why, after a short period of Olmec cultural ascendancy in many parts of Mesoamerica, the various tribes broke away from a homogeneous Preclassic culture and went their several ways. But before discussing the Olmecs themselves in detail, it is necessary to consider the end of the Preclassic period in the Valley of Mexico, and the transition to a theocratic form of society.

The culture of Tlatilco was unquestionably moving towards decadence. For unknown reasons, the place was abandoned between 500 and 300 BC. Perhaps the lake flooded or, possibly, fresh tribes drove out its happy inhabitants. At all events, the site remained unoccupied until the present century. The cultural emphasis shifted to Cuicuilco, Tlapacoya, and later to Ticoman.

> Yet the full impact of Mesoamerican religion on those central Mexican villagers is symbolized by the great adobe mound of Cuicuilco. On the skirts of the volcanic range of Ajusco, at the south-west of the Valley, they built a massive oval mound, approximately 369 feet in diameter and 60 feet high, to the top of which led a wide ramp. They faced the sides with river boulders to guard against the erosion of seasonal rains and, perhaps, to add to the effect of rugged majesty. They reared no stately temple on the summit but instead constructed an altar, open alike to the sky and to the eyes of the congregation (Vaillant).

Twice people added to this ceremonial site, the oldest pyramid in Mesoamerica, which, *pl. 9* round about 400 or 300 BC, was buried by lava erupting from the Xitli and Ajusco volcanoes. Copilco, a neighbouring, older Preclassic settlement, met the same fate. (Today, on the deep lava field of Pedregal, covering many square miles, stands the most up-to-date university in Latin America.)

In the south, likewise, on the opposite side of the old lake, the ceremonial site of Tlapacoya has only recently been discovered and excavated. The whole structure consists of several square platforms and an arrangement of steps composed on a grand scale. The pottery found in Tlapacoya, a continuation of the Tlatilco style, frequently exhibits Olmec features. The layout, too, of this place stands in direct contrast with Cuicuilco's peasant-archaic method of building, and could be traced to Olmec influence, although irrefutable proofs are lacking.

From pottery, the chief means of expression surviving from this period, it is evident that Ticoman, not Tlapacoya or Cuicuilco, was at the forefront in the transition from the Preclassic to the Classic periods. This site confirms the return to a simple, peasant mode of life, and material found is in direct contrast to the decadent art of Tlatilco and Tlapacoya in their latter stages. Although Ticoman can lay claim only to a pottery that is somewhat clumsy and misshapen, there nevertheless appears here for the first time the figure of the 'old god' of fire, Huehueteotl, which, like a landmark, may be followed through the entire history of Mexico up to the Spanish Conquest. This pottery, and the figure of the 'old god', provide proof of the transition to the later Classic Teotihuacan culture which, even in the early stages, was apparently strong enough to withstand Olmec influences. Had these two centres, Ticoman and early Teotihuacan, been weak, the history of Mexico would, perhaps, have seen an Olmec empire or, at least, an alliance of tribes under Olmec supremacy, for at the time only the latter culture seemed sufficiently mature for the purpose. But so long as the mosaic of Mexican cultures remains incomplete, such a train of thought must remain hypothetical.

3 Theocracy: the Early Classic

The fascinating culture of La Venta and other sites on the Gulf coast, usually known as Olmec, lies at the origin of the Classic or urban cultures of Mesoamerica. Its features are already evident, among others, in the 'pretty ladies' of Tlatilco and Tlapacoya, in the incense burners belonging to the first period of Monte Alban, and the ceremonial site of the later Zapotecs, as well as in the plaster masks that adorn the oldest building of the Maya culture at Uaxactun in Guatemala. When they do appear, they stand out from the uniformity of Preclassic culture and are associated with a sudden cultural flowering. The more material is found concerning Olmec culture, the more clearly is the latter's influence on other peoples and races confirmed. A surprising stylistic discipline in its art reflects new religious ideas and customs, and shows traces of a far-reaching change in society. But who these 'Olmecs' were, to which people they belonged, whether they formed a tribe or group of tribes, what language they spoke, is all entirely unknown.

By 'Olmeca' the Aztecs meant 'rubber folk', the dwellers in the 'rubber country' (*olli* = rubber), which lies along the southern Gulf coast of Mexico. Its legendary reputation lasted until the Spanish Conquest. By this time, however, the culture which we call Olmec and which, as the Olmeca known to the Aztecs were certainly not the people responsible for it, is also recorded as the La Venta culture, had already been extinct for a thousand years. La Venta and its other ceremonial centres lay hidden under the thick vegetation of this region, but the torches that the Olmecs had lit continued to cast their light on those who

27

Danzante. Monte Alban I

came after them. Hieroglyphic writing, calendar science, and fundamental conceptions of the gods were discoveries of this culture that has vanished into nothingness. The Maya, Totonacs, Zapotecs, Mixtecs, Toltecs, and lastly the Aztecs, all had a share in the heritage of this 'mother culture'.

Nothing more than this would be known of this strange people had not their artists, builders, and priests themselves erected, in the mangrove forests of Tabasco and southern Vera Cruz, immense monuments that have withstood the course of two thousand years. In these mysterious relics we repeatedly encounter a child's chubby face with protruding lips and a broad nose, somewhat reminiscent of a Bavarian baroque angel. We might also be tempted to detect in it a resemblance to a portrait of the Buddha as a child: but under no circumstances would we assume it to be an ancestor of the peoples who today inhabit this land. What is this child's face with its pouting lips – the homely archaeological designation is 'baby-face' – supposed to represent: the royal *infante* of a dynasty suffering from thyroid deficiency, a gnomelike deity, or, perhaps, this culture's ideal of beauty? We do not, and never shall know. What we do see, again and again, not only on the Gulf coast but also in the Valley of Mexico and the barren mountains of Oaxaca, is the unmistakable, pouting, child's mouth with corners like those of a sparrow's beak. Wherever this face appears it announces the end of the Preclassic cultures and testifies to an awakening. The vague primitive conception of the gods disappears along with the loose social order. During this time magic turns into religion.

pls 17–38
figs 1–2

Men now came to worship capricious agrarian gods, not, as in Christianity, wholly good or wholly bad, but possessed of both qualities. Like the powers of nature, unfathomable and untamed, which they personify, they can be won over only by sacrifice. Temples must be built and special ceremonies performed in their honour. It is they, or rather their human representatives the priests, who determine the important days for agriculture and the time of sowing. This new priestly class drew up a calendar, thereby obtaining the strongest hold over the common people, for, in these zones, periods of rain and drought maintain a regular rhythm with only minimal variations. If an order was given to burn the forests, for example, a few days too late, so that the rainy season intervened, then a whole year had to elapse before the corn could be sown again, with resulting famine for the community. This responsibility fell to the priestly élite, which is why the Classic cultures are so often described as 'theocratic'.

The Olmecs were the first to recognize the immense significance of the calendar. The two earliest written dates recorded in the New World are of Olmec origin. Stela C from Tres Zapotes bears a date which corresponds to 31 BC, and is the earliest recorded on the American continent. Another inscription, carved on a small jadeite sculpture, gives a date corresponding to AD 162.[14] Stylistically, neither discovery has any connection with the early periods of Olmec culture. (The C-14 datings put La Venta between 1454 BC ± 300 and AD 126 ± 250). The Olmec calendar, together with its system of recording, was later adopted by the Maya and improved to such an extent that it became the most accurate calendrical system in the world. The peoples of Mexico proper also based their various alternative calendars on the Olmec 52-year system.

The Olmec culture gives every sign of being a culture with a high degree of social organization. The background is still obscure, but it is certain that here, in a comparatively short space of time, an élite was formed that rejected tribal tradition and imposed its new ideas on all those who lived within its sphere of influence. Monumental Olmec art and architecture (there are few architectural remains, although we know of some pyramids, extensive tombs and other sites) surely presuppose a collective effort under the leadership of specialists. This could only take shape within a population that was no longer fully engaged in the production of food and other staples. Only a division of labour could make possible an established religion, an active calendrical science, the development of the applied arts, and the erection of large ceremonial, and later even urban, structures. The specialists were supported by the tributes of the cultivators.

When not required for agriculture, labour was employed on the erection of ceremonial buildings. Since neither the Olmecs nor the later theocratic societies of the Classic period seem to have used slaves, it may be supposed that the people's willingness to work was the sign of a strong religion. A man introduced to this new society which, by its security, made his life easier, no longer felt his existence to be fortuitous; it acquired a deeper meaning through faith, the community, and fear of the gods.

By its creative energy the priestly élite which wielded spiritual and temporal power in the Olmec culture roused the other peoples of the Mesoamerican territories from an archaic state that had lasted for thousands of years. During recent years, it has become apparent that the designation of the Olmec culture as 'Archaic' or Preclassic may now be outmoded. The manner in which this early advanced culture came into being can be roughly reconstructed, but where and when it did so is not precisely known, in spite of much evidence.

La Venta, the largest religious (and perhaps political) centre, was not a city in our sense of the word; these were to appear much later in Mexico.[15] La Venta, Tres Zapotes, Cerro de las Mesas, and several others were ceremonial centres with temple buildings and meeting places, as well as dwellings for priests, architects, artists and artisans. The tombs of high dignitaries were also to be found here. Robert Heizer estimated the numbers in the hinterland at about 18,000. They built La Venta, enlarged the city, and supplied its inhabitants with provisions. It was only on appointed days that they flocked towards the priestly centres to sacrifice to the gods, to pay tribute, and, not least, to attend the markets.

La Venta was dominated by a large, four-sided pyramid of earth. Scholars have estimated that, with two thousand workers, the erection of this building took four hundred working days. In front of the pyramid there extends the plaza, measuring about 160 × 200 feet, from where the peasants could watch the ceremonies of the gorgeously robed priests on the steep steps of the pyramids, and where they could exchange their goods either before or after the ritual. La Venta's stone-lined tombs were, if anything, more carefully built than the rest of the city. Both here and in Cerro de las Mesas, where no less than 782 highly polished jade figurines were found as offerings in one grave, they testify to an established cult of the dead.

Anyone who has seen the swampy tropical vegetation of the two states where the Olmec ceremonial sites lie abandoned would be able to confirm that there could hardly be a more hostile environment for man. As with the Maya of the Classic period, it was the isolation on the one hand, and the continued demands of the pitiless tropics on the other, that spurred them on to such immense achievements. The most prominent deity in this *pl. 28* jungle culture is a being with a human body but with arms and the region of the mouth having the attributes of a jaguar. Had this jaguar god not been so predominant, we might have supposed a change in climate over the last two thousand years. The environment is not the only proof of pious humility and an unflinching determination to suffer willingly all manner of discomforts. Whoever has seen the stone monuments, including colossal human heads weighing many tons, will be able to judge how disciplined the organization *pls 19, 36* must have been that transported these basalt blocks to La Venta from a quarry over sixty *fig. 1* miles away, unassisted by draught animal or wheel. One of the basalt heads has a circumference of over 18 feet and an estimated weight of about 60 tons. The other monuments are but little smaller.

The most astounding feature of Olmec art is the incredible artistic talent that asserts itself in objects irrespective of their size. It enlivens an essentially monotonous art that restricted artists to religious subjects and a few clearly prescribed forms. The proportions are always true, whether in a large effigy or in a jade sculpture or piece of pottery no more than a few inches high. Good proportion means that sculpture, whether large or small, is equally expressive. There is an instinctive and confident balance of sculptural emphasis between softly rounded forms and carefully smoothed planes. Absence of detail gives a heightened sense of realism to what are already realistically graceful sculptures. The restless opulence of the art of the Maya and Totonacs was unknown to the Olmecs. A similar combination of sensibility and integrity does not reappear in pre-Columbian Mexican art until the time of the Aztecs, 1500 years later. There is not the least trace of any influence of other styles on Olmec art, although the latter's forms are perhaps discernible in other stylistic trends. To judge by the impressive material hitherto so freely yielded by Mexican soil, this art must have evolved spontaneously out of Olmec man and his tradition.

In every portrayal we encounter the same emphatically mongoloid human type. In many sculptures of this constantly recurring and ever changing 'baby face', a vertical cleft in the forehead suggests the ritual mutilation of the person portrayed. This is the one thing that the burial offerings attest, for otherwise they tell us little of manners and customs.

Body stamp. San Andres Tuxtla, Vera Cruz

In contrast to the splendid hairstyles of many of the women depicted in Preclassic art, it was fashionable to shave the head. The small clay figurines also display wart-like tattooing and many-tiered turbans. In most cases, headdresses were more elaborate than other clothing, which usually consisted of a small loincloth at most. The helmeted warriors wore armour of leather and cotton.

The fearsome visage of the jaguar forms an antithesis to the innocent face of the child. Was the jaguar god the embodiment of the chthonic powers that threatened light and life, and was the child with an incision in its head a sacrifice intended to pacify him?

The bearers of the La Venta culture were not a peaceful people. Their monuments portray well-armed warriors in a profusion encountered at a later date only among the Aztecs and Toltecs. It is possible that the Olmec view of life was imposed on other tribes, even by force of arms, for monuments have survived of their victorious campaign. By contrast, nothing is known of their decline. Perhaps the younger peoples, who had grown tired of these warriors, were as yet insufficiently mature to record their victories by monuments as impressive as those of the Olmecs; or perhaps repression of the people led to a revolution which destroyed the élite, thus leaving the cultivators to revert to their previous existence. At La Venta, the most powerful centre of Olmec culture, as well as at Tres Zapotes which flourished some centuries later, there are signs of violent destruction. The rest is nothing but a silent exit from Mexico's historical stage. The traces of this dominant culture are lost
pl. 25
in the thick forests and inaccessible mountain valleys of Mesoamerica. The southernmost monument in the style of La Venta stands in a coffee plantation in El Salvador, and small jade ornaments, bearing the unmistakable Olmecoid child's face, have even been found in graves in Costa Rica. Was it trade that spread these ornaments so far southwards, or are they evidence of a migration? Perhaps the archaeologists of the next decades will be able to solve this riddle too.

4 Theocracy: the Classic

Prior to the formation – with a course that was similar in both Old and New Worlds – of early high cultures, many communities had already made impressive discoveries for the advancement of human society. These centuries witnessed the cultivation of domesticated plants, the origins of pottery, local calendars and archaic deities; all of them discoveries that, directly or indirectly, influenced human existence.

We do not know why the founders of the La Venta culture were prevented from developing and consolidating their early promise, and ultimately establishing an urban metropolis. Another, equally anonymous people, the builders of Teotihuacan, were to succeed in doing so. In the latter case the process was in its initial stages at about the time of Christ's birth and preceded the Olmec La Venta culture. Cuicuilco and Tlapacoya were the ritual gathering places for small, autonomous, sedentary communities. The arts and crafts of these closely neighbouring places remained confined to the locality. Teotihuacan was to change this picture fundamentally. From the numerous independent village communities of the Mesa Central there gradually emerged a unified, comprehensive culture under the control of a theocratic ruling class. This transformation was undoubtedly occasioned by the rapid increase in the population of the fertile areas, for at almost the same time similar concentrations of intellectual forces were establishing themselves in the valley of Oaxaca, the Guatemalan lowlands, and the central Gulf coast. These social reforms ousted the shamans. Their place was taken by a far-sighted, well-organized priestly caste, relying on a complicated religion and a perfected calendar, and who, by all accounts, assumed secular leadership as well. A diet based primarily on maize permitted two or three days to be set aside each year during which the cultivators could be used for the erection of ceremonial buildings and of dwellings for the élite. Surplus foodstuffs maintained those classes not employed in agriculture. In this manner the ceremonial centres could be enlarged, so that over the course of centuries they acquired an urban character. The most important urban centre in this new age was Teotihuacan, a city in the true sense. The small valley where it gradually arose must certainly have been settled in the days before the pyramid of Cuicuilco lay under a mass of lava. No writer has given us any information as to how Teotihuacan slowly came into being, or how it acquired wealth and influence. Our knowledge of the rise, the zenith, and the passing of this city and its culture is often dependent on small details. Hence no discovery is so insignificant as to be unworthy of consideration. It has only recently been realized that a small piece of charcoal, or the carelessly discarded remains of a corn cob, can reveal more of chronology than the noblest building of an unlettered culture.

Body stamp, owl. Teotihuacan

Teotihuacan was, from the beginning, planned on a grand scale, and was deliberately intended to become a cultural, religious, economic, and political centre. From the start, the metropolis prevented the formation of numbers of small, mutually competing groups. Even though in ruins, Teotihuacan, which lies about thirty miles from the capital, is one of the most impressive places in Mexico. For a generation, archaeologists of all nations have been attempting to interpret its history through weapons and implements, through secular and sacral buildings, and last but not least, through the hundreds of thousands of small votive offerings. Today, the austere monumental architecture still bears witness to the departed power and stature of the priestly rulers as well as to the people's overwhelming fear of the gods. The frescoes painted in delicate pastel colours exemplify the beauty of the divine portraits and testify to the wealth of the priests.

pls 80–2

pls 85, 89, 100

'It was by far the largest and most wonderful city of pre-Hispanic America. Larger in extent than Athens, larger than Rome', said Jorge Acosta who, in 1962, with 550 workmen and 37 archaeologists, set about excavating the metropolis of the theocratic culture. (The President of Mexico placed 1,320,000 pesos at the disposal of the project.) Acosta put Teotihuacan's population at 250,000 at the period of its prime.

Of the bearers of this Classic culture, we know more today than did the Aztecs before the arrival of the Spaniards; but do not know nearly enough. Neither the history nor the name of a single priest or ruler survives; neither do we know what the city itself was called by the inhabitants, nor what language its builders spoke, nor to what group of peoples they belonged.

The Aztecs told the Spaniards on their arrival in the country that the builders of this deserted city had been giants, a race that had met its end at the end of a former age of creation. Many Europeans for long believed this, finding proof in the outsize bones of extinct animals that are found from time to time in this region. The Aztec name Teotihuacan means 'the place where they became gods'. The Franciscan friar Bernardino de Sahagún wrote soon after the Conquest: 'They called the place Teotihuacan because it was the burial place of kings; and the ancients said of them, whoever died became a god. If one were to say that he is now *teotl* (god), then it is as much as to say he is already dead.' Sahagun took

33

Body stamp, fire god Xiuhtecuhtli. Teotihuacan

down the information on indigenous culture provided by his Indian informants in their own language, the Nahuatl of the Aztecs. Perhaps the friar sensed that a European language could never adequately convey the imagery of Mexico.[16]

'The place where they became gods' – the whole name is expressed in the few syllables – 'was a shining city, shining red like blood, and if blood had run down over the steps, one would not have perceived it' (Jorge Acosta). And indeed blood did flow in Teotihuacan, in honour of the gods. The excavators found paintings of human hearts and, nearby, obsidian sacrificial knives; they brought into the light of day flat plates made from brain-pans, and unearthed red and yellow pots containing the hip and thigh bones of humans, signs of ritual cannibalism. The Teotihuacanos, like the Maya, also practised self-mortification. They cut off their fingers and eyelids, and steeped *amatl* (the Nahuatl term for paper made from plant fibres) in their own blood. But without doubt, the Teotihuacanos' greatest offering to the gods consisted in the building of their city with its vast pyramids, wide streets, and spacious palaces. As a product of a 'stone age' culture that knew neither draught animal nor beast of burden nor wheel,[17] these buildings, and indeed the whole layout of the city, represent an enormous achievement both mental and physical. The driving force could only have been a religion that was real and comprehensible to the entire population, for archaeological discoveries, both large and small, reflect a peaceful view of life which suggests a theocratic, agrarian society very different from that of the warlike Olmecs or that of the Toltecs who followed later.

At Teotihuacan the fire god, Huehueteotl, 'old god', or Xiuhtecuhtli, 'the lord of the turquoise' who is already known to us from the Preclassic period, was joined by other important deities: the rain god Tlaloc, 'he who makes things sprout', the water goddess Chalchiuhtlicue, 'our lady of the turquoise skirt', and the god of seedtime Xipe Totec, 'our lord, the flayed one', who wore the skin of a freshly flayed human victim to symbolize earth's mantle of Spring. An earth goddess portrayed in the shape of a toad formed a link with the underworld and the land of the dead. The most amiable god in Teotihuacan's pantheon, however, was a small, fat deity whose name has been forgotten. No magic attaches to him. In all likelihood, the Fat God was the god of intoxication and happiness, the pulque god.

pls 83–4

34

Body stamp, rain god Tlaloc. Teotihuacan

This pantheon grew from century to century, for not only did new gods have to be invented to meet new requirements but foreign ideologies and deities infiltrated into Teotihuacan with the expansion of culture and trade. It also claimed an ever growing number of priests, for whom seminaries came into being. A polytheistic religion and a cult that grew ever more complex produced the new classes of artist and builder, artisan and trader, all of whom had to be supported by the peasants.

Before concerning ourselves with the rise and fall of a culture so important to ancient Mexico, we shall take a look at its centre. Teotihuacan was built in a series of concentric rings. In the middle were the pyramids and the temples as well as the market and places of assembly. These were surrounded by the citizens' dwelling-houses, which in turn were encompassed, to a distance many miles from the city centre, by the peasants' fields and *pl. 80* farms. Today, it is still the Pyramid of the Sun, with its vast dimensions, that repeatedly draws the visitor's attention. Standing alone, it vies with the mountains that enclose the valley to the north. Its front faces east and is next to the 140 foot wide Camino de los Muertos, the Avenue of the Dead, which traverses the town like a *via sacra*. The Swedish archaeologist, Sigvald Linné, discovered that the Avenue of the Dead, together with all its adjacent buildings, is orientated at an angle of 17 degrees to the meridian, so that on two days each year, the equinoxes, the east-west axis of the buildings forms a line with the setting sun. Here, as in other cities of the Classic period, the orientation of the buildings and most of the larger monuments was deliberate, for these structures were at the service of the calendar in determining times so crucially important if man was to be fed. The priests, who made a close study of the calendar, gave the peasants orders to clear the land and told them when to sow. They decided when the harvest should be gathered, and in return demanded tribute for the gods and for their own livelihood.

On the broad steps of the Pyramid of the Sun, less steep than those of the Classic structures of the Maya, and in full view of all, there was enacted in early times the impressive ceremony of divine worship. The bottom platform comprises two separate stairways, while the next is formed of one wide stairway. The third platform has two, and at the top there is one. Incorporated with austere magnificence into the powerful structure, they help to interpret

35

a striving towards the stars and heavens, lending vitality to the inert mass of the base of the pyramid. The Pyramid of the Sun may be found prosaic by an observer who sees it in passing, but a longer examination will reveal the excellent proportions of the whole structure. There is nothing here of a confined, mystical striving towards God, as in the Gothic cathedrals; rather it is an attempt to achieve a harmonious transition to heaven through the basic power of the soil. The red stucco with which the building was originally covered must have presented an impressive spectacle in the light of the rising and setting sun.

To the north, the one and a half mile long Avenue of the Dead is barred by the Pyramid *pl. 81* of the Moon, which is 130 feet high; to the south it leads nowhere. Perhaps this side of the city was kept open for pilgrims? European builders, as Paul Westheim points out, would never have thought like that, but would have erected a pendant. Small temples and buildings, fronted by terraces, lined both sides of the Avenue of the Dead. One small temple, famed for its mural paintings, was dedicated to agriculture, or rather to the powers that protected it. Unfortunately it was left exposed to the weather after its excavation at the beginning of this century, so that an idea of the paintings can be had only from copies made at the time. To the south, at a right-angle to the Avenue of the Dead, there is a complex erroneously called the Ciudadela ('citadel'); this is not a fortification but a row of platforms in a rectangular walled precinct. The eastern end of the complex, its main frontage, too, facing the sunset, constitutes Teotihuacan's most elaborate structure, the Temple of Quetzalcoatl. (The *pl. 82* traditional name, like those of the Pyramids of the Sun and the Moon, is of Aztec origin.) For unknown reasons, the west front was later built over, so that its magnificent façade was covered and largely saved from destruction. The temple takes its name from the god Quetzalcoatl ('feathered serpent'), whose sculptured likeness stands out from the façade in bold relief. We shall often meet this deity, who played so fateful a part in Mexico's history. In the Postclassic period, he became the god of learning, who, on assuming the mask of the wind god Ehecatl, stands at man's side to give him help. Many sources go so far as to call him the creator of the present human race (after the cataclysm which was supposed to have destroyed the giants of Teotihuacan). Historic personalities among the Toltecs used his name in order to demonstrate their divine origin.

On the Temple of Quetzalcoatl in Teotihuacan the feathered serpent is displayed in alternation with the mask of the rain god Tlaloc. The snake's body undulates horizontally in relief between the individual ledges, the remaining spaces being filled with shellfish and sea-snails. This opulence is unusual in Teotihuacan, for its sober, monumental, austerely proportioned architecture is predominantly disposed to the bold use of flat surfaces.

The sculpture on the Temple of Quetzalcoatl undoubtedly has a deeply symbolic basis. Theories about its interpretation are not always in agreement. The German scholar Walter Krickeberg saw in the heavily stylized masks, not the rain god, but the images of butterflies symbolizing dead warriors, while the body of the feathered serpent represents the night sky. This was the Aztec conception, which Krickeberg believed he had traced far back into the past. The method is correct in principle, for Teotihuacan's culture did indeed honour many gods whom Cortés was still able to find on his entry into the Aztec capital. Yet we must not forget that ancient American religion resembled a luxuriant growth, proliferating from century to century, and that, during Teotihuacan's flowering, it

Body stamp, wind god Ehecatl. Teotihuacan

did not as yet display the abundance of the Aztec pantheon. In Teotihuacan, the simpler explanation, that of the rain god Tlaloc, would appear to be the more illuminating, for the religion of this culture was that of a peaceful agrarian society. It was only in a later period that the warriors became the object of such high and excessive esteem. There were still no fortifications in this Classic city, and excavations have not brought more than a few weapons to light.

Besides the numerous small temples, functional architecture also helped to mould the city's appearance: schools and food stores, dwellings for the priests and their numerous acolytes, workshops for the artists and builders, rest-houses for merchants from foreign lands, perhaps, too, a small group of barracks round the temple precincts for some form of guard. The people visited the city only on feast days, in order to join in worshipping the gods, and no doubt afterwards to exchange their ware in the markets. They also came when ordered to work on the construction of sacred buildings.

Very little secular architecture remains. It is apparent from the ruins that the buildings were single-storied, windowless and long. Light and fresh air only came in through the door. In most cases, the houses were arranged in a rectangle and equipped with a stone gutter to convey precious water to the central courtyard where it could collect. All palaces and temples were plastered with layers of a red stucco made with lime and volcanic rubble mixed with iron oxide, the walls polished to a dull gleam with jadeite. The façades of the secular buildings were almost exclusively covered with white stucco. All the streets and squares within the seventeen square miles comprising the ceremonial area were paved with a layer of rock-hard cement four inches thick. Compared with Teotihuacan, the European cities of the Middle Ages with their unpaved streets would have looked like dirty little villages. George C. Vaillant draws a fascinating conclusion from the presence of street-paving and the large number of structures:

> The modern Maya Indians burn ten times as much wood as the quantity of limestone to be reduced, and they have the advantage of steel axes. It is not too fanciful, therefore, to assume that the Teotihuacan masons, lacking metal of any kind, found it easier to

Body stamp. Guerrero

use hearths of charcoal, obtained by burning over the forest, than to try to obtain the requisite fuel by chopping out their logs with stone axes. If this interpretation is correct, the hills must have been widely denuded of timber, with a consequent drying up of streams and erosion of fields.

Thus must Teotihuacan, that splendid and brilliant centre, have destroyed its own agrarian economy.

The largest city of ancient America was abandoned by its inhabitants and left empty. This presents archaeologists with a most difficult puzzle. Acosta places no credence in plague and famine, and writes: 'a suffering people would have emigrated, yet there is no evidence of an exodus'. There are no signs, either, of conquest by foreign tribes; and yet conquerors throughout the course of history have always contrived to leave their mark. The only signs in the abandoned city providing evidence of its end are charred beams and soot-blackened walls. Perhaps a great fire, fed by straw from the roofs and wooden beams from walls and floors, destroyed this splendid place.

Whether it came about through external causes or through a revolt against the priestly caste by the dissatisfied and hungry, the fall of Teotihuacan ended the theocratic Classic culture. In the same way that at one time successive waves of productive energy from this city had been absorbed by the hinterland, so now the destructive spirit of rebellion appears to have been carried into the farthest corners of the land; at almost the same time, the Classic culture of the Maya collapsed in the lowlands of Guatemala. A new ruling class, of a rather more secular outlook, brought different ideas and processes of thought to fruition; and a different art and architecture matched these conceptions that were new in relation to the Classic period.

In terms of Old World development, the technical achievements of the American Indians were roughly at the level of the Neolithic period. The huge contrast between the inhabitants of Mexico and the people of the outgoing Stone Age in Europe lies in the aesthetic quality of their arts and handicrafts. By the expressive power of their forms as well as by their artistic sensibility, American Indian sculptures, paintings, and pottery vessels, created with the technical resources of the Stone Age, are to be numbered among the world's most perfect works of art. As C. A. Burland has pointed out, Mexican art has its framework within the tribal society. It is highly organized, more on a communal than on an individual basis, everyone's place in society and his social duties being regulated by tradition.[18]

The stages in a culture's development, as well as the insidious signs of its degeneration, are most clearly manifested in its small-scale art. With the Teotihuacan culture, as with many others in ancient Mexico, there is no answer to the questions 'whence' and 'whither', although between these extremes the 'how' and 'why' can be largely answered by archaeological discoveries. On the basis of technical, stylistic, and cultural differences the culture may be divided into four sections.

Teotihuacan I and Cuicuilco both reveal a pottery that is simple, awkward, and rustic. Artistically, the products of this still Preclassic period are far below the level of those of the Valley's other places of settlement. Potsherds and fragments are most plainly in evidence in the builders' rubble of the mighty Pyramid of the Sun, since all the earlier buildings were pulled down in order to provide the 35,000,000 cubic feet needed for the construction of the 200-foot-high 'heavenly mountain'.[19] Besides bones and stone implements, the interior of the pyramid yielded fragments of notably inexpressive pottery figures. A small globular or heartshaped lump of clay constituted the head, while the eyes and mouth were indicated by sketchily drawn lines. Frequently, nose and mouth ran into one to give the impression more of an animal's snout than a human face. The picture presented by these figures points to the unpractised hands and vague religious conceptions of an undeveloped society in which every man was his own master, and which lacked both disciplined social organization and clearly defined ideas. Its artifacts do not remotely bear comparison with the much earlier figures of Tlatilco. The functional pottery shows a relationship to Ticoman pottery. It is either brown or red, and often bears yellow or whitish geometric patterns applied by the negative process. Nothing in Teotihuacan I suggests that it marked the beginning of the upward trend culminating in the Classic period, or gives a hint that the old dwellers in the Valley were also the bearers of a developed culture.

The transition from Preclassic to Classic culture in Teotihuacan is so abrupt that many scholars suspect outside influence. Seen anthropologically, the human remains found in the city suggest lowlanders rather than highlanders. The chronicler Torquemada (1723) mentions that the Totonacs living on the Gulf coast boasted that their ancestors had built the great pyramids in the highlands. Whatever its origins, Teotihuacan in its flowering disseminated its culture from the Huaxtec country in the north-east to the Maya highlands in the far south. Kaminaljuyu, on the outskirts of Guatemala City, shows influences so strong that it might almost have been a colony; over a long period its architecture was modelled on that of Teotihuacan and the style of its pottery was typical of the city that lay some six hundred miles to the north. For one short moment in history two major cultures joined hands, that of the Maya and that of Teotihuacan.

While not even the smallest building survives from the first Teotihuacan period, the second was to boast two of the mightiest. The Pyramids of the Sun and the Moon both arose at the very beginning of the Teotihuacan II period.[20] Having regard to their extent it may be assumed that at this time, about AD 200, there was in existence a powerful theocratic

Statue, water goddess Chalchiuhtlicue. Teotihuacan

social structure. The lateral length of the almost square Pyramid of the Sun, 213 feet high, amounts to 730 feet, and it is estimated that 3,000,000 tons of earth had to be moved for its construction. The pyramid, erected in one continuous operation, remained, apart from a small later frontal addition, untouched throughout the centuries, in contrast to sacred architecture elsewhere that was constantly being built over and enlarged.

As the early cultivators grew into a theocratic society, the simple black and brown pottery in turn shows evidence of the desire for better quality and a greater variety of forms. Bowls with incised decoration and the typical cylindrical, tripod vessels were both popular. In Teotihuacan II the distinction between functional pottery and the much finer variety intended for religious purposes is clear. The tripod vessels, decorated with polychrome paint which was applied to a thin plaster coat, bear a family resemblance, both in subject and technique, to the large wall paintings. Priests or a rain-dispensing deity are nearly always *pls 96, 101* in the centre of the pictures.

Even without other proof, the distinctive style and technical assurance of this pottery would suffice to mark the arrival of the so-called Classic period, as would the gracious and lively clay idols that portray gods as well as men. Curiously enough, the conventionalized heart shape, from which the human head shape developed, was retained throughout the *pls 87, 94, 95* four phases of Teotihuacan's culture.

The formal composition based upon the heart shape is apparent, not only in the countless ceramic artifacts that were an intrinsic part of the culture – for the Teotihuacanos literally filled the land with them – but also in the stone masks. Simple, for the most part life-size, and always boldly worked, they have an intriguing similarity to a portrait. 'With what mastery – despite simplification and stylization – have these sculptors succeeded in reproducing Indian racial characteristics which no camera can really capture', wrote Sigvald Linné about these sculptures, whose practical purpose is still unknown. In all probability they were used in the death rites of important personages. A possible explanation may be found in Peru. There, in the coastal areas, the dead were bound before burial into mummy bundles and provided with a false face. Conclusive evidence is unavailable since no trained archaeologist has yet found one of these masks *in situ;* for the many masks in private collections and museums have been placed on the market by grave robbers, who are understandably reluctant to divulge their sources of supply. In all probability the burial site of the kings and high priests, of which Sahagún spoke, lay outside Teotihuacan, for hitherto only a few unimportant graves and foundation sacrifices have been found within the area of the ruins. The simple and expressive power of these masks, the feeling for material, the sensibility of their makers, all, except for the features, are reminiscent of *pls 90–3* the Olmec pectorals worn by high dignitaries. Fashioned with tools of obsidian and bone, smoothed and polished by patient hands, they, as much as the pyramids, bear witness to deep faith.

The esoteric mode of expression of the masks and clay figurines has its counterpart in one having an almost abstract effect, and which is used chiefly in frescoes and the decoration of pottery. Here the central theme is the rain god, Tlaloc, who is reduced to an abstract geometrical formula. The artist seeks, by means of an alienation effect, to separate the invisible and the divine from the visible and human. In Teotihuacan culture there are two particularly striking examples, somewhat reminiscent of the ancient Peruvian culture of Tiahuanaco, which attempt to apply architectonic rules to monumental sculpture. At the foot of the Pyramid of the Moon there stood a 13-foot high statue of the water goddess, Chalchiuhtlicue, translated into geometrical forms by some disciplined mind. This sculpture is in itself a piece of sacred architecture, fashioned in accordance with rules similar to those that dictated the construction of the buildings that once surrounded it. In form, it is deliberately remote from the sculpture of harmonious realism. The figure of the goddess was carved from a single block of stone squared off on six sides. As a pyramid is composed of horizontal platforms, so too is the organization of this statue, apart from the somewhat prominent front. Even here the artist avoids a rounded plasticity, not through lack of ability but out of obedience to his own conceptual world; he resists the temptation to endow the divine countenance with the softness of human forms. In spite of her strangeness, however, the water goddess does not, curiously enough, create a frightening impression, as do perhaps the monumental sculptures at San Agustín in Colombia and Tiahuanaco in Bolivia. By architectonic methods alone, the protectress of the water, undoubtedly a friendly deity, is translated from the natural to the supernatural plane. In this form the work acquires an awesome monumentality comparable with the much larger statues of the gods of ancient Egypt.[21]

In a quarry near Texcoco, there has been found another even larger (23 feet high), partially completed sculpture, conceived in accordance with the same architectonic principles. When it was uncovered, scholars found sacrificial bowls belonging to the twentieth century. Reverence and divine awe in the face of these mighty images must indeed have had deep roots in the Indian mind if 450 years of Christian religious influence had succeeded in making so little impression. In the Temple of Quetzalcoatl the serpents' heads and, even more so, the masks of the rain god, are fashioned in accordance with these same rules. This is an example of the harmonious interplay of building and sculpture.

Teotihuacan III is divided into two phases, each named after a place investigated by Linné. Xolalpan (Linné 1934) is the earlier, and is followed by Tlamilolpa (Linné 1942) which ended with the destruction and abondonment of the city. The ideas that permeate the Classic flowering are still those of the preceding early Classic Teotihuacan II phase, although here is a greater abundance of detail and sumptuousness of execution. At the time of the greatest territorial expansion of the culture of Teotihuacan III, these ideas are found as much as eight hundred miles further south, in architecture and handicrafts identical in style to those of Teotihuacan. These discoveries point to peaceful expansion; perhaps it was missionaries who carried the Teotihuacan view of life to the most remote areas.

A surprising number of frescoes survived the city's destruction; yet even these can only be a fraction of what might have been seen by a pilgrim of the time. The Temple of Agriculture, with its all too prematurely discovered frescoes, has already been discussed. The wall paintings which were discovered later have been largely preserved from further damage by protective structures, and the appointment of official custodians.

The Teotihuacan mural paintings are true frescoes. As in classic Italian wall painting, the paint is applied to the plaster while it is still fresh, i. e. before it dries. The frescoes of Tepantitla, which lies somewhat outside the main ceremonial zone, are of two different styles. To convey the difference by analogy, it might be said that one room could have been done by a Gauguin, the other by a Henri Rousseau; or so the naive representation of the paradise of the rain god suggests. A great stream of water gushes from the heart of a mountain in two directions. A crowd of happy, singing people throngs the painting. There are luxuriant trees, plants, and butterflies; people bathe, dance, rest beneath the trees, sing. (In the mural paintings, and later in picture writing, speech and song are indicated by a scroll in front of the face.) Everywhere in the rain god's heaven, pleasure and harmony reign. 'In the rain god's domain, Tlalocan, neither famine, nor sickness, nor poverty prevails', goes the old saying. This naively humorous work falls right outside the context of the otherwise formalistically stylized art of the Teotihuacan culture. The picture is different even in its colours, which are appreciably stronger than those of the other frescoes. To illustrate this paradise the artist used mainly soft pink, pale blue, pale green, indigo and ochre, along with an Indian red background.

In an adjoining room of the same palace, we find a painting more in keeping with an austere theocratic culture. Priests in splendid raiment and gorgeous headdresses proceed in file holding a ritual implement in one hand and a wide, curling scroll bearing pictographic signs – perhaps the text of their prayers – in the other. By reason of their emotional aura, C. A. Burland named the old wall paintings 'poems in fresco'. At Tetitla, another structure *pl. 85* outside the ceremonial zone, the main subject is a water-dispensing deity, probably Tlaloc, who, exceptionally, is portrayed without a mask. Here the work differs from all other ancient American wall paintings, in that the front of the figure is displayed in its entirety, whereas it was customary to show the body in front-view and the head in profile as in ancient Egypt. Water falls to the ground from the deity's outstretched arms; in its stream we see again precursors of the written character. The extravagant ornamental headdress, with spreading quetzal feathers and a quetzal bird's head in the middle, speaks not only of wealth but also of trading relationships with the tropical countries where this gorgeously feathered bird had its habitat. In another room jaguar gods or their priests stride across the frescoes, singing *pls 99–100* and shaking rattles. Again, in Atetelco the main subjects of the wall paintings are jaguars and coyotes, with scrolls in front of their heads to indicate speech. The tradition of these pictures was carried on in the pictographs of historical times. For us they are difficult to understand because we encounter them out of context.

pls 98, 105   In the pottery of Teotihuacan III, which is in direct line with the preceding period, figurative representation became more realistic, emulating that of the stone masks. Particular care, often extending to the minutest detail, is characteristic of the modelling of the clothing. Clay dolls with articulated limbs also belong to this period. Moulds were used for the production both of figures and of the projecting borders of cylindrical vessels which were often decorated with a frieze of small heads of gods.

The moulds give evidence of the culture's gradual decline into decadence. At first there was still the desire to put finishing touches by hand to figures made in moulds, but later these moulds were to lead to a mass-production that lacked the faith-inspired vigour of the past. If pottery burial offerings are intended to please the gods and to convey to them man's wishes, and this is certainly their purpose here, there can be no clearer sign of flagging religious fervour than pottery that is both repetitive and industrialized. The signs of decadence in Teotihuacan III are still slight, but they are there. The causes of the catastrophe that put an end to this third phase, and to the existence of the city, are lost in the mists of time. All that is discernible is a flagging religion and the inability of the élite to halt the decline. Arts and crafts are the seismograph of this unlettered society. They mark its individual trends, the rise and fall of its culture, and after many centuries they still reveal much of their creators' thoughts.

There was yet to be a short epilogue to the culture of Teotihuacan: certain neighbouring sites reveal a style known as 'Teotihuacan IV' (Ahuizotla-Amantla period). The style is enervated, decadent, and devoid of conviction. Gone are the gracious terracottas, or the delicate cloisonné reminiscent of a butterfly's wing. Gone, too, the dully shining stone masks with half-open mouths. What remained was the mould that produced the same thing day in day out. When the barbarians from the north overran the high plateau, they found nothing of this theocratic community's former greatness. But we shall return to this later, for in order to grasp the Classic culture in its entirety, we must look southwards to the Puebla plateau and the Oaxaca valley, and eastwards to the shores of the Gulf of Mexico.

Situated geographically between Teotihuacan and Oaxaca lies a structure that in terms of volume is the largest ever made by man. Today it appears as an overgrown hillock crowned by a small Catholic church, yet over the course of generations 141,000,000 cubic feet of building material went into the construction of the Pyramid of Cholula, more than into that of the Pyramid of Cheops in Egypt. The place was still an important religious centre at the time of conquest, but even the little town's 365 churches cannot erase the memory of the blood-bath staged here by Cortés during his march on Tenochtitlan, the Aztec capital.

Cholula, which lies at the foot of the extinct volcano Popocatepetl, must have occupied a continuously important position from Preclassic times through the Classic period up to the collapse of Indian culture (1521). It is situated on the most important lines of communication that pass through the Puebla plateau on their way from the Valley of Mexico to the tropical Gulf coast. The first tangible pieces of evidence of a human community are the 'pretty ladies', closely related to the contemporaneous clay figures of the Valley, although lacking their neighbours' plastic subtlety. In general, their closest stylistic affinity is to that of the 'pretty ladies' of Cuicuilco. They lack entirely the softly rounded forms favoured by Olmec sculpture and by the graceful pottery of Tlatilco.

pl. 11

The central structure of this site was erected, and on several occasions extended, under the influence of Teotihuacan. The pyramid was evidently built in at least five stages, all widely separated in time. The interior passages so far opened up measure some three and a half miles. On the walls are death symbols in the manner of the Mixtec and Aztec cultures. Their artistic value is far inferior to that of the Teotihuacan frescoes.

This pyramid, like all other Mexican pyramids, shares only its designation with those of Egypt. Whereas the Egyptian pyramids were built as burial places for kings, the most intensive excavation in Mexico has revealed only one tomb of a high dignitary in the interior of a pyramid; this is at Palenque, a city of the Classic Maya culture. With the exception of Palenque (which proves the rule), the Mexican pyramids served as sub-structures for temples and altars.

In addition to the bearers of the La Venta culture, a people that developed a true grave architecture were the Zapotecs, whose home was in the sub-tropical valley of Oaxaca. At first they built rectangular shaft graves with well-constructed walls whose plan in course of time became T-shaped, and later, shortly before the Conquest, cruciform. The many graves of the region contained particularly valuable and impressive ceramic burial offerings portraying the gods of this ancient and idiosyncratic culture.

THE ZAPOTECS

> I have been unable to find any information concerning the first appearance of this people that had the semblance of veracity, nor any concerning the origin of their rulers . . . To vaunt their courage, they lay claim to be the sons of jaguars and other wild beasts. The great leaders of ancient lineage consider themselves the scions of ancient, shady trees, and those who pride themselves on their invincibility and steadfastness say they have been born of crags and cliffs.

That was all that the Spanish chronicler Burgoa was able to learn about the origins of the Zapotecs at the beginning of the sixteenth century.[22] To us, four hundred years later, the origins of this people are still a mystery, and problems multiply when we excavate their ancient cities.

Whereas the builders of La Venta, Teotihuacan, Cholula, and Xochicalco (a ruined city near Cuernavaca) merged with other peoples, the Zapotecs, like their south-western neighbours, the Maya, their northern ones, the Mixtecs, and the Totonacs on the Gulf coast, today still form self-contained communities, clinging to their ancient languages.

Like a spectral city, Monte Alban casts off each morning the veils of white mist that rise out of the fertile valley and, for a moment, swirl through the sacred place of the Zapotecs. Reminiscent of an island round which the sea has gone dry, this ingeniously planned seat of priests and gods, with its temples, squares, sunken courtyards, tombs, and ball court, towers above the floor of the valley, 1,300 feet below, and commands a view over mountainous terrain. 'If that isn't a wonder of the world, I don't know what is,' remarked Egon Erwin Kisch, the 'roving reporter', when he saw this bold and impressive structure.[23]

pls 111, 113–4, 126

Danzante. Monte Alban I

The Zapotecs were a people of great architects who, in their overall planning as in their detail, paid great attention to the basic design, the ground-plan, and showed a command of the all-important element of spatial organization. They exploited Monte Alban's existing features so as to lend it a sacral character by their arrangement of buildings on the summit. They had no need for ornamental detail since the maximum effect was achieved by the simplicity of their buildings. Few architects anywhere have possessed so much feeling for landscape and the part it can be made to play in their work as did the creators of Monte Alban. The very choice of this site, itself the primary building consideration, promotes a harmonious interplay between environment and architecture. The difference between European and ancient American architecture is nowhere in Mexico so pronounced as it is on Monte Alban. Despite continual extensions and alterations, the architects were never to do anything that would detract from the harmony of the whole, a fact all the more astonishing in that this ceremonial centre was to remain active for nearly two millennia. Although the faithful repeatedly extended and enlarged the sacred site throughout this long period, its homogeneity nevertheless gives the impression of being the creation of one genius.

At the outset, few buildings appear to have stood on the range of hills, for it was only over the course of centuries that the summit became levelled to accommodate this great site. To the north and south, the square, some 2,300 feet in length and 820 feet wide, is bordered by the main building complexes. The temple on the north side, standing on a platform with an area of about 180,000 square feet, has the widest flight of steps (142 feet) in ancient America. There are fragments of the twelve columns, constructed of rubble, that once supported the roof of the gallery. Along the west side, the structures stand close together, their only feature being impressive flights of steps. On the other, east, side, three sizeable building complexes flank the square. They enhance the symmetry and, for that very reason, impart an even more pleasing appearance to the whole. On their own in the middle of the plaza stand four buildings, the ancient Monticulo J and three later structures, laid out along an axis. Monticulo J served as the observatory. Its ground-plan forms an acute angle, a feature in which it differs from all the other buildings whose ground-plans

Danzante. Monte Alban I

are either square or rectangular. It is one of the oldest structures on the site, if not indeed the oldest. The whole of the later complex lovingly enfolds this ancient relic of the past. Monte Alban is thus a mighty amphitheatre, differing only in its rectangular layout from those of Roman and Greek antiquity. The smooth plaster façades, which lend an air of perfection to Teotihuacan, were not favoured by Monte Alban's builders. The platforms of their pyramids were built with rough hewn stone and adobe (sun-baked clay); their forbears were indeed 'born of crags and cliffs'.[24]

The Zapotecs, who handled stone so well when building steps and temples, were, *pls 113–4* curiously enough, among the worst stone-carvers in Mexico. Their stelae inscribed with hieroglyphs are overshadowed by the more artistic products of the Maya culture. Only the so-called *Danzantes* (dancers), drawn with great boldness on smoothed stone with stone implements, have any individual artistic value. However, the people who created the 155 'dancers' – less than one third of these have remained intact – do not seem to have been *pl. 110* Zapotec. The accompanying pottery as well as the style of the reliefs point to the Gulf coast and the La Venta culture.

Clay was the Zapotecs' favourite material, and it was with clay that they created their most individual and personal works, the effigy vessels which are often referred to as 'funerary urns'. As in other fertile and densely populated places, so too in Oaxaca and in Monte Alban, its spiritual centre, evidence of good and bad times is at its plainest in pottery burial offerings.

Monte Alban I produced a simple but impressive pottery which would appear to have long since outgrown the experimental phase. Animated forms and simple, incised geometric decoration were coeval with its founding. The typical cylindrical vessel bears a human face that is anthropologically different from the 'Zapotec' type which is found in later Monte Alban art. The chubby countenance with protuberant upper lip enables us to recognize without difficulty its relationship to Olmec culture. In this presumed deity, with its childish *pls 107–9* face and Jaguar's features, Miguel Covarrubias sees the ancestor of Cocijo, the later Zapotec rain god. He also refers to the *Danzantes,* those degenerate, simian daemons of the primeval forest, who likewise display characteristics of the Gulf coast. Monte Alban I poses the

46

Unknown glyph from Monticulo J. Monte Alban

question – which came first, the chicken or the egg? Was it the Zapotecs who, on their wanderings, met and drew inspiration from the Olmecs, or was Monte Alban a creation of Olmec culture? Pottery found in other parts of Oaxaca provides little information on the subject. Thematically, these earliest inanimate witnesses belong to the large family of fertility goddesses of Preclassic cultures and are typical of the whole of Mesoamerica. In Oaxaca, as elsewhere, most of them are broken, that is 'killed'. One difference is technical and lies in the harder firing, the other, a stylistic one, consists in deeper carving in the region of the eyes and in greater emphasis on the nose. The latter detracts from much of the feminine charm of these 'pretty ladies', especially as several from this district go so far as to bare their teeth.

The calendar is unquestionably the highest achievement of ancient American abstract thought. The earliest dates that it has been possible to decipher so far belong to the La Venta culture; but the Monte Alban glyphs that accompany so many of the *Danzantes*, and decorate so many of the vessels of the earliest period, probably anticipated them. It has not yet been found possible to correlate them with our own calendar. Perhaps it was here that, for the first time, dots were used to denote single quantities and a bar, the numeral five. Other, undoubtedly earlier, inscriptions on the mountain exhibit a primitive form of counting in which numbers are indicated by fingers. It was not until later that the vigesimal system (counting by fingers and toes instead of fingers alone, in contrast to the Peruvian culture's decimal system) came to govern Mesoamerican mathematics. With the additional invention of the zero, making possible a positional notation, the Maya raised this system to such perfection that they were able to write down values to the order of millions, using a minimum of space, long before the Old World managed to replace the cumbersome Roman numerical system with the positional 'Arabic' system. Although no one has yet managed to decipher with certainty a Monte Alban inscription, there is no doubt that here, too, writing served the calendar and was the prerogative of the priestly caste.

Monte Alban II was a comparatively short but nevertheless fruitful period. Elegant pottery employing the cloisonné technique further enriches the preceding period's wealth of forms and is reminiscent of the vessels of Classic Teotihuacan, although here in the south

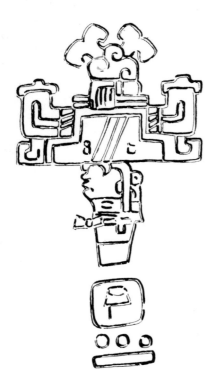

Unknown glyph from Monticulo J. Monte Alban

other forms and colours were used. This time also saw the appearance of the effigy vessels which were to become typical of the Zapotec culture, maintaining their characteristic form for over a thousand years. The earliest examples of these cylinder-shaped vessels, whose front view with a large applique figure, standing or seated, makes one forget that they are containers, still exhibit an archaic severity. Later the style becomes ornamental and more relaxed. The term 'funerary urn' often applied to these vessels is inaccurate; none has been found to contain human remains. In fact, they are burial offerings, found in chamber graves which, unlike those of the first phase, were provided with niches and roofed with a corbelled or false vault. This latter, an acquisition from Maya architecture, was formed of horizontal overlapping slabs and was familiar to the Old World's Mycenean culture. The true vault was unknown to the pre-Columbian cultures.

pls 112, 115–9

Monte Alban II is coeval with Teotihuacan II and the Chicanel phase of the Maya culture. Although it was obviously influenced by both of these very different cultures, it says much for the inventiveness and self-sufficiency of this culture that there is no sign of plagiarism. Everything that is made here carries an individual stamp, a style that was to become typical of the whole area. The Monte Alban II phase marks the gradual dawning of the Classic period, which covers the first centuries after the birth of Christ.

The Mexican archaeologist and excavator of Monte Alban, Alfonso Caso, has divided, on grounds of artistic quality, the third phase into A and B. Monte Alban IIIA was the 'golden age', golden in name only, however, for excavation results suggest that the art of metalwork did not reach Mexican cultures from Peru by way of Panama until Postclassic (or Historic) times. Both in small-scale art and in architecture, powerful artistic forces were at work. The style is extremely versatile, drawing its inspiration from the gentler, pliable Maya peoples no less than from the tough, reserved tribes of the Mesa Central highlands. But the essential Zapotec character is always apparent. Teotihuacan influence is most plainly demonstrated in the grave frescoes; yet the Zapotecs' work lacks the sure touch and harmonious colour gradations of that of their northern exemplars: it is less gracious, less disciplined. Again, the mural paintings are different in that they have writing in the form of name glyphs surrounding the figures.

Danzante with glyph. Monte Alban

In their remarkable urns the Zapotecs have left us a comprehensive account of their gods. Although they do, in fact, resemble divine figures – natural forces in abstract form – found in other parts of the country, these monumentally conceived clay portraits from Oaxaca stand out by virtue of the noble expression of their humanized faces. It is not the squat figure of Tlaloc with his broad-rimmed eyes and slavering mouth that meets us in pl. 118 the Zapotec Olympus but an aristocratic-looking gentleman, recognizable as the rain god Cocijo only by his long, forked snake's tongue. The corn god, too, with his snout-like, turned-up nose, as well as the old god of fire, and the jaguar and bat gods, proclaim their divine functions through rich clothing and opulent head ornaments. The creators of these sensitive figures never attempted to achieve complete realism. In spite of the wealth of ornament (technically possible only by reason of the clay peculiar to Oaxaca and of an improved method of firing), the works are subject to a strict figurative norm of rhythm and symmetry. The bearing and facial expression of many of these figures gives the impression of an expectant repose already overshadowed by grief. There is no laughter, no smirk of malice, no expression of pain or pleasure, in this art. There is a strange radiance about these calm faces that accompanied the dead into the underworld. This countenance with its human features is the constant, the central point from which the eye of the observer is drawn towards the riot of head-ornaments and the gorgeous clothes. The head-ornaments, garments, and jewellery of these divine portraits proclaim the wealth of the country – that wealth of costly textiles, glittering colours, and valuable semi-precious stones, because of which, in later times, the country was to find no peace. It was coveted and conquered by the Mixtecs, by the Aztecs and, finally, by the 'white gods', as the Spaniards were known. Not for nothing did Cortés, Mexico's conqueror, demand this region as his fief from the Spanish crown. Cortés, the would-be viceroy of New Spain, has gone down in history as the Marqués del Valle ('Marquis of the Vale [of Oaxaca]').

The transition from Monte Alban III A to III B took place between the fifth and seventh centuries. While Monte Alban III B undoubtedly entered upon the inheritance of the preceding period, signs of decadence were already present. As with the culture of Teotihuacan, the cause of its loss of artistic vigour can only be sought in the decline of religious ideas.

However, it has not been possible to explain the reasons for the ending of the theocratic era in Monte Alban. The Zapotecs' great ceremonial centre was abandoned at about the same time as were Teotihuacan and the centres of the Classic Maya culture. Unlike the latter, Monte Alban shows no signs of violent destruction. In the following period, the sacred mountain served as a necropolis, a cemetery for high dignitaries. Zaachila, which became the new capital, is nowadays hardly more than a village, with little or nothing to recall the ancient past. On the other hand, Mitla (its Aztec name, Mictlan, 'abode of the dead' means the same as its Zapotec name, Yoopaa), a later Zapotec foundation, was to be recorded in archaeological annals as the best preserved ruined site of ancient Mexico.

It speaks for the Zapotecs' architectonic ability that at Mitla, where the environment was of an entirely different nature, no attempt whatever was made to copy the Monte Alban layout. From a technical aspect, moreover, the architecture at Mitla is somewhat more advanced. Thus the rubble columns of Monte Alban have become monolithic supports. The architectonic emphasis on uncluttered surfaces is here reversed. Whereas in Monte Alban interiors were of secondary importance, the vast palaces at Mitla contain long halls and small, square, inner courtyards. In contrast to the great open plaza of Monte Alban, the later foundation has more the aspect of a medieval monastery. The whole architecture has become more introverted, more secular. By contrast with Monte Alban, where thousands could assemble, Mitla's paved courtyards were unable to accommodate more than several hundred. The buildings here do not stand exposed to the vibrant light, nor is the overall plan immediately apparent. From the outside, the only distinguishable features are the unusual windowless façades, on which the sun on its journey makes a daily play of light and shade. Their numerous geometric designs, built up of tiny blocks of stone, have no equal in Mexico. Only at Chan-Chan on the north coast of Peru do we encounter a similar predilection for geometrically decorated walls which, however, are of clay and hence lack hardness and durability; these are in any case much inferior to the works at Mitla, where the panels of ornamental friezes that line the walls and fill in the horizontal surfaces have the liveliness of an oriental carpet. Nevertheless, the walls themselves give an impression of the unapproachability of a reserved, possibly fearful, ruling caste.

I do not know how many geometric designs are used on these walls, but it almost seems as though every possibility has been exhausted. Here may be found patterns familiar from the history of Greek art alongside Peruvian textile motifs; almost Germanic designs mingle with Oceanic ornamentation. Indeed the geometric invention of the entire world is recapitulated on the walls of the palaces, both outside and round the inner courtyards. The whole effect is highly dramatic. What imparts life to this otherwise dead city is not a spectacular skyline but the continually varying reliefs, now recessed, now projecting, arranged in *pls 122, 124* obedience to the strict rules of a controlled surface.

The second peculiarity that meets the eye in Mitla is the use of simple, monolithic *pl. 123* pillars. On entering the interior of the 'Building of the Columns' they are encountered in military array dividing up a long, undecorated room. Today the roof no longer exists, so that the effect of this windowless, once gloomy hall has been reversed. Dazzling sunlight bathes the roof's stone supports which, depending on the time of day, cast their shadows on the paved floor. In the days when the pillars were shrouded in darkness, one small fire

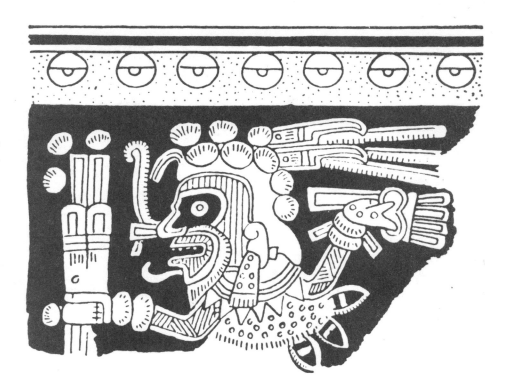

Fragment of mural painting,
Mixcoatl, god of hunting.
Mitla (after Eduard Seler)

must have created a mysterious spatial effect with the indistinct shadows cast by its flames.

Mitla was in fact a complex with cellars beneath it. No chronicler has given any information as to what the Spaniards found in these chambers; in the present century archaeologists have only discovered empty rooms.

THE MIXTECS When Mitla was built is not known with certainty. Probably it arose during the so-called Monte Alban IV phase, the transition period between the abandonment of Monte Alban and the arrival of the Mixtecs in the valley of Oaxaca. The final period (Monte Alban V), which, both in Mitla and in the Monte Alban necropolis, displays features alien to the Zapotecs, was one of Mixtec supremacy. Frescoes, in the style of the Mixtec pictographic manuscripts, are ranged in a frieze beneath carved geometric reliefs. Had the Mixtecs been summoned to Mitla as artists, or were they also the masters of its palaces? At all events, these ferocious warriors and gifted artists used the Zapotec tombs of Monte Alban for the interment of some of their highest dignitaries. We know that these were originally Zapotec, not Mixtec, tombs, since the newcomers did not even attempt to remove the former's burial offerings. When in 1931, Alfonso Caso opened Tomb 7, he was not aware that before *pls 128–35,* him lay the richest discovery of modern times in the New World. Over five hundred precious *138–42, 146* burial offerings – gold and silver work, bone carvings, ornaments of pearl and semi-precious stones, rock crystal sculptures, mosaics inlaid with shell and turquoise, as well as the finest polychrome pottery in Mexico – testify to the Mixtecs' all-embracing artistry. In the graves of both Mixtecs and Zapotecs weapons are entirely lacking. Thirty-one years later Caso presented a sensational report to the International Congress of Americanists on a grave he had discovered in northern Oaxaca whose extraordinary ornaments and earthen vessels were, in his opinion, the work of the same artist who had made those found in Tomb 7 at Monte Alban. Moreover, he thought the dead could even be identified, as the 'lords of Yanhuitlan', on the evidence of Mixtec pictographic writing. It is only fifty years ago that our knowledge of American prehistory put away, as it were, childish things and became a man, indeed a growing man, for this knowledge increases year by year, slowly filling in the many awkward gaps in the overall picture.

51

With the Mixtecs, who prepared the way for Aztec knowledge and art, we have already advanced far into historical times. Rather than leave the region, we shall anticipate the course of history and cast a glance at this important and seminal culture. There is not much information relating to the tribe either at the time of the Conquest or during the early colonial period. The centre of their territory, which they still occupy today, was La Mixteca Alta. Very little pre-Columbian architecture remains, for the conquerors, to an extent even greater than elsewhere in Mexico, used the stone from the ancient temples for the erection of their churches and monasteries. It was the Dominicans who set to work with the greatest zeal, building magnificent monasteries such as those at Yanhuitlan and Coixtlahuaca, as well as numerous churches on the foundations of the old temple buildings, in order to celebrate the victory of the new religion. Now, four hundred years later, most of the Spanish houses of God have fallen into ruin; the saints of the Spaniards never quite succeeded in obliterating here the distinctive characteristics of the ancient Mixtec gods.

'Don't go to La Mixteca Alta, murderers live there'. As late as 1960 I heard this several times, both in the capital and in other parts of the country. The assertion was false and the warning in vain. La Mixteca Alta, the highland home of the Mixtecs, is among the most important cultural areas of the New World and is still relatively uninvestigated; the contact of Americanists with Mixtec culture has mostly been outside the latter's territory.

La Mixteca Alta, 'land of the cloud people', lies like some mighty fortress beside the ancient routes that join North and South America. (Today the Pan-American Highway cuts across the area, touching Yanhuitlan and Nochistlan, two important ancient settlements. On either side of the main artery, only small tracks are available to the traveller seeking entry to the interior of this secluded country.) It was no coincidence that the Mixtecs, more than any other Mexican people, became proficient in the metal-working techniques which reached Mesoamerica from Peru by way of Panama. Mixtec gold ornaments, which look like filigree, were in fact cast by the 'lost wax' *(cire perdue)* method. The wax model was enclosed in clay, dried, then finally displaced by the molten metal, hence 'lost'. 'Like dreams, yet fashioned by man's hands' was Las Casas' description of the Mixtecs' treasures; and Albrecht Dürer marvelled 'at the subtle *ingenia* of the men in foreign lands' when he

pls 128, 138–42

52

had the opportunity of seeing works of the Mixtec and Aztec cultures in the course of his journey through the Low Countries.

pls 129–32 The Mixtecs' bone-carvings rank almost equally with their goldsmith's work. Mythological subjects, dates, and astronomical symbols, carved on jaguar bones with a confident hand, served as burial offerings and as ritual implements. They can even bear comparison with early Chinese ivory carvings.

pls 145–6 Mixtec pottery has no equal in the whole of Mexico. Typically characteristic are the spheroidal tripod bowls with feet often ending in jaguar's claws or birds' heads. Painted in bright colours whose vivacity is enhanced by a brilliant slip, the vessels portray gods and historical personalities in the style of the pictographic manuscripts. Others again are decorated with patterns and symbolic designs combining attributes that are partly animal, partly human. This idiosyncratic style was late in appearing, certainly after AD 1300, and was still in use when the Spaniards arrived. Another technique developed by the Mixtecs in the decoration of their plates and bowls was the combination of painting and relief. This method of incised decoration at the bottom of a bowl was later to be copied by the Aztecs, although they never achieved the quality of the originals.

Culturally, the Mixtec élite's most important achievement was undoubtedly the independent development of a pictographic script fundamentally different from the hieroglyphic writing of the Mayas. Almost two thousand years separate the earliest written and calendric symbols on the *Danzantes* from the Mixtec codices. It is with these books, made of long folded strips of deerskin or *amatl* (a paper manufactured from plant fibres), that the written history of Mexico begins. Real people, whose names have come down as well as their histories, emerge from the anonymous throng of gods, priests, and rulers. By good fortune, some of the most important historical inscriptions dating from the beginnings of this culture escaped both destruction by the soldiery and incineration by the Inquisition.

Pictographic script is writing by pictures; in contrast to the Maya hieroglyphs, Mixtec symbols were still tied to concrete subjects. As with medieval European book illumination, American picture writing was the prerogative of the various priestly castes. Whereas the Aztec codices often appear naive, those of the Mixtecs give evidence of an advanced stylization that supposes a long tradition. In these portraits of gods and people, face-paint, clothing and jewellery, as well as gestures, were prescribed down to the last detail so that there was little latitude for artistic freedom, despite inevitable variations in artistic quality. Unlike the book illuminators of medieval Europe, the Mixtecs, and the Aztecs who succeeded them, both strove to achieve a purely decorative effect without being distracted by a desire for naturalistic expression.

This is a two-dimensional world that tells of rites, lays down instruction for ceremonial procedure, and records mythical occurrences as well as historical incidents relating to tribal princes. Its pictographic character is easier to grasp than the hieroglyphic inscriptions of the Maya, yet the difficulties of reading should not be underestimated, since the historical constituent of these original documents is pervaded by mythical, cultic conceptions which are foreign to us.

The *Codex Vindobonensis*, the Vienna Codex, was brought to Europe in 1520. It contains *pls 106, 143* a sacred sequence of pictures extending over fifty-two pages, the reverse side of which was originally left empty. The successive pictures tell of earliest times, of the genesis of the gods, and of the origin of the Mixtec nobility from a tree high in the mountains of La Mixteca Alta, at a place that is now the village of Apoala.

The sequence resembles a musical score, parts of which can still be neither read nor played, although the form, the division by sections, and the main themes are already known. The sequence of pictures comprises ten sections, five of which are main sections, one introductory, two episodes, and two final sections. The latter include historical matter on the subject of temples in Mixtec territory and their correlative role in the service of the gods. Every section concludes with a representation of a ritual fire-drilling.

The section (section I, ff. 52–47) begins with a preamble enumerating the priests' ten most important duties and contains ten place hieroglyphs, the first of which, a black wall, is that of Tilantongo, the Mixtec royal city.

Then follows the genesis of the gods from earliest times. Each individual is known by the glyph corresponding to his date of birth. Thus, 'One Deer' and his wife produce a long line that ends in the year 5 Flint. Some of this pair's children, peculiar tree and stone creatures, are again repeated with the tree of Apoala. Further repetitions follow and fresh people appear. Finally there is a portrayal of the god Quetzalcoatl, whose calendar name is Nine Wind, being born of a stone knife. The stone knife is one of the children of One Deer and his wife. In the guise of the morning star, Quetzalcoatl Nine Wind, the grandson of this divine couple, fetches the tribe's sacred objects down from the heavens: the sacred bundle of sticks, the conch shell trumpet, the five lances disposed in a quincunx. Beside him the sun and moon hang from the heavens. Eventually Quetzalcoatl Nine Wind raises the fallen heavens out *pl. 143* of the water.

As in any archaic tradition, what has gone before is always repeated and to some extent supplemented in the following sections. It is only after this mythological preparation that history slowly emerges, beginning either with the birth of the chief Four Crocodile, the founder of the Tilantongo dynasty, or with the somewhat earlier birth of the princess Seven Flower, which is depicted in the Codex Teozacoalco. In Europe this would have been AD 692. By consulting other sources it becomes evident, therefore, that the dynasty

Body stamp, rain god. San Andres Tuxtla

existed without interruption until 1580, the year in which the ruler of Tilantongo was christened Francisco de Mendoza by the Spaniards. Like history books everywhere, those of the Mixtecs tell of wars and treaties, of fire and murder, of births and sacrifices. The codices also record intimate matters. We learn, for instance, of marriages between brothers and sisters and other blood-relations, and of the marriage of a man of sixty with an eight-year-old girl. The lives and deeds of named personalities, Five Reed (or Five Alligator), the calendar reformer, and his famous son Eight Deer being examples, cover whole pages of these books that often measure twelve yards or more. Eight Deer, the Mixtec culture hero, was known both by his calendar name and by that of Jaguar Claw.

As with the Zapotecs and their riches, so the artistic gifts of the Mixtecs brought about their downfall. The Aztecs living to the north set great store by the subtle, brightly coloured pottery and the delicate goldsmith's work. After many battles, the Mixtecs were finally defeated and made tributary by the Aztecs in 1494. Numbers of artists were compelled to make their way to the Aztec capital to place their talents at the disposal of the foreign rulers. Only a few generations earlier, between 1340 and 1350, this gifted people of highland peasants had themselves toyed with the idea of expansion. Partly by diplomacy – we know of Mixtec noblemen successfully marrying into Zapotec princely families – and partly by force of arms, the tribe spread southwards. Today Mixtec-speaking islets in Zapotec territory still testify to this expansion. Archaeological confirmation may be found in the graves at Monte Alban and in the style of the frescoes at Mitla. In the north the evidence is not so clear-cut. Nevertheless, the Mixtecs must have had the effect of a 'cultural fertilizer', as Linné put it, on all the peoples, and they were many, with whom they came in contact. Traces of these highlanders may be followed as far north as the coast of Vera Cruz. Pottery found on the Isla de Sacrificios is closely related stylistically to that of the Mixtecs. The main centre of manufacture, at least in the years before the Conquest, of this much coveted pottery was at Cholula, on the Puebla plateau, the 'Meissen' of the New World. At Guasabe on the Rio Sinaloa, over a thousand miles to the north, Gordon Ekholm discovered pieces of the Mixtecs' treasured pottery in a mound-shaped burial site. We also know that this pottery graced the boards of Aztec kings.

55

A different kind of world, today largely inhabited by the Totonacs, greets the traveller when he comes down from the infertile Mixtec highlands into the subtropical region of the central Gulf coast; merry songs, cheerful dances, clean, well-fed people dressed in white, the fragrance of vanilla – all are in complete contrast to what he has left. Furthermore, if he delves into the past he will find laughing deities and an almost baroque temple architecture. Of the many faces presented by ancient Mexico during the pre-colonial period, that of the Gulf coast is the only one to register both joy and love of life.

Since it can only be assumed, but not proved, that the people now known as the Totonacs were already in occupation of the region during the Classic period, scholars find it helpful to distinguish the 'Tajin Totonacs' from the Totonacs proper, who were the first tribe whom the Spaniards encountered after landing in Mexico, and who, weary of their tributary obligations to the Aztecs, joined forces with the conquerors.

At that time, the Totonac capital, Cempoala ('the place of the twenty waters'), was governed by the 'fat chief', who treated with the Europeans and offered them help. According to the chroniclers, the population of this city, lying on the southern boundary of the state of Totonacapan, numbered about 25,000. The estimate was probably exaggerated, but even if the figure is halved, Cempoala was a large city by sixteenth-century standards. The friendly encounter with the Old World must have cost it dear; eighty years later, the city once described as splendid and flourishing had to be abandoned by reason of the diseases brought in by the white men. Today it is a ruin of minor importance, only the foundations of the largest buildings being visible.

El Tajin, another site in Totonac territory, arouses more admiration; even in decay, *pl. 148* it is still a place of overwhelming beauty. Excavations have revealed that its inhabitants deserted it in the thirteenth century for reasons that are not known. Neither the conquistadors nor the friars heard anything of El Tajin, a circumstance the more remarkable since the ruins lie only some eight miles from the market-town of Papantla which figured prominently in the Aztec tribute rolls.

El Tajin, 'lightning' in Totonac, was for long an active ceremonial centre and was probably the only one in the whole of Mexico to survive the collapse of the Classic period.

Body stamp. Vera Cruz

The first buildings went up in the fifth and sixth centuries, and the city retained its own architectural idiom, uninfluenced by other tribes, until about the twelfth century. Only then did the building style of the Tajin Totonacs undergo a stylistic change undoubtedly attributable to the Toltec tribes then moving through the region. Meander patterns and rectangular niches, typical features of Tajin construction, were superseded by large, flat-surfaced façades. Following a short hiatus between 1130 and 1180 or thereabouts, this city, too, was abandoned for unknown reasons. Excavations have revealed signs of fire and of extensive destruction, but there is nothing to identify the destroyers. Perhaps new gods disputed the seniority of the old, or the peasants, grown tired of the exactions of the priestly caste, rebelled.

In the history of its art Totonac culture presents a strange phenomenon. The pottery reveals Maya traits, the later sculpture was influenced by the Toltecs, but the architecture is, with very few exceptions, all its own. This culture had no part in the great development of Maya architecture, nor did it take after its southern neighbour in matters of the calendar, of writing, or of other branches of science.

pl. 154

The Tajin Totonacs' stone sculpture is laden with mysterious symbols, while the pottery, lacking the mysticism of the highlands, seems by contrast almost immature. Three specific sculptural forms, each having its individual character, were widely disseminated but are known to have originated from the central Gulf coast. These three creations of the Totonacs are carved from hard stone and served the cult of the dead.

pls 155–6

The *yugo* (yoke), a horseshoe-shaped object (sometimes closed to form a ring), could have been a stone reproduction of a ball player's hip guard. This item of dress, familiar to us from reliefs and small earthen sculptures, was probably of padded leather and would be unlikely to have lasted long in the damp climate. As has been confirmed in the course of a fairly recent dig by the University of Vera Cruz, the purpose of these stone reproductions was to banish into the earth the evil spirits of the dead. The motifs on these strange functional objects attest to their association with the nether regions: toads, the symbol of the earth goddess; owls, the embodiment of the evil spirits of the night; eagles which, according to mythology, bore dead warriors up to the heaven of the sun god. The function of the ornament

57

bordering the *yugos* is virtually that of writing. At once eloquent and withdrawn, the symbols surround and embellish the representation itself. Male figures are often portrayed on 'yokes', their heads carved full-face at the centre of the curve and in profile at the ends. The choice of hard stone – the easily workable volcanic rock was never used – and the careful execution betray the immense ritual importance of these sacred objects. If he was to endow them with power, the artist must not make things easy for himself.

pl. 153

The *palma* derives its name from the palm frond it resembles. Here again these objects can only have been copies of a ball player's sacred insignia and his lucky charms. The many ball courts to be found at all the larger Mexican ruined sites as well as in the areas of the Maya culture bear witness to the importance of the Mesoamerican ball game, *tlachtli*. In this team game, an elastic rubber ball, that might be struck only with the hip or buttock, had to be passed into the opponents' court. The following account is given by Christopher Weiditz, the Nuremberg draughtsman, who encountered some Indian ball players in 1529 and recorded in his diary: 'In like manner do the Indians play with a blown up ball using their hands or hinderparts to move it along the ground; they also have stout leather for the hinderparts to receive the counter blow of the ball, likewise they have leather gloves.' The ball would certainly not have been inflated but made of solid rubber. The highest religious importance was attached to the ball game, which is clearly based on a system of cosmic symbolism. High priests conducted the games in courts situated within the temple precincts.

One of the reliefs in the ball court at El Tajin portrays a clearly recognizable player wearing *yugo* and *palma*. Whereas the representations on the stone *yugos* are usually invested with symbols, those on the *palmas* suggest scenic treatment, or are confined to masterly and highly realistic depictions of animals that undoubtedly had a totemistic significance for the ball players. A *palma* discovered in Totonacapan, ranking by virtue of its expressive power as a major work of art, portrays a head, half skull, half living. The work symbolizes a ball player's alternatives, victory or defeat, survival or death by sacrifice. The reliefs in the city's ball court reveal to us the progress of such a player. Before the game he is consecrated by a priest garbed as an eagle; on losing the divine contest he submits to sacrificial death.

pl. 149

pl. 151

pls 176–7

The third typical form, the *hacha* (axe), is easily recognizable as the ceremonial battle-axe. It was very widely distributed. *Hachas* have been unearthed at Palenque, a Maya city in the Guatemalan highlands, abandoned during the ninth century, and also in the Huaxtec country on the northern Gulf coast. Representational themes alternate with abstract motifs. Whether the subjects are animal heads, human heads or skulls, all are adapted to the axe's pointed shape and are carved with great skill.

pls 150, 157

pl. 162

Both on the Gulf coast and elsewhere, it is pottery that takes us farthest back into the past. At the outset there were, besides ugly and strikingly inept portrayals of fertility goddesses, also male figures in the so-called Remojadas style. For centuries they conformed to stereotyped patterns, and it is exciting to observe how a sensitive, rounded sculpture gradually evolved from the formless mass of clay. These little burial offerings lacked neither ornaments, necklaces, earplugs, nor carefully arranged hairstyles. Bituminous facial paint made an early appearance and is a characteristic of the region. Articles extraneous to the district are the pouting child faces of the Olmecs in the bottom layer and, in the upper layers, a

pl. 163

polychrome pottery which is influenced both in form and in decoration by the Mixtecs. Remarkable are the *cabezas sonrientes* or laughing heads which resemble Asian deities rather than the bloodthirsty gods of Mexico. With their benevolent aura and cheerful, welcoming gestures they stand distinctly apart from the rest of theocratic art.

In order to discuss Totonac architecture it is necessary to return to El Tajin. The very site is in utter contrast to that of Monte Alban. El Tajin lies concealed in a depression surrounded by hills and by green hostile walls of tropical vegetation. An Amazon Indian proverb runs: 'The gods are mighty but the jungle is mightier'. This is just as true for El Tajin as it is for the Classic cities of the Maya culture. The city is held in an almost tender embrace by its relentless adversary which still conceals large sections of it. The most noteworthy structure is the seven-stepped Pyramid of the Niches, built in a highly individual style that finds no counterpart elsewhere. The niches give the impression of windows, and it is perhaps for this reason that the building, which marries geometrical austerity and baroque opulence, looks so un-Mexican. It could be that each of the 365 niches contained a day god of the year or his symbol, and that at night there burned in them the flames of sacrificial offerings, for *tajin* can mean 'fire' or 'smoke' in Totonac.

Beside the largest structure, which, blending harmoniously with the hilly landscape, avoids the monumentality of the highland pyramids, there stands Tajin Chico, 'little Tajin', a structure remarkable by reason of its design. In this somewhat higher-lying complex the niches are adorned with meander patterns. Cornices, which by their perspective give the illusion of defying the laws of gravity, as well as unusable flights of steps whose purpose is purely decorative, are other distinguishing features of the architecture. Ladders, and not the projecting, massively constructed stairs, were used to reach the terraces and the interiors of the upper rooms; a unique masterpiece of the impractical!

The builders showed practical ability, on the other hand, in the roofing of their rooms, for which they used a cement of pounded shells mixed with sand, pumice, wood, and plant fibres. The task was a wearisome one, for the rooms had first to be filled with stone, wood, or earth before the light building material could be poured on, layer by layer. Depending on span, roof thicknesses measured between thirteen and thirty-five inches. This method,

unique in ancient America, made possible the roofing over of an area up to eight thousand square feet, with a span of over sixteen feet. It is a remarkable fact that, whereas many discoveries spread like wildfire throughout a continent, an achievement of such importance to building – for roofing problems invariably presented themselves in the massive works of Mexican cultures – should have been confined to such a small area, lying though it did in a region through which traders and migrants were continually passing.

The Aztecs decried the Huaxtecs, describing them as 'drunkards' and 'sorcerers'. For over three thousand years these north-eastern neighbours of the Totonacs formed an homogeneous community, and it was not until shortly before the Conquest that they became tributary to the Aztecs. Up to this day they have preserved their language as well as many pre-Hispanic customs. In numerous Huaxtec districts, for example, the dead are still 'sent on their way' wearing sandals; a large bowl, the *jicara*, is supposed to help them in crossing the river. Nor do those left behind omit to supply the dead with provisions for their long journey or to include a handful of corn to humour the turkeys which, according to mythology, attempt to bar the way of the departed. Another custom still observed in the present century forms an ethnological link with the Lacandon, the only Indian tribe as yet unconverted to Christianity, who live withdrawn in the jungles of Chiapas and Peten. Like the Huaxtecs, they use the water in which the feet of the dead have been washed for the preparation of tamales (maize cakes) which the bereaved family then distributes among the guests.

The Huaxtecs' relationship to the large family of Maya peoples (to which the Lacandon also belong) is not only evident from ethnological similarities but has been confirmed by linguistic research. The separation, which came about very early, probably between the eighth and fifth centuries BC, was caused by a group thrusting coastwards from the highlands and driving a wedge between the two. While the mother culture in the south experienced a great advance in scientific knowledge, the Huaxtecs long remained at the archaic Preclassic stage, taking no part in the development of hieroglyphic writing or calendric science. Maya architectonic features such as the corbelled vault never reached them. Like castaway islanders, those cut off gradually created their own culture, no more than superficially touched by outside influences. In the history of their art, these comparatively unambitious people developed a personal style which they retained for nearly three thousand years. Olmec, Totonac, Mixtec, and Toltec traces are little in evidence in the various culture sequences (Panuco 1 to 6 in the archaeological table). On the other hand, Huaxtec ideas, disseminated peacefully by way of trade, are evident in the Valley of Mexico. The Huaxtecs also had an influence that was primarily religious on the Aztecs and the other Nahuatl-speaking peoples as they moved down from the north to settle in central Mexico.

She, our mother,
Came from Tamoanchan,
She, our mother, came from there,
She, the goddess Tlazolteotl.

In the early Mexican sacred books Tlazolteotl ('filth goddess') is described as the goddess of dirt, perhaps because of the sins men unloaded onto her, but also as the fertility goddess. A turban of cotton material, strands of spun cotton in her perforated ears, a spindle whorl in her hair, all proclaim her home to be the land of the Huaxtecs, 'the land rich in cotton'.[25] The Aztecs confessed their acts of adultery to Tlazolteotl, eater of filth, and hoped that the goddess would absolve them.

Teteoinnan ('the gods' mother'), who is another aspect of Tlazolteotl; Xilonen ('young maize mother'), the corn goddess; Xochiquetzal ('flower feather'), the goddess of love and flowers; and Ometochtli (Two Rabbit), the pulque god: all these ascended to the high plateau, where they took their places in the Aztec pantheon. The entity worshipped as the creator of humanity by many tribes, Quetzalcoatl, is also venerated in the guise of Ehecatl ('wind'), the wind god, who owes many of his essential attributes, and perhaps even his original form, to the Huaxtecs. It is with his cult that the spread of circular buildings throughout the whole of Mexican architecture is most closely connected. At Cempoala and Calixtlahuaca, as well as Malinalco and Quiengola, temples of this type were erected in honour of the wind god. The circular platforms of the pyramids at El Ebaño (San Luis Potosi) are possibly as old as the structures at Cuicuilco.

Archaeological investigation of the Huaxtec country, 'La Huasteca', has up to now been no more than superficial, but the region will undoubtedly produce some surprises in the future. At Tantoc, not far from Tamuin, two pyramids await excavation, one of which may even surpass the Pyramid of the Sun at Teotihuacan both in height and volume. An ancient and in this context frequently disputed tradition according to which 'The settlers from the Rio Panuco who dwelt in Tamoanchan undertook to erect the pyramids of the Sun and the Moon in Teotihuacan' (Sahagún) may well be confirmed by excavation.

Palms, tree stumps, river boulders, and baked clay were the customary raw material used by the Huaxtecs for the construction of temple platforms, ball courts, houses, and courtyards. As in Teotihuacan, the ceremonial centre was coated with lime plaster (here, on the coast, made from seashells), which was then painted in brilliant colours. The altars were decorated with frescoes, but of the rest nothing can be described until all the structures dating from this era are examined in detail. Only then will it be possible to form a complete picture.

pl. 202

No region in Mexico is so remote from civilization as to be exempted from occasional visits from grave robbers, whose discoveries find their way into private collections and museums abroad. These, together with legitimate finds, enable us to reconstruct a culture's external image. In stone sculpture as well as in pottery, the Huaxtecs contrived to remain faithful, for nearly three thousand years, to a style that was all their own. They eschewed both the baroque exuberance of their southern neighbours and the expressionism of the highland tribes along their eastern borders. Even their life-size sculpture is in no way self-assertive, maintaining an individual, calm beauty. Out of a rhythmic sequence of almost flat surfaces there arises the plastic unity of a well-balanced sculpture in which the static predominates and sculpture in the round is dispensed with. By contrast there are the lively scenes on the reliefs, and frescoes that are more 'drawn' than painted. The latter are reminiscent of Mitla in the arrangement of the figures, and of Maya painted pottery of the Tepeu period in their virtuosity and immediacy. This is 'cubist' painting. On vases, too, *pl. 184* this original style may occasionally be seen.

The motifs, in common with those elsewhere in Mexico, are exclusively religious. Whereas pottery developed over three millennia from the archaic fertility goddesses to *pls 182–4* 'popular' vessels in the form of corpulent women and zoomorphic creatures, stone sculpture was the expression of complicated religious concepts. One monument, now in the Brooklyn *pls 179–80* Museum, portrays on one side a young, handsome god with noble, human features, on the reverse a skeleton with the most important internal organs plainly recognizable. According to Herbert J. Spinden this work represents Quetzalcoatl's apotheosis as the morning star. Other representations of this deity about his ritual affairs are incised on shells worn as pendants *pl. 181* by high dignitaries and have been preserved in graves in the damp coastal area. This decorative shell-work had its corollary – not so much in style as in craftsmanship – in the bone carvings of the Mixtecs.

The Huaxtecs lost their independence shortly before the Conquest, when this most northerly province of Mexican culture was made tributary to the Aztecs. A land that could produce three corn crops in a year, that possessed the coveted wealth of the tropics, and whose inhabitants were manufacturers of gorgeous textiles, was too tempting, even though the naked Huaxtecs, with their blackened, pointed teeth and rough customs, had an awesome reputation as warriors. In 1521, after Cortés had captured a settlement on the Panuco, he came on the skin of one of his soldiers, Alonso Alvarez Pinedas, hanging as a trophy in one of the temples; Pinedas had fallen into the hands of the Huaxtecs two years before.[26]

The only inhabitants who took no part in the rise and fall of the theocratic Classic WESTERN MEXICO cultures, and who persisted in an archaic mode of existence that knew few gods, were the early settlers of the north-west coast. The modern states of Colima, Jalisco, Nayarit and Michoacan are now largely inhabited by people known by the Spanish name of Tarascos or 'Tarascans'. We know of a number of Tarascan chiefs who put up a bitter resistance to the Aztecs, and of their last king who was asked by an emissary of the haughty Aztec ruler Moctezuma II to help his people against the white invaders. Fortunately for the Spaniards the Aztec emissary met his end on a Tarascan sacrificial stone. Had these two warlike nations joined forces, the Spaniards might even have been driven out of Mexico.

The Tarascans were for long thought to have been the creators of the anecdotal pottery that makes the north-west coast so popular with treasure-hunters. Accounts of their migrations, however, similar in pattern to those of the Aztecs, confirm that the Tarascans were late immigrants, so that the original pottery can once more be classified only by the names of the place of discovery and the state where it was found.

By contrast with the god-centred art of the theocratic Classic cultures, the art of the

pl. 46

north-west coast might be said to constitute a 'human comedy'. It tells lovingly of pregnancy and childbirth, babies at the breast, older children at play. Nowhere else in the Americas is the subject of mother and child so frequently and lovingly handled. The harsh rigidity of theocratic art took no root here. Unencumbered by religion, this art concentrates on the everyday, often with humour and earthy irreverence, sometimes even to the point of

pls 41–79

caricature. It tells of proud warriors and of the diseased and dying, of dreaming men and tattooed women. The portrayals of birds and snakes, fishes and crabs, mussels and sea snails, show both representational talent and an acute observation of nature. A favourite subject, and one of the few with religious connotations, is the dog, which, according to the beliefs of many early peoples, is supposed to accompany the souls of the dead. Sahagún wrote:

> For companion he had a small dog, a yellow one that wore a strand of slackly spun cotton for a collar. Men say that he takes [the dead] across the ninefold river to Mictlan . . . There the waters are wide, dogs are the ferrymen, and when one recognizes his master he leaps into the water in order to take him across. It is for this reason that the natives breed so many dogs, for it is said that the white dog and the black dog are unable to cross over to the land of the dead. It is held that the white one says: 'I have just washed myself', and the black one says: 'I have just painted myself black.' Only the yellow one, and none but he, can cross the river.

Here the colours of dogs are related to various divine functions, yellow, in Aztec religion, being the colour of the god of death.

pls 74–7

Colima pottery has left a captivating memorial to the native Mexican breed, a grey dog not unlike a dachshund. This mute and hairless animal, also known in ancient China and now virtually extinct, was called *techichi* ('stone dog') or *tepexhuitl* by the Mexicans. Likenesses of these dogs in all manner of true-to-life situations and attitudes were fashioned by the artists of the north-west coast as burial offerings to accompany the dead into the underworld. In one well-known example the dog is actually wearing a human mask; more often he is portrayed as a corpulent beast with a maize-cob in his mouth.

It was not only as companions of the dead that these animals were valued by the Indians, for they were also fattened for eating. 'Small, plump, and delicious to eat' was how the Franciscan friar Sahagún described the Mexicans' most important domestic animal.

pl. 60

We must turn to the Mochica culture on the north coast of Peru in order to meet with pottery that is as life-like and life-loving. The Colima groups have their counterpart in no other place but this, many hundreds of miles to the south. In the north-west of Mexico, nothing was too insignificant to serve as model for lively and animated representations to accompany the dead. The groups of ball players and cheering spectators, the houses overflowing with drunken guests, are evidence of a vigour more spontaneous than consciously artistic. Preserved in a lively impressionist style, the representations in the graves have survived the actual houses.

Since this is a 'Preclassic' art, innocent of gods, having at most daemons, there is little evidence of a sacred architecture that would have corresponded to the pottery. (The *yacata,* a Tarascan term for cult structures of earth and rubble, usually with rectangular, T-shaped or circular ground-plans, did not appear until the period of the small Tarascan kingdoms whose last seat was at Tzintzuntzan, 'the place of the humming-birds'). The only religious buildings in a broader sense before the appearance of the Tarascans were the spacious tombs. Accessible only by way of a narrow shaft, the dome-shaped burial chambers were as much as forty-five feet below ground level, usually connected severally or in pairs by a small passage. Placed beside the remains of the dead to accompany them on their journey to the underworld lay the animated and worldly pottery, which remained 'alive' and intact, not broken as was usually the case with most Mexican cultures.

One of the peculiarities of the north-west coast culture is that we know little or nothing of those who created it, in spite of the descriptive nature of its art. Not until scholars are given the opportunity to undertake systematic excavations will the situation change. The only certain knowledge we have acquired from the representations of this life-loving community is that of their social ranks. The naked, or the scantily clad, contrast with those who wear rich clothing and ornaments; a world so uncomplicated when revealed in its small-scale art was obviously complex in reality. This people's relatively secular mode of existence, associated with the fact that they were loosely organized into village communities, accounts for an almost entire absence of change in their art over a long period. Their view of life seems to have remained fixed at the Preclassic stage and to have altered little throughout the Classic period until the arrival of the warlike, well-organized Tarascans. In this region, largely without an established religion such as ensured artistic conformity elsewhere in the country, the observer will today see creations of genius alongside work that is bad or indifferent. The freely-conceived, exuberant idiom of these modellers in clay, who for the most part took their subjects from life, although occasionally from mythology, is sometimes conventional, sometimes daring and unrestrained. Much of it still lacks form, yet there is little that is incompetent; some of the work, indeed, betrays the highest degree of formal sensitivity and awareness. The scene as a whole, however, stays always the same, revealing work that is the original, personal inspiration of its creator, rather than that of an artist commissioned by an élite. In Mexican art as a whole, this specialized art of the north-west represents the extreme in worldliness, a 'barbarian' art, it might perhaps be called, rooted in everyday life. It knew neither the fascination with death nor the acceptance of death as an ever-present factor in life which are important characteristics of Mexican religion even to this day.

In most instances the art of the north-west coast was a folk art, naive, happy, altogether impulsive and unrestrained by narrow spiritual or secular directives. Consequently it moved rapidly ahead of its time in many ways, while in others it lagged far behind. Although over a thousand years have elapsed since its inception, this pottery – the artists were unable to acquire much liking for stone – is unbelievably modern in appearance and in many examples anticipates some of the art of the twentieth century. It is not surprising that its discoverers were not archaeologists but artists, chief among them Diego Rivera.

Body stamp. Guerrero

Among these vigorous sculptures are the only works in pre-Columbian Mexico – again the parallel with the Mochica culture in Peru comes to mind – to break the modesty tabu.

pl. 45 Effigy vessels in the shape of seated youths with penises of extreme length that serve as spouts give the impression of intruders in early Mexican art, which always sought to avoid the portrayal of the naked human body. In the figures of the north-west coast, the subject is taken to the point of caricature and is probably without any deep religious significance.

Techniques, materials, and themes identify the individual stylistic trends, which do not always necessarily correspond exactly to the states whose names they now bear.[27] In

pls 64, 70, 79 contrast to the monochrome red pottery of Colima, a typical feature of of Nayarit is the detailed painting of face and body. The patterns of the woven materials, too, comprise several colours. These for the most part very ugly shapes lack affection for the small and insignificant. The Jalisco style, like that of Nayarit, is primarily concerned with the creation of human figures, usually women. At first compact and only a few inches high, their size increased

pls 68–9 over the course of centuries. These are the ladies with the long, narrow, aristocratic heads whose only occupation appears to be sitting or standing. A few of these introspective creatures, with their air of bored dignity, carry a child or dog which is disproportionately small by comparison with themselves. This was no aberration but a deliberate distortion of perspective, perhaps to make the child appear more helpless and the mother a more imposing primeval mother.

pl. 62 Seldom in the pottery of Jalisco does action claim the observer's attention, but when it does, the result is most striking and expressive; a fixed instant in a gesture or a movement is intentionally recorded by means of a 'still'. Colima's pottery differs from that of Jalisco

pls 65, 67 and Nayarit by being rounder and more dynamic. It eschews the static. But the most obvious difference in stylistic trends is to be found in the conception, for whereas the Jalisco seated figures are portrayed in a rigid attitude mainly attributable to the set of their backs, Colima artists found their inspiration in the curves of the human form.

If only for reasons of size, the manufacture of these clay figures demanded manual skill, speedy operation, and a firmly preconceived idea of form, since the damp clay tended to sag easily during modelling or to crack if it dried too quickly. In ancient America the use

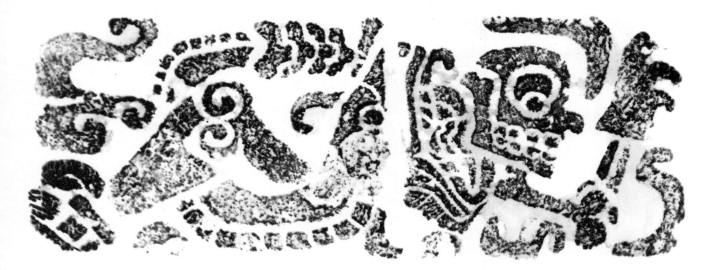

Rubbing of a relief. Tula (cf. *pl. 181*)

of armatures was either unknown or despised. The vessel shapes of the larger figures were the result of practical experience; besides fulfilling the functions of a container, they owe their hollow form primarily to the risk of fractures during baking. It was only smaller figures that could be fired when made of solid clay.

The prehistory of the state of Michoacan is also veiled in darkness. Covarrubias refers to it as a 'chaotic puzzle'. Only the Preclassic Chupicuaro style has an individual character in its 'pretty ladies', usually smaller than the 'ladies' of Tlatilco, whose flatness is relieved by noses, eyebrows and necklaces in applique modelling. The mask-like faces, with eyes surrounded by geometric patterns and with no more than the nose and mouth modelled in low relief on the outside of the vessel, have an almost uncannily reptilian appearance.[28] The vessels are coloured an intense red, of a consistency not unlike lacquer. The process was *pl. 39* apparently a closely guarded secret of this culture, for otherwise it would have certainly been used elsewhere.

During the Classic period the stimulation received from the Teotihuacan culture found its chief expression in vessels decorated with cloisonné. As in the case with the rest of Mexico, these traces are lost towards the end of the ninth century, and it is not until hundreds of years later that history reasserts itself. Michoacan became Tarascan territory and marked the northern boundary of the Aztec sphere of influence.

Further south, and still on the Pacific side, Mexican art achieved the utmost simplicity of form and line, often to the point of an abstraction hitherto unknown. The present state of Guerrero is once again virtually a blank page for scholars; all that is known of Guerrero architecture, for instance, has been learnt from stone models of pillared temples, found in graves. Opinions differ as to the chronology of the discoveries; so many objects have been found, however – though far outnumbered by the fakes offered to tourists on the way to Acapulco – that an attempt must be made to classify them on the basis of stylistic comparison.

The small number of clay figurines so far discovered at San Jeronimo, north of Acapulco, are members of the large family of 'pretty ladies' of the Preclassic period, all of which, from El Opeño in the north to El Salvador in the south, display related features. The shapely, high-domed forehead reflects the region's ideal of beauty, but the large surprised eyes seem

66

Hieroglyph of the city of Tula (Tollan, 'the city of rushes')

little related to the art of the Valley of Mexico. For over two thousand years pottery had to take second place to stone sculpture, and it was not until the end of this period that earthenware returned to fashion. Nor does the polychrome pottery of Tepuxtec – showing, curiously enough, more affinity to that of Nicaragua than to that of its neighbours the Mixtecs – give any indication of being connected with another culture. Yet there must be other links in this field between the San Jeronimo figurines and Tepuxtec ware. The pottery was of little or no interest to the *huaqueros* or grave robbers who found a readier market for the sculptures of grey or greenish stone which were not uncommon in the area.

pls 102–3   The 'ceremonial axes' of Guerrero are often carved into a human likeness with fewer than ten lines, and there are also numerous elaborate masks with exaggerated 'de Gaulle' noses. Whether they are stylized, executed with cool detachment, or lovingly worked by an artist down to the smallest detail, and whatever their size, Guerrero masks are always smooth and boldly original. They embody elements of Teotihuacan mixed with the enigmatic style of the Olmecs. Over the course of centuries the full lips become clear-cut and ascetic. Perhaps the Teotihuacanos even found the pattern for their masks in Guerrero. (Covarrubias refers to the various types as Olmec-Guerrero, Olmec-Teotihuacan, Teotihuacan-Guerrero).

The unmistakable child's face on the one hand, and the absence of Olmec monuments and buildings on the other, give reason to believe that the Olmecs, the 'bringers of culture', occupied this region *before* they came to the southern Gulf coast. The two cultures share one iconographic theme, the 'stargazer', but the relationship is one of subject, not of style. At La Venta there stands a sculpture of a priest – though some believe it to represent a monkey – many feet in height, with face turned heavenwards. The same effect is given by the ceremonial axes from Guerrero, for they are always carved in the image of a squatting, and equally simian, priest, with upraised face. The experience gained from the observation of the stars enabled the La Venta culture to establish a calendar. In Guerrero, up till now, nothing like this has been found.

The surprisingly 'modern' feel of the art of the north-west coast is again encountered here. The ceremonial stone axes, invariably carved with a few sure lines into a figure, are closer to some sculptures of the twentieth century than they are to many works of the Classic

67

Body stamp, Quetzalcoatl as the wind god Ehecatl. Texcoco

period. They are austere and unapproachable like the rugged, barren landscape, withdrawn and taciturn like its inhabitants. It was not through chance that hard stone was the most favoured material. There is little in this art that might reflect the people's wealth, and there is no sign whatever of its northern neighbours' dionysiac zest for life. Guerrero art is cryptic and carries with it an aura of daemonism. It knew no gods with clearly defined attributes, but no one who has ever held these lovingly polished sculptures in his hands can possibly be in any doubt that here is the heritage of a god-fearing, deeply religious society.

It was Covarrubias who first drew attention to the unity of this characteristic style which preferred stone to clay, and whose defunct culture he named after the Mescala river, on the banks of which most of the objects were found.

The god Tezcatlipoca ('smoking mirror'), *Codex Borgia* (cf. *pl. 215*)

5 Militarism: the Toltecs

In Tula, the highland metropolis of the Toltec culture and the heir to that of Teotihuacan, we encounter a situation very different from that prevailing on the Pacific coast. When the Spaniards arrived in Mexico, the Aztecs still spoke in awed tones of the Toltecs, the race of 'artists and master builders'. Aztec noblemen traced their descent back to them, and according to the legends that surround Tula or Tollan ('city of rushes'), many of their gods dwelt for a time on earth. Early travellers' tales and other sources contain more allusions to Tollan than to any other place. All the nations and dynasties with any pretensions to civilization claimed to originate from this ancient seat of the gods, known to posterity as the 'land of promise'. In earlier days, not only had the plants of the torrid zone ripened in these cold, barren highlands, they had also grown to a fabulous size. Gorgeous tropical birds flew about hills that were said to contain precious stones and metals. In other words, Tollan was the earthly paradise; and, as we shall see later, expulsion inevitably came.

This old tale, like many others, contains a grain of truth. Before deforestation, the climate of the region had in fact been favourable. It was not until later that periods of drought, combined with strong winds sweeping across the plateau, caused the erosion of the layer of soil, no more than a few inches deep, upon which men depended for their food, clothing and shelter. Moreover, as we have seen, the theocratic cultures, obsessed with erecting countless pyramids to the gods, may well have hastened the process of deforestation and brought the Valley's economy to the point of collapse.

Following the decline of Teotihuacan and the city's destruction by fire, warlike nomadic tribes from the north poured unhindered into the Mesa Central. Among them were the Toltecs. They mixed with the original inhabitants, assuming their higher cultural level. The *Historia Tolteca-Chichimeca* speaks of two tribes: the Tolteca-Chichimeca and the Nonohualca, the 'dumb ones' or the 'differently spoken', who had settled alongside each other at Tollan. In the view of Mexican research scholars, the 'dumb ones', who were on a higher cultural level, are the Mixtecs, for when stock is taken of the Mexican peoples, they alone remain unaccounted for. The Mixtecs left their traces in Cholula as early as the Classic period and carried their culture northwards to Sinaloa on the Pacific, and to northern Vera Cruz on the Atlantic. Southwards their influence extended even further. On the far boundaries of Maya territory, now Quintana Roo and Belize (British Honduras), stylistic elements of this culture have been found. It is a tempting theory, but not altogether plausible, for Mixtec sherds are absent from Tollan (Tula) itself.

The Tolteca-Chichimeca have a history which is easier for us to trace. This people, who spoke an ancient form of Nahuatl, dominated the original inhabitants, gradually ousting their language, which is now totally lost. The two conflicting elements, the warlike nomads on the one hand and the peaceloving sedentary population on the other, combined over the course of centuries to form an aggregate that was given shape by Toltec culture with its centre in Tula. Early reports of Tollan are so riddled with myth, and often so unreal, that prior to the excavation of Tula (Hidalgo) many scholars had consigned the Toltec metropolis to the realm of folklore. Since 1940, when archaeologists started digging in the neighbourhood of the present town, and when it became certain that here, below ground, no more than forty miles from the capital, lay the oft-described Tollan, there has followed a series of events that, from an archaeological viewpoint, are almost miraculous. Still more unexpectedly came the discovery of a rock relief confirming that the hitherto mythical priest-king Quetzalcoatl Ce Acatl Topiltzin was in actual fact a ruler of the city. Stone carvings give the date of his accession as 980 and the year of the city's fall as 1171. The latter is slightly inaccurate, for other sources show the correct date to be 1168.

According to the *Historia de los Reynos de Colhuacán y México* the Toltecs had ten kings.

The red and the black Tezcatlipoca on the ball court, *Codex Borgia*

Their fifth was Quetzalcoatl Ce Acatl, the king of the priesthood, who had assumed the name of the ancient Mexican god and who, according to tradition, built his remarkable palaces with seashells, turquoise and feathers. In the course of his conflict with Tezcatlipoca ('smoking mirror'), a rival who identified himself with the eponymous tribal god of another Chichimec group, Quetzalcoatl was defeated and fled with his followers over the sea to the east. The trail is taken up in the *Book of Chilam Balam of Chumayel*, a record of the traditions of the Maya jaguar priests of Yucatan, far to the east, and confirmation is found in the

figs 3–5

architectural style of Chichen Itza. This city in the middle of Maya territory, more than seven hundred miles from the home of the ruler Quetzalcoatl Ce Acatl, was rebuilt by the Toltecs in the style of ancient Tula. The reliefs of Toltec warriors and of heart-devouring

pl. 185

eagles and jaguars might almost be copies. The so-called god Chacmool, a typically Toltec reclining figure holding a bowl, and the sculptures of feathered serpents, furnish further proof of Toltec immigration. In Maya tradition the principal religious innovator is known by the name Kukulcan, which is a literal translation of Quetzalcoatl, 'feathered serpent'; Maya chroniclers put the time of his arrival between 977 and 999. In addition to their similarity in point of time, these pieces of information are also of immense significance through the fact that they were handed down by a different people.

Since this Quetzalcoatl (his calendar name Ce Acatl means 'One Reed') is the first historical Mesoamerican personality we encounter, it is worth our while to take a look at some of the early books and to find out more about this man of exalted rank. In the legends, Quetzalcoatl and his adversary Tezcatlipoca are identified with two of Mexico's more important gods. They are thesis and antithesis, forming the framework of a religious philosophy whose dualism is most clearly symbolized by, on the one hand Quetzalcoatl, contemptuous of human sacrifice, and, on the other the blood-thirsty Tezcatlipoca. Their conflict epitomizes the entire religion: the warlike view of life prevails, the peaceful succumbs. Human sacrifice is introduced (or rather reintroduced), and reason gives way to power politics. For centuries men looked back nostalgically to the rule of Quetzalcoatl, the days of peace when art and culture began. This was particularly the case with the Aztecs, in spite of, or perhaps because of, the fact that their tribal god Huitzilopochtli bears many of the features of Tezcatlipoca. Apparently the Aztec kings were at pains to keep on good terms with all these earlier gods, for their enthronement was accompanied by the following speech:

> *From today, O lord,*
> *thou sittest on the throne,*
> *on the chair that first*
> *Ce Acatl Nacxitl Quetzalcoatl*
> *did establish*
> *and in his name there came*
> *Huitzilopochtli,*
> *the true creator of the throne*
> *as it is today,*
> *and in his name*
> *came first Acamapichtli. . . .*

Then follows an enumeration of the preceding kings of Tenochtitlan.[29] According to legend, Quetzalcoatl's banishment and the end of the earthly paradise were his own fault. One day, the sick and ageing king, who because of his ugliness kept himself hidden, was approached by his adversary, Tezcatlipoca, accompanied by the latter's younger brother, Huitzilo-pochtli, with the pulque god for ally. They extolled the medicinal benefits of white pulque, saying: 'If you drink it, it will intoxicate you and will make your body light. You will weep and be troubled. You will think of death. You will think of where you are to go.' Allowing himself to be persuaded, Quetzalcoatl drank, continuing to do so until the fifth cup, the 'one too many', as had been planned. In his intoxication he forgot the rites, failing to observe the vows of fasting. 'Then he wept and was overcome by a deep melancholy. Only then did he accustom himself [to the idea of departure] . . . it was the work of intoxication, wrought by the demon of the sorcerers'.[30] Another source, the *Anales de Cuauhtitlán*, describes the broken vow of fasting in clearer terms reporting that the priest-king called for his sister 'that we may become drunk together'. They committed incest, and by forgetting the gods they enacted their own doom and that of their people.

> *And when he came to the shore of the lake,*
> *he made for himself a bier of serpents,*
> *placed himself upon it, and that was his ship.*
> *He was borne away over the water,*
> *and no one knows how he came to Tlapallan.*[31]

Early sources are all more or less in agreement about the departure of Quetzalcoatl, the king of the priesthood. In the *Memorial Breve* is written:

> *In as much as he sought out the region of the sunrise,*
> *which henceforth is named*
> *for the fact that he vanished in redness [blood],*
> *vanished into smoke.*
> *So it is said*
> *that one day he will return.*

Roller stamp, the death god Mictlantecuhtli. Central Mexico

'But from then on there is no more peace in Tollan', report the writers of the *Codice Chimal-popoca*.[32] Hundreds of years later the Aztecs still went in fear of Quetzalcoatl's return. According to Sahagún, Moctezuma II is said to have told Cortés: 'I was troubled throughout the days that I looked towards the unknown land whence thou camest, the land of clouds, the land of mists, for the kings, my forefathers, have told us that thou wilt come to visit thy city, and that thou wilt place thyself upon this throne, and that thou wilt return'. When Cortés landed on the shores of Mexico in the year of Quetzalcoatl's birth, *Ce Acatl* (1 Reed, also the date of his death one calendar cycle later), the prophecy seemed to have come true.

Many modern writers have persisted in repeating Moctezuma II's understandable mistake of identifying Quetzalcoatl Ce Acatl, whom the traditions describe as white-skinned and bearded, with a visitor from Europe. Foolish hypotheses have been put forward in an attempt to identify him with the Vikings, with the crusaders, with Irish monks, and with St Thomas the apostle, no less. Very recently one author even 'discovered' that the 'white god' of Mexico was an immigrant from Mycenae. All this is nonsense. The god Quetzalcoatl, whose mother died after four days of torment when giving him birth, was a Mexican deity, a 'culture hero' who taught men how to grow corn and to weave cloth. 'Four in number were the houses he built, his house with beams of turquoise, his house of seashells, and his house of quetzal feathers. And his sacrifices consisted in serpents, birds, and butterflies that he killed. And there he called out to the place of duality, to the nine-layered heaven. And he found himself in a meadow of precious stones, a meadow of quetzal feathers.' There is no doubt that such a god as this springs from Indian soil and from the Indian mind. It was only later that he was translated into the image of a person with historical origins. Such glorifications of historical personages are common to all world religions.

The great difficulty in understanding early American religion in general, and the Aztec religion, which was based on the Toltec and even earlier cultures, in particular, lies in the many-sidedness of their divine figures. The conflict between the gods undoubtedly reflects, and is associated with, a spiritual and social conflict among their votaries. The gods and their cults were propagated by an élite in an endeavour to secure power for themselves. The gods' form and essence derived from the views and experiences of this formative élite.

Compromise with other ideas combined with a millennial tradition effected a blend of often contradictory features into a single image. Thus, the basic Christian concept of wholly good and wholly evil powers was unknown to the Indians. As in nature, of which the gods are an abstract symbol, and as in man himself, unpredictability and disaster are inherent in even the most benevolent of influences. Quetzalcoatl is a typical example of the two-sided nature of the ancient American deities. To the uninitiated his ways were mysterious and unfathomable. The initiated, on the other hand, the priests, knew, or professed to know, how to keep at bay, by propitiatory sacrifices, the hostile powers inherent in the gods. Inevitably, the gods became ever more exigent; in Aztec times men were sacrificed even to Quetzalcoatl.

The god Quetzalcoatl also has other names, and appears in many different forms. According to one myth, he descends into the underworld as the 'creator god' and steals from Mictlantecuhtli, lord of the land of death, the bones of men from an already departed age from which to create a new race of men.[33] Fleeing with these, he is pursued by the birds of the god of death. He stumbles and falls, and the bones are broken, but he succeeds in reaching the upper world with the pieces. There he sprinkles the bones with his own blood; and because the broken bones were not of equal size there is now man and woman.

Literally translated, Quetzalcoatl means 'serpent with the feathers of the quetzal bird', and thus he is represented in art. *Coatl* (or *cohuatl*) means 'twin' as well as 'snake': and the feathers of the rare quetzal are an emblem of what is precious. As 'precious twin' the creator god is linked with his twin brother Mictlantecuhtli, who appears in pictographic manuscripts as a skeleton, and whose task it is to escort the sun through the underworld every night. The cosmic counterpart of this two-faced figure is the planet Venus, the morning star which, at another time of the year, has its place in the firmament as the evening star.

The concept of the heavens themselves is illustrated by a semicircular, double-headed serpent which personifies the day sky, the night sky being expressed by the snake's mirror image. Together they form a circle; this cannot be purely accidental, and was, in my opinion, based on the theory of a spherical earth, although at the time the earth was generally believed to be a flat disc floating on the sea.

The creator god, Quetzalcoatl, not only created men, he cared for them. Again he had to steal from the powers of evil in order to help his creatures. This time, according to the myth, it was ants who were the evil daemons, and who kept and concealed maize, man's valuable food. By cunning, Quetzalcoatl appropriated several grains which he gave to man.

In Aztec religion, about which we know most, men honoured this deity as a culture hero who brought them art and knowledge, who taught them how to work precious stones, to weave and dye cloth, and who imparted the techniques of mosaic and leather work. He instructed them in writing and in calendar science; he laid down their holidays, and demanded prayers and sacrifices as food for the gods. In his projecting mask he became the wind god Ehecatl, one of the rain god's most important companions. As Quetzalcohuatl, 'precious twin', he is the patron of twins, although freaks are also associated with him; and pictographs show him, certainly the most human of gods, as a sinner, 'eater of filth', filth being symbolic of sin.

Tezcatlipoca, who often appears as his 'brother' and adversary, embodies the night sky, the moon, evil, death, and destruction. The elected patron of witches and bandits, it is

said of him that he is the god 'who will never grow old'. He is Yaotl, the enemy. His manly virtues make him the patron of warriors. Tezcatlipoca is called 'smoking mirror' because his face is smeared with soot containing metallic flecks. The natives also use the same word for these. His qualities, however, were not wholly evil, for like a Prometheus of the old New World he brought men fire, although this really came within the province of the physically and historically 'old god', Xiuhtecuhtli or Huehueteotl.

Is it through mere chance or through a universal, primeval image in the human subconscious that Tezcatlipoca is associated with Satan, by his club foot even more than by his connection with fire? This appendage forms the end of a scroll-shaped figure that surrounds his ideogram, the 'smoking mirror' of the god. Had these representations not been familiar from pre-Hispanic pictographs, one would have been inclined to attribute to the Spanish missionaries the recasting of this heathen god in the role of Satan. It is easy to imagine how much the parallel must have facilitated their task of converting the Aztecs. But again, as history has shown, similarities between the characters of many of the ancient gods and those of the Catholic saints could ultimately represent an impediment to conversion to Christianity. No sooner has the Indian left church after praying to the Holy Virgin than he will invoke the ancient gods. Although he may light candles to the Madonna in a Catholic place of worship, he will, shortly afterwards, burn copal resin before an early pagan image.

The bloodthirsty Tezcatlipoca's emblem is a flint or obsidian knife. Lord of cold and ice (the north), god of sin, protector of princes and slaves, he rules over the warriors and is the patron of bachelors; his calendar name is Ome Acatl, Two Reed. One of his aspects is Tepeyolohtli, 'heart of the mountain', the jaguar with the wild cry; another, as depicted in the *pl. 214* *Codex Borbonicus*, Chalchiuhtotolin, a jewel-encrusted turkey. He is encircled by the rainbow snake, symbol of sin and incertitude. He bears two vessels, one of fine pulque, the other filled with gold.

The entire conceptual world of the Indians was invariably linked with their topography and, to a lesser extent, with the historical past. Even historical personages who had succeeded in achieving divine status became before long no more than a reflected image of nature's boundless powers.

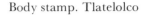
Body stamp. Tlatelolco

To archaeologists, Tollan and the Toltecs mark the beginning of the most exciting chapter in Mexico's long history. For the first time, information that had been passed down by word of mouth or in writing can be supplemented by actual discoveries. Conversely, artifacts vouch for the accuracy of many old traditions. Henceforward words, even though they are, unfortunately, ambiguous, are to accompany both art and history. Much is still indistinct and many secrets will only be revealed in course of time. Many misconceptions, too, that have crept in will have to be put right.

The beginnings of Toltec culture are somewhat obscure. It starts with Mixcoatl ('cloud serpent'), the half mythical conqueror who, about 900, rather in the fashion of Attila the king of the Huns, penetrated into the cultivated region of the Valley of Mexico and in all likelihood put an end to what remained of the decadent Teotihuacan culture. On the collapse of theocratic culture, the region became accessible to nomadic tribes from the infertile north who were known to the cultivated peoples by the collective name of Chichimecs, 'those of the race of dogs'.

In the Valley, history is of a somewhat repetitious nature. To those in the barren north, the area surrounding Lake Texcoco was an oasis, a constant temptation to the 'barbarians' to invade the region and exchange their insecure hunting life for the secure existence of cultivators. As the Ostrogoths profited by Rome's decadent culture, so in Mexico the new arrivals drew advantage from the existing inhabitants' cultural achievements. The great past of the earlier cultures, however, no longer exists in the consciousness of the Aztecs, or of the other tribes that were to flourish five hundred years later. Their historical memory went back no further than the great days of Tula which, embellished by memory, became a golden age for later generations. Yet historically speaking it represented nearly two and a half centuries of turmoil and disorder.

Conflict between the gods, no doubt reflecting tribal feuds between two chiefs, was not the only problem. Weaker immigrant groups were driven out either for religious reasons or simply through the desire for expansion of stronger elements. Toltec refugees had an influence on both the Mixtec and Zapotec cultures, and also left their traces in Cholula. In their sacred book, the *Popol Vuh*, the Quiché, a Maya group who lived still further to the

76

south, indulge nostalgic memories of Tollan. The Pipil of western Guatemala and eastern El Salvador belong to the Nahuatl linguistic family and are probably descendants of a community that was expelled from Tula. On the Pacific coast of Guatemala there are stelae that display Toltec stylistic features, and in Nicaragua, even today, there are stylistic and linguistic indications which are attributable to Toltec emigrants, while admittedly displaying little evidence of Tula's cultural excellence. Only in Maya territory, in Yucatan, did those refugees under the leadership of Quetzalcoatl Ce Acatl, also known as Topiltzin, succeed in erecting a new and more brilliant Tula, in the shape of the rebuilt Chichen Itza. But here, too, fratricidal wars between rival dynasties disrupted the land. Chichen Itza was abandoned centuries before the arrival of the Spaniards, and the Toltec minority, which for a short while had enriched its culture, was absorbed by the Maya.

The last ruler of ancient Tula, up to its fall in 1168, was Huemac. Recent excavations as well as early inscriptions give us reason to suspect that the Mexica, or Aztecs, as they were called after their mythical place of origin, Aztlan, played an important part in the destruction of the city. For centuries afterwards the first metropolis of historical times lay in ruins, and, although it subsequently became an apanage of the Aztec nobility, it never succeeded in regaining its former size of status. The convert Don Pedro Montezuma, a son of Cortés' irresolute adversary, had his residence there. Excavations indicate that the recently revealed structure, the Cielito ('little heaven'), which is situated four miles from the one-time seat of Quetzalcoatl, was in occupation as late as the first years after the Conquest. Toltec and Aztec sherds lay side by side beneath those of the early colonial period.

Unlike their religion, the Toltecs' art has no connection with the culture of Teotihuacan. It sprang from a worldly, indeed military, spirit and gives no sign of having any antecedents. Rather than with the endeavour to make emotionally manifest the driving forces of nature – the nature gods – this art is concerned with demonstrating the secular power of its rulers. Whereas during the Classic period the immaterial often assumed abstract forms that were incomprehensible to the people, no one could fail to understand the ideology of Toltec art. Stone now became the preferred material for architectural embellishment, and was no longer reserved for statues of gods. Warriors or warlike tribal deities are portrayed in reliefs on pillars and again in free-standing sculpture which is also used for architectural decoration.

pls 188–9 The reliefs at Tula and all the sculptures radiate a virile and untamed energy which has banished all evidence of the theocratic artist's sensitive hand. Like those of the much earlier La Venta culture, the Toltec artists show an astonishing feeling for material, although they neglected semi-precious stones, such as jade, obsidian and rock crystal, that are difficult to work. No use was made of the alabaster and pale nephrite whose natural veining had cast its spell on Teotihuacan's artists, and which imparts a lifelike aspect to their staring masks. In this militaristic culture, the introversion, spirituality, and patience of its predecessors gave way to the inclination for a monumental and intemperate display of grandeur, almost reminiscent of the proverbial ostentatiousness of the newly rich. Blankly staring

pl. 186 warriors nearly sixteen feet high – some say they personify Quetzalcoatl as the morning star – were at one time supports for the roof of Tula's famous ruler. (Four of these colossal atlantean figures still stand among the ruins; the fifth, as the emissary of ancient Mexico, spends its time travelling from exhibition to exhibition throughout the world.) A similarly massive style is displayed by the standing figures with upraised arms which at one time supported stone table-tops. These figures, as well as the colossal atlanteans (pillars shaped like men) and the square pillars with the incised reliefs of warriors, illustrate a spirit both in Tula and in Chichen Itza that is contrary to that of the Classic period.

Toltec art, like any other, exists within a social context. Its sculpture embraces three aspects of reality: representational, based upon the living model; intellectual, deriving from the conceptual world of the creative mind; social, determined by the existing ideology. Under the Toltecs, Mexico underwent a fundamental change as a result of emancipation, first from the animistic magic of the early hunters, gatherers, and cultivators, and then from the ritual preoccupations of the theocratic priest-kings. Of course, this transition from the theocratic state to the political was not complete or definitive; nor were the Toltecs to be the most powerful representatives of this 'new age'. Folk art, religious art, and art in the service of the state still went hand in hand; but there was nevertheless a decisive shift of emphasis. Whereas in earlier cultures priests and secular rulers – church and state – had been embodied in one person, and the main purpose of art, irrespective of its technical level, had been to mediate between the living on the one hand and the gods and the dead on the other, in Toltec culture the main emphasis was on worldly things. The gods, although in no sense deposed, were nevertheless used in the service of secular policies. Warlike astral deities superseded the vegetation gods of the preceding era. Religion was now subservient to the warrior caste, an instrument for the glorification of war. 'Then began the time of human sacrifice.'

It is precisely in this connection that a remarkable apparent paradox emerges from the old reports. Quetzalcoatl Ce Acatl, who identified himself with a god to whom in Tula only butterflies, birds, flowers, and small animals were sacrificed, and who opposed the bloodthirsty Tezcatlipoca, was, according to early Maya sources, the instigator of a marked increase in human sacrifice in Yucatan. Among the Toltecs' successors, and more especially among the Aztecs, these warlike proclivities, as well as the harsh practice of human sacrifice, were to assume considerable proportions.

But let us return to Toltec art which, as a medium of this unlettered culture, speaks in very clear accents. Its stone sculpture is static; even the gigantic snakes that once formed the entrances to the temples of Chichen Itza evince none of the mobility of their live counter-parts. Nowhere in this monumental art is there any sign of the impressionistic conception so evident in the large-scale sculpture of La Venta. With the Toltecs, most sculpture is rigid, uniform and deployed in military fashion. The reliefs at Tula are an exception. On the thrones, warriors, both living and dead, march towards an unknown destination; on the walls, great cats, puma and jaguar, prowl with lowered heads along the friezes, while eagles, and more cats, hold human hearts in their claws. Representatives of the warriors feed these daemons with the hearts of sacrificed captives. Sometimes there sits between them, crouched in a toad-like attitude, the figure of the culture hero, Quetzalcoatl. Another wall frieze depicts recumbent figures with larger than life human skulls and crossbones. In terms of death, and things inhuman and animal, Toltec art is dynamic; in terms of its warrior élite, and things human, it is static. Then as now it gives the impression that the warriors would lose some of their dignity if they abandoned their rigid posture and behaved more like human beings.

fig. 5

Rubbing of a relief on a *teponaztli*. Aztec (cf. *pl. 136–137*)

This spirit is more plainly apparent in the Toltec renaissance at Chichen Itza in Yucatan, where even more warriors in ceremonial dress are carved on the pillars. These pillars, a hitherto unknown architectonic element, permitted the construction of high, roomy halls, a practice unknown to the preceding culture of the Maya. The contrast between the understatement of the roof supports and the turbulence of the lively reliefs on the walls produces a singular tension.

As in ancient Greece, the buildings of the period and their decorative detail were resplendent with bright colours. Ancient Tula and the later Chichen Itza of the Toltecs must have made an unforgettable impression on the pilgrims who came to visit them.

The soft medium of clay was of no more than secondary importance to the Toltecs. Their pottery, whether for practical use or for the purposes of the cult of the dead, never attained the standard of the Classic period. In all their portrayals of the ancient gods, which are somewhat reminiscent of the rain god, Tlaloc, they confined themselves to forms inherited *pl. 192* from the culture of Teotihuacan. Domestic pottery, vases, cups, and plates were generally decorated with linear patterns that do not quite cover the entire surface. The impression is superficial and devoid of any deeper symbolical implication. This pottery, which is to be found almost throughout central Mexico, is known to archaeologists as the Mazapan style. One innovation was a long-handled incense burner, probably an import from Maya territory. *pl. 191* Another type depicts Toltec personages in relief, in a style which is reminiscent of the paintings in Maya pictographs. It is only stylistically that these very rare vessels, of high artistic merit, unidentifiable with any precise place of discovery, can be attributed to the Toltecs. Possibly they were made to Toltec specifications by the Maya of the Yucatan peninsula, who were especially proficient in this technique.

A pseudo-vitreous ware – known as 'plumbate' from its resemblance to a lead glaze – had its source in Chiapas or in the Guatemalan highlands, and was distributed, but not manufactured, by the Toltecs. The leaden sheen derives not from a glaze but from the nature of a clay peculiar to the locality and from a special method of firing. The Toltecs were further responsible for the wide dissemination of metal work consisting entirely in articles for decorative use, as also of clay tobacco pipes.

Next to the warriors it was above all the merchants who brought about the social revolution and, in so doing, helped to diminish the ascendancy of the priests. Moreover, they disseminated the products of the various Mexican cultures, so that even after the fall of the metropolis, the refugees never quite lost touch with their ancient home.

Neither the clues furnished by the excavation of the city, nor the knowledge we possess of the historical figures of that time, are sufficient to solve all the riddles presented by this people, described by the Aztecs as 'artists and master builders' but, by their own account, soldiers. Yet the Toltec culture provides an emphatic affirmation of one historical principle: that expressed in Arnold Toynbee's admonition to the effect that militarism is suicide. In Yucatan, in the valleys of Guatemala, on the high plateaux of central Mexico, this culture vanished into nothing. All that remained, along with the ruins and the stone memorials, was their successors' reverential, but spurious, memory of an age of peace.

In the long chain formed by Mexico's cultures we find links that are particularly lustrous flanked by others whose function is purely ornamental or, better, structural. What lies between the brilliant Toltecs and the last shining link, the Aztecs, is unimposing, indistinct. After Quetzalcoatl Ce Acatl came five Toltec rulers, the last of whom, Huemac, apparently fell into disfavour with his people because he married a woman whose posterior measured one fathom across. For this he was deprived of his priestly office. But even as a secular prince fortune deserted him, for newly arrived nomadic tribes stormed the northern bastion of Mexico's culture, and in 1168 the same fate overtook Tula that centuries before had overtaken Teotihuacan. The Nonohualca, the 'dumb ones', 'took the black colour, the red colour, the books, and the picture writing' and moved off towards the east. 'They took knowledge, they took everything, the songs, flute playing' (Historia Tolteca-Chichimeca). Huemac then attempted to establish a new city at Chapultepec. If we are to believe early sources, he took his life after failing to do so.

The destruction of Tula's political power brought utter chaos throughout the land. Bands of civilized warriors were dispersed in all directions by barbarian nomadic hordes. The period was marked by disunity, even among linguistically related peoples. Discord among the Nahua tribes had the effect of a chain-reaction on other cultures. The consequences of Tula's fall were widespread population migrations.

New Chichimec groups led by Xolotl penetrated into the Valley and took possession of the most important localities. Their capital was set up first at Tenayuca, later at Texcoco. The other main participant in the ensuring political trial of strength was the city-state of Azcapotzalco. Archaeologically speaking, the situation at this time is confused. Valuable early sculpture of the Toltec culture has been found in Colhuacan, the last refuge of those expelled from Tula, as well as in Cholula. Toltec sculptures, relics, perhaps, of Huemac's ill-fated stand at Chapultepec, have even been found in the area of Tenochtitlan, the later Aztec capital.

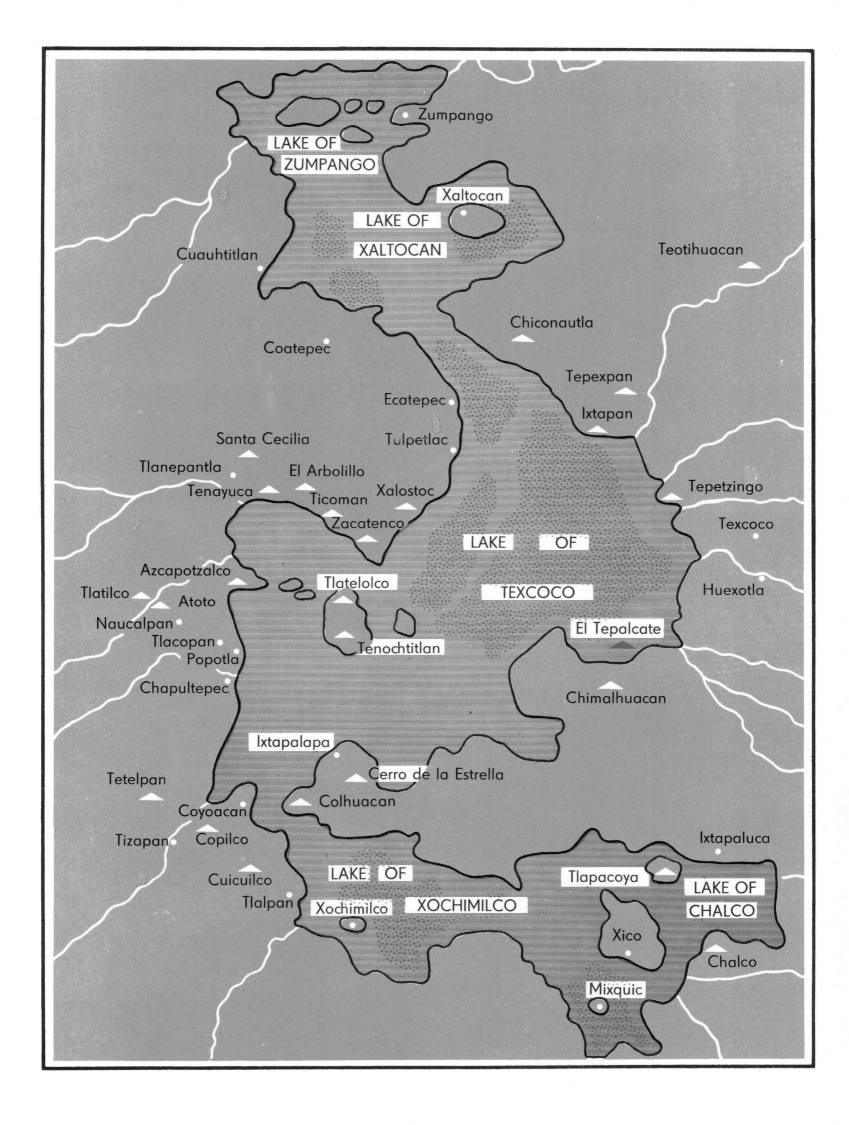

Acayacatl
('water face')

6 Militarism: the Aztecs

When the Aztecs appeared on the stage of the Mesa Central, they were a very minor tribe, whose migrations were dependent on the whims of others more powerful than they. Tired by their long wanderings and spent by battles with other tribes, they established themselves on an island in the middle of Lake Texcoco (which now no longer exists). The small infertile island was the only place left available to these humble late arrivals by the peoples who had arrived before them. According to legend, the Aztecs were supposed to settle on that spot where they saw an eagle with a snake in its beak, perched on a nopal cactus. Whether or not this happened in 1325 (more plausibly, recent investigation would appear to suggest 1370) in the swampy region that was to become the 'Venice of the New World', we do not know. At all events, the ancient ideogram of eagle, snake and cactus has become the arms of the present day Mexican republic, and the modern capital stands above the ruins of the one time Aztec metropolis of Tenochtitlan.

We shall now open out the strip, many feet in length, of the manuscript known as the *Tira de la Peregrinación Mexica,* and follow the wanderings of this sorely tried people.[34] On a small island, surrounded by six palaces, there stands a temple, Aztlan, their mythical place of origin, the 'land of the white colour'. In the year 1 Flint (1168?)[35] it is abandoned by its inhabitants. Two persons, one with the name glyph 'fishing net' *(matlalin)* the other 'reed' *(acatl),* personify the two rulers. Unfortunately the picture chronicle is reticent about the reasons for the migration. Forther on it tells of wanderings that last for centuries. The first

Acamapichtli
('handful of canes')

Chimalpopoca
('smoking shield')

halting-place after leaving the island is Colhuacan, where the groups expelled from Tula found shelter. Here, in a cave, the Aztecs find the stone image of Huitzilopochtli, 'humming bird on the left'. They choose him as their tribal god.

In terms of real life, this picture conveys nothing more than the meeting of incoming nomadic tribes with the long established inhabitants who had already reached a higher cultural level. The Aztecs visited Colhuacan once again at a later stage in their history in order to ask a legitimate 'Toltec prince' to become their king. It would appear that they obtained Acamapichtli, who was related to the Toltec ruling house on his mother's side.

From Colhuacan, the 'place of the grandparents', they took with them the image of Huitzilopochtli. Other tribes accompanied the Aztecs. The pictograph shows their names in the form of rebuses. These names mostly reappear in later history, and are still encountered today in small villages. There are the Matlatzinca, 'those with hips like fishing nets'; the Tepaneca, 'who live on the stone', the later inhabitants of the volcanic desert of Pedregal; the Tlahuica, 'bow and arrow [makers]', who settled in the more remote parts of Morelos; the Malinalca, 'who twist', and have their seat in Malinalco; the Acolhua, 'who live by the water' and are citizens of Texcoco; the Xochimilca, 'who grow flowers' and live in Xochimilco; the Chalca, 'dealers in precious stones' from the city of Chalco; the Huexotcinca, 'those with the clothed legs', who established themselves at the southern end of Lake Texcoco.

All these tribes, each of which had established its own small city-state, later came under Aztec supremacy, either peacefully or by force of arms. In his *Los Veinte i un Libros Rituales i Monarchia Indiana* the Spanish chronicler Torquemada explains the next momentous occurrence illustrated in the *Tira* as follows:

Incited by the devil, the wanderers rested beneath a large tree and built a temple in honour of Huitzilopochtli. One day, precisely at noon, the tree broke asunder with a fearsome crash. This the Aztecs attributed to the anger of their tribal god, and they summoned the other six chieftains to a conference. Huitzilopochtli bade the tribes disperse and go their several ways. Only one was to bear the name 'Mexica' or 'Azteca'. The place where this happened is called Cuauhtlipoztequiayan, 'the place where the tree broke'.

In the pictograph the high priest of 'the chosen people' announces the dispersal to the other tribes. With tears in their eyes, the other tribal princelings take note of the god's decision. In the next picture, the footprints of those sent away disappear into nothingness.

For long the Aztecs enjoy no rest. Bearing the idol of their tribal god, they continue their wanderings. The chief Black Serpent bears Huitzilopochtli on his shoulders and receives the god's commands. He first demands the sacrifice of three people. This is carried out by the high priest, Acatl, whose name we already know from Aztlan. Above the victims the pictograph indicates that the sacrifice favours the fortunes of the chase. Later the tribe passes through Chocoyan and Coatlimac, after which we learn of a prolonged stay in an uncivilized region. The passage of time is denoted by calendric hieroglyphs beginning with *Ome Calli* (2 House), until the next New Fire ceremony, also in the year 2 House, one calendar cycle or 52 years later. In the following year, *Vei Tecpatl* (3 Flint), another exodus takes place.

The wanderings of the Aztecs in search of a home are plotted by no fewer than forty-two place hieroglyphs, among them that of Tollan, the 'city of rushes'. Chapultepec, the hill on the shore of Lake Texcoco, then swarming with fish, is also no more than a temporary halting-place, for the envy and hostile actions of all the other tribes soon put an end to their stay. Coxcox, king of Colhuacan, defeats the Aztecs, who for many years lead a life of slavery. Then, on the outbreak of a war between Colhuacan and Xochimilco, Coxcox sends his slaves as conscripts to the front, where they acquit themselves well. As a proof of their bravery they cut off the Xochimilca warriors' ears, bringing them back by the sackful to their master. In the pictograph the macabre scene is not without a certain absurdity. One of the sacks lies before King Coxcox, who points at it and asks what it contains. In the next scene he finds out. Horrified at the unseemly conduct of the barbarians, the king turns his back on them in disgust. Nevertheless, the Aztecs regain their freedom in return for the service they have rendered. Barely has this happened when two warriors armed with obsidian knives sally forth in order to retail these heroic feats of arms throughout the Valley, and to offer the tribe's services to the other city-states. Here the *Tira de la Peregrinación Mexica* breaks off, for the remaining portion of the manuscript is no longer in existence. Its content, however, written in Nahuatl, in Latin script, shortly after the Conquest, survives.

Moctezuma I, Ilhuicamina ('he who shoots at the sky')

To what extent these episodes are based on truth is difficult to say, although there is no doubt that the Aztecs were feared by other tribes because of their military competence, cruelty, and the bloody ritual they practised. The Aztecs' arrogance reached its height when, with a view to the founding of a ruling dynasty, they asked Coxcox for one of his daughters. Upon their request being granted, not only did they, instead, sacrifice his daughter to their tribal god, but they invited the king to the ceremony as well. Enough was enough. The king of Colhuacan called for war against the murderers of his child. The Aztecs were defeated, and fled to an island in the middle of the lake, the same where Huitzilopochtli is said to have vouchsafed his portent. They shared the island with another, earlier community, Tlaltelolco, which for nearly 150 years contrived to maintain its independence in the immediate vicinity of these ferocious warriors. Only fleeting mention is made of the founding of the Aztec capital in the *Historia de los Reynos*: 'There, at Mexico-Tenochtitlan, was the beginning in the year 8 Rabbit [1318].³⁵ At first the Mexitin [Aztecs] built no more than a few huts.'

Like that of Rome, the founding of the Mexican capital belongs to the realm of myth, for little or no historical information remains. The Aztecs, upstarts in the midst of historically much older tribes, had good reasons for drawing a veil over their brief and recent past in the Valley. Historians differ as to whether the chieftain, Tenoch, who, as its founder, is reputed to have given the city its name, did in fact exist. Early sources are unanimous only in describing the region as one of the poorest in the whole of the highlands. The building of the city was unquestionably a pioneering operation on the part of the Aztecs, who to their skill at arms now added a technical competence which they were to develop to levels unusual in the Indian race. To increase the area of arable land they constructed artificial islands, the *chinampas*. These man-made fields based on rafts of woven reeds appear later in the Aztecs' tribute rolls.³⁶

The rise of this minor tribe came about through the choice of a military commander. Acamapichtli (1375–95), a Toltec nobleman from Colhuacan according to one source, a refugee chieftain from Cuauhtitlan according to others, reorganized the people and trained standing armies who fought as mercenaries in support of the Tepanec city of Azcapotzalco

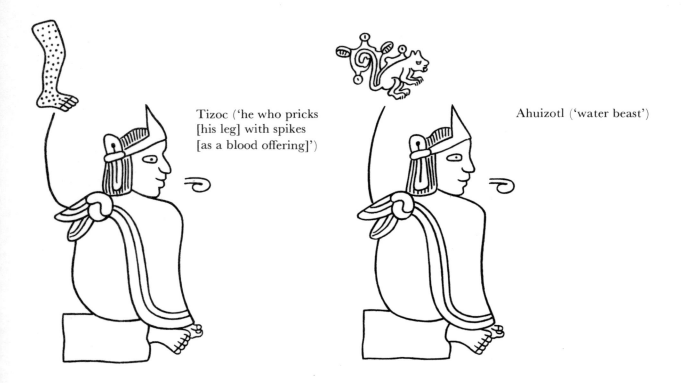

Tizoc ('he who pricks [his leg] with spikes [as a blood offering]')

Ahuizotl ('water beast')

against other rival city-states. This military aid was of advantage to the Aztecs, in that they were regarded favourably, or at least tolerated, by the most powerful city on Lake Texcoco, and also because mercenary service was a welcome source of revenue, the island being much too small to supply the agricultural needs of the people. Under the succeeding ruler, Huitzili-huitl (1395–1414), the tribe continued to fight for Azcapotzalco. But on the death of Tezozo-moc, the king of this city-state, his two sons began a fratricidal war – a political situation which the Aztecs are thought to have promoted by their intrigues. Thereupon Maxtla, one of Tezozomoc's sons, engineered the murder of the Aztec ruler Chimalpopoca (1414–28), with the result that war broke out between the former mercenaries and their one-time masters. Nezahualcoyotl ('hungry coyote'), the rightful king of Texcoco, whom his adversary Tezozomoc had exiled, resumed control of Texcoco and readily offered the Aztecs his support. Azcapotzalco was destroyed and the Tepanec tribe lost its supremacy in the Valley. Only Tlacopan, a Tepanec city in the neighbourhood of Azcapotzalco which had allied itself with the Aztecs and Texcoco, survived. For strategic reasons the Aztecs were invited after the victory to become part of a triple alliance which henceforward was to dominate the Valley. This alliance, Texcoco on the eastern shore, Tenochtitlan in the middle of the lake, and Tlaco-pan on the western shore, straddled the whole of the fertile region.

It is said of Itzcoatl (1428–40), who brought about this alliance as much by diplomacy as by military power, that his mother was a concubine and that he had made away with the legitimate heir. Whether or not this slur is historically accurate cannot be proved, never-theless it was he who gave instructions for the old pictographs to be burnt and for the hitherto not altogether creditable history of his tribe to be rewritten in terms more appropriate to the 'chosen people'. 'They kept an account of their history but this was later burnt during the rule of Itzcoatl. The lords of Mexico decreed it. The lords made it known that it was not permissible that our people should see such pictures. Our people would be lost and our city would be destroyed. for these pictures are full of lies.' So runs an old legend. Strengthened by the alliance and at last free from tributary obligations, the Aztecs began to expand.

Itzcoatl did not yet dare to penetrate into the fertile lands of the Gulf coast, but instead moved his troops to the south and south-west where he laid the local inhabitants under

86

Moctezuma II, Xocoyotzin ('the younger'; the glyph is a rebus)

tribute. The concept of a war of conquest as a means of securing *Lebensraum* was unknown to the Aztecs, nor did they wish to incorporate defeated tribes into their 'empire'.

In the development of Mexico, as in that of Peru, a small minority group, through its military and administrative ability, quickly succeeded in subduing large parts of the country. But whereas in Peru the Quechua-speaking Inca dynasty and people encountered at first only the relatively poorly organized Aymara-speaking tribes, and only in the last phase of their history came to grips with the united empire of the Chimu on the north coast, the Aztecs, on the other hand, everywhere found established communities, resembling their own, and with a longer cultural tradition. Consequently, there never existed in Mexico, as there did in Peru, an empire in the true sense of the word. Another reason for this is undoubtedly to be found in religion. Looked at as a whole, Mexican religion gives an impression of unity, but closer examination reveals a situation in which even different quarters of a city might have their own idea of the divine hierarchy. The Toltecs attempted to establish a state religion that supported the secular rulers, but they, too, repeatedly came up against the varying opinions of individual groups. While the members of the Inca dynasty in Peru succeeded in establishing themselves as the legitimate descendants of the sun god, the Aztec rulers were but insignificant subjects of an unpredictable pantheon, insistent in its demand to be 'nourished' by man. In order to keep their gods alive by continual sacrifices, and thus ensure success in war and husbandry, they dissipated their most essential resources. In 1440, Itzcoatl was succeeded on the throne by Moctezuma I (1440–69). Montezuma or Moctezuma is a Spanish corruption of his true name, Motecuhzoma ('wrathful lord'); his second name, Ilhuicamina, means 'he who shoots at the sky'. He began his career by confining himself to limited campaigns. The city of Chalco, on the south shore of the lake, was conquered by the Aztecs after its refusal to supply them with stone for the erection of a large temple at Tenochtitlan. The next operation, against the neighbouring city of Tlatelolco, was a failure, and although its ruler was killed, the city that stood near Tenochtitlan remained independent. 'He who shoots at the sky' then turned his attention to the lines of communication that led to the wealthy eastern coast, advancing with his army to the shores of the Gulf of Mexico.

Totonac communities, as well as Huaxtec settlements further north, were made tributary. To the west, the people of what is now the state of Guerrero learned to fear the Aztec warriors, while to the south Moctezuma I's troops penetrated into La Mixteca Alta. The Aztecs were not invariably capable of holding what they had conquered, and many of the 'conquests' credited to Moctezuma Ilhuicamina and his successors were really re-conquests. One punitive campaign under Moctezuma brought the warriors for a second time to Totonacapan, the country of the Totonacs, on the pretext that Aztec merchants had been murdered in these lands. Official accounts had it that traders from Tenochtitlan and Texcoco had been robbed, waylaid or killed and 'therefore war ensued'. The booty was shared out among the members of the alliance of three cities; two portions each went to Tenochtitlan and Texcoco, while Tlacopan had to be content with only one. In nine chronicles written by natives of the country immediately after the Conquest, there is mention of ninety-five different places either conquered or reconquered by Moctezuma I.

Fourteen years after the establishment of the expansionist triple alliance, its economic consequences began to be felt. A terrible famine descended on the inhabitants of the Valley of Mexico, and particularly on the Aztecs who were very short of land. The famine was the result partly of a prolonged drought and partly of agricultural neglect brought about by continuous warfare. Old records tell of thousands who starved and of countless numbers who had to sell either themselves or their children into slavery with the Totonacs. If we are to credit men's memories, it was then that human sacrifice, hitherto kept within modest limits, assumed abnormal proportions. Thousands of slaves and captives gave their blood to the Aztec gods. Their sacrifice, a blood-bath unexampled in the earlier history of the land, seems to have had the desired effect of instilling new strength into the exhausted gods, for shortly afterwards came the rain. Up to the time of the Spanish conquest the great majority of prisoners of war continued to be sacrificed for religious reasons.[37]

The system of enfeoffing the bravest warriors with conquered territories, begun in the rule of Itzcoatl, was perfected under Moctezuma I. The original agrarian clan order was abolished and from it a new class, the warrior nobility, grew up. When Moctezuma I died in 1469, Axayacatl (1469–81) was chosen as his successor. Of all the Aztec rulers he was the most warlike, almost as though he had foreseen his early death – he died of wounds at the age of thirty. It was Axayacatl who subjugated the neighbouring city of Tlatelolco, that thorn in the side of the Aztecs. In 1473, Aztec nobles assumed the city's leading offices.[38] During his twelve years' reign, Axayacatl was mainly preoccupied with quelling Totonac and Huaxtec revolts on the Gulf coast and with reimposing upon the rebels their obligations to the victors. His attempts at fresh conquests in the north-west came to nothing in the face of the united Tarascan tribes, who had banded together a short time before. For the first time the Aztecs encountered a unified and more powerful people, who put them to ignominious flight. Even in the later course of their history the Aztec rulers never succeeded in conquering any part of the Tarascan dominion, which formed an invincible obstacle to expansion towards the north-west.

Axayacatl was succeeded by his brother Tizoc (1481–86), who is depicted in most chronicles as an incompetent king and a weakling, perhaps because he did not succeed in subjugating new territories. After a short reign, Tizoc is reputed to have been poisoned by

his own followers. From the point of view of the history of art this shadowy personage is commemorated by one of the finest Aztec monuments, the Stone of Tizoc.

His successor, Ahuizotl (1486–1502), who was also a grandson of Itzcoatl, devoted all his energy to restoring the fortunes of an empire whose decline was attributed to Tizoc's weakness. 'Ghostly water beast' as his name reads in translation, was, next to Moctezuma I, the most successful of the Aztec conquerors. In 1487 thousands were sacrificed on the occasion of the consecration of the great temple begun by his predecessors. Ahuizotl and his ally Nezahualpilli ('hungry prince'), ruler of Texcoco, are supposed to have performed this grisly operation in person, tearing out the hearts of twenty thousand prisoners on the steps of the pyramid. (Supposing we assume that each prisoner took one minute to immolate – with the stone implements available it could hardly have been done faster – this means that the two of them would have been occupied without respite for 180 hours, or seven nights and eight whole days, in opening up the thoracic cavities of their victims. While the extent of human sacrifice among the Aztecs must not be underrated, it would be unwise to accept the assertions of Spanish sources uncritically.)

There was little relaxation for the warriors during the seventeen years of Ahuizotl's rule. To the north the rebellious Huaxtecs had to be dealt with; in the south the Aztecs penetrated as far as the border of what is now Guatemala; on the Isthmus of Tehuantepec there was fighting against the Zapotecs; in the south-east Ixtlilxochitl tells of a drive towards the Pacific Ocean. (This chronicler, however, credits the victories to his native city, Texcoco.)

In Tenochtitlan the population rapidly increased for, like every other capital, it constituted a magic attraction to countryfolk. Supplies of fresh water were ensured by the construction of an aqueduct from Chapultepec. At that time Tenochtitlan was without doubt the busiest city in the New World. Valuable cotton reached the market from La Huasteca; the fertile valleys of Oaxaca supplied dyestuffs derived from a small louse; semi-precious stones and precious metals came from Guerrero, beautiful brightly coloured pottery from Cholula; La Mixteca Alta provided artists who worked precious stones and gold; Chiapas on the Pacific coast sent cocoa beans, valued both as a drink and as currency, while from the

Gulf coast fragrant vanilla, feathers of rare birds, and the valuable skins of jaguars, found their way to the capital. Tenochtitlan was the seat of the mightiest dynasty, a place of the most gruesome ritual, and a centre of trade, although it was never the capital of a united empire, as was, say, Cuzco of ancient Peru.

The neighbouring city of Texcoco played a different role. This was a place of culture, of philosophers and scholars, and the home of poets. Here also was the largest library. Nahuatl as spoken in Texcoco was held to be the language at its most elegant. Other peaceful works have preserved its rulers' names for posterity, since it was the great Nezahualcoyotl who divided the lake with a dyke in order to separate the fresh and the salt water. He was also concerned about the multiplicity of gods, and strove to establish a monotheistic religion. Known to his subjects as the 'poet prince', his mournful songs in the midst of all the glitter presaged the approaching end of Indian culture.

It was militaristic Tenochtitlan, rather than learned Texcoco, that left its stamp on early American culture in its last phase. As in Tula centuries before, it was now the peaceful view of life that suffered. The earlier conflict between Tezcatlipoca and Quetzalcoatl was re-enacted in a dispute between the votaries of Huitzilopochtli and the disciples of the philosophic monotheism of Nezahualcoyotl. This conflict, however, was not a physical struggle, since the opinions of one side were eclipsed by the power and prestige of the other. The year 1500, in which the Aztecs assumed political leadership of the alliance, was a decisive one. Tlacopan, the third member of the alliance and very much the junior partner, had to some extent maintained the balance between Tenochtitlan and Texcoco; it now became a satellite of the Aztec capital, its native rulers being replaced by officials from Tenochtitlan. Fifteen years later the Aztecs succeeded in placing one of their own people on the throne of Texcoco also.[39]

In 1502 the successful ruler Ahuizotl met his death by drowning at the height of his fame when a disastrous flood overwhelmed the palace. (Flooding was to remain a perennial problem until Lake Texcoco was finally drained around 1900.) One of his sons, Motecuhzoma Xocoyotzin ('Moctezuma the Younger' or Moctezuma II), inherited the throne. The fate of this ruler (1502–19) is recorded in perhaps the most inglorious page of Aztec history. A codex in the Vatican shows Moctezuma II before his accession to the throne as a warlike and very successful general; however, his subsequent behaviour led to accusations that he was fickle and dilatory. Perhaps it was the reports of great 'water houses' that converted this young warrior into a religious fanatic, since it is hardly conceivable that news of Columbus' caravels, sighted in the Gulf of Honduras in the year of Moctezuma's coronation, had failed to reach the court of Tenochtitlan. As ruler he participated in only one major campaign, leaving all other military operations, of which there were many in the course of his reign, to his brother Cuitlahuac (also his successor; he died of smallpox in 1519).

Moctezuma II will always remain a controversial figure in early American history. Early sources and Mexican poetry provide a background against which his behaviour is perhaps explicable. Thus Sahagún's Aztec informants told of a series of unusual events that were said to have taken place in the years prior to the arrival of the Europeans. Ten years before Cortés set foot on Mexican soil, 'there manifested itself for the first time in the heavens a kind of ominous portent, like a cluster of fire, like a flame of fire, like an aurora that was long visible, and, as it were transfixed the heavens . . . It was seen in the east, rose to its full height at midnight, and only with the coming of the rosy dawn did the sun then thrust it aside'. The second ominous portent in Mexico is described as follows: 'Of itself without having been kindled, the temple of the devil Huitzilopochtli set itself alight. . . .' Other temples were struck by lightning at this time. A comet, too, appeared in the heavens: 'It came from the region of the sunset and went to the region of the [sun]rise.' A wailing woman foretelling disaster was often heard in the night. And when trappers on the lake shore discovered an ashen grey bird in their nets and brought it to their ruler, Moctezuma II interpreted this too as an evil omen. The eighth portent the chronicler describes as: 'people who had two heads but only one body'. In all these out-of-the-way occurrences, the pious monarch discerned a message from his gods.

Men redoubled their efforts to appease the divine wrath. More and more victims were sacrificed to the tribal deity and war god, Huitzilopochtli, who, according to their belief, daily re-enacts his struggle for existence with the underworld. Every morning, having been reborn, he conquers the moon and the stellar gods, and every evening, after his passage through the firmament, he dies and travels through the land of the dead. As one of the dead he makes his way back towards the day, so that on the next morning he can again join battle with the powers of the night. It was the duty of men, the beneficiaries of light and warmth, to provide him with nourishment, and this they did with the most valuable thing they had, their 'jewel water' *(chalchihuatl)*, as they called their blood.

Moctezuma II, whose pomp exceeded that of any of his predecessors, and who was the first to assume the title of *tlacatecuhtli* or 'chief of men', was himself no more than a wretched captive of his people's cosmic religion. Frequently he would withdraw for days at a time for the purposes of fasting and self-mortification. No mortal was permitted to look him in the face.

Bernal Díaz, who saw him almost daily when the Aztec ruler was a prisoner of the Spaniards, writes:

The great Montezuma was about forty years old, of good height, well proportioned, spare and slight, and not very dark, though of the usual Indian complexion. He did not wear his hair long but just over his ears, and he had a short black beard, well-shaped and thin. His face was rather long and cheerful, he had fine eyes, and in his appearance and manner could express geniality or, when necessary, a serious composure. He was very neat and clean, and took a bath every afternoon. He had many women as his mistresses, the daughters of chieftains, but two legitimate wives who were *Caciques* in their own right, and when he had intercourse with any of them it was so secret that only some of his servants knew of it. He was quite free from sodomy.[40] The clothes he wore one day he did not wear again till three or four days later. He had a guard of two hundred chieftains lodged in rooms beside his own, only some of whom were permitted to speak to him. When they entered his presence they were compelled to take off their rich cloaks and put on others of little value. They had to be clean and walk barefoot, with their eyes downcast, for they were not allowed to look him in the face, and as they approached they had to make three obeisances, saying as they did so, 'Lord, my lord, my great lord!' Then, when they had said what they had come to

Plan of the city of Mexico-Tenochtitlan (attributed to Cortés)

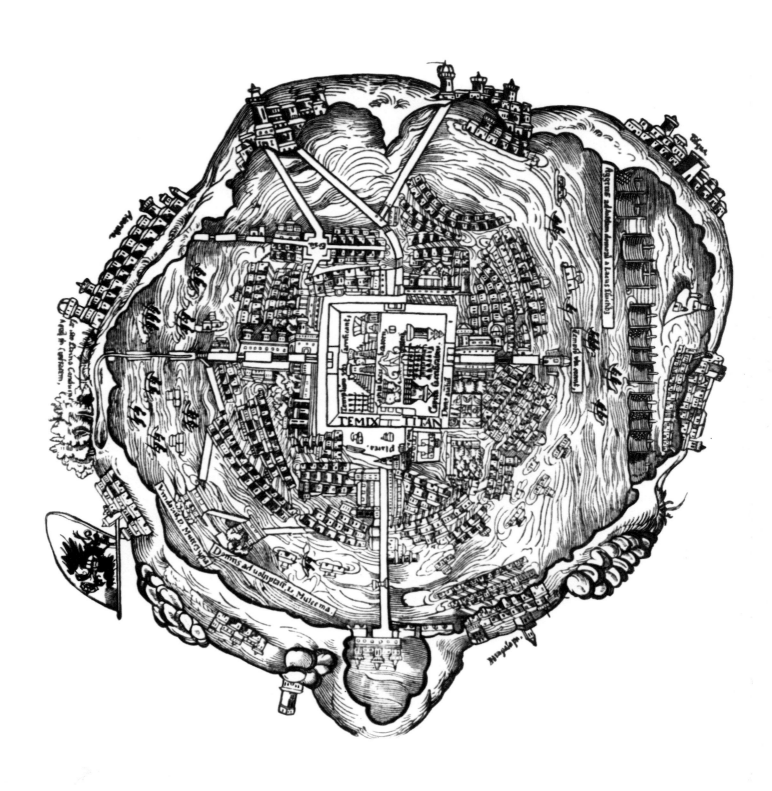

say, he would dismiss them with a few words. They did not turn their backs on him as they went out, but kept their faces towards him and their eyes downcast, only turning round when they had left the room. Another thing I noticed was that when other great chiefs came from distant lands about disputes or on business, they too had to take off their shoes and put on poor cloaks before entering Montezuma's apartments; and they were not allowed to enter the palace immediately but had to linger for a while near the door, since to enter hurriedly was considered disrespectful.

Bernal Díaz devotes many pages to the choice dishes enjoyed by the monarch, and to the ceremonial at his table. The veteran soldier, who did not exchange the sword for the pen until he had attained a great age, tells of the palace library consumed in the holocaust of books, of the arsenal that remained unused, of the apartments with their statues of the gods that fell victims to the wrath of the Spaniards, of the cages of exotic birds and wild animals whose fate he does not record. The Spanish soldier does not forget to mention the beauty of the gardens. His account leaves no doubt as to the splendour evolved by the royal household, which could have vied with the courts of kings and emperors in medieval Europe; nor any doubt as to the personal power of a civilized monarch whose people, only a few generations previously, had been among the poorest and most backward in the country. In Moctezuma's time there took root in Mexico a belief already current for some generations among the Peruvian military aristocracy, namely the myth of the divine origin of secular rulers. The 'chief of men' in Mexico was still the mortal descendant of mortal forbears, but had the Spaniards not appeared, Moctezuma's heirs would perhaps have started to trace their direct lineage back to their tribal gods, as did the Inca dynasty of Peru, who proclaimed themselves the legitimate offspring of the sun god.

Tenochtitlan, the Aztec capital, presents the inevitable question as to how it was possible that a small, swampy island, used as a hiding-place by a persecuted minority, could have grown in so short a time into a metropolis comparable only, in the eyes of its conquerors, with the opulence of Venice. This comparison is instructive and not wholly superficial. Venice, too, was founded by a minority, which had retreated before the Huns to the relatively inaccessible lagoons. But whereas the city of Venice took nearly a thousand years to develop, an analogous process in the New World was completed in less than two centuries. Similar circumstances were at the root of both cities' rise to power and the wealth that came with it. Venice with her fleet commanded a large portion of the Mediterranean, and was thus enabled to achieve a position of monopoly in trade. In Mexico the Aztec warriors overran the country from coast to coast, exacting tribute from those they defeated. They also stationed garrisons at strategically important points in order to protect the trade routes used by their merchants. The army served both the secular and the religious require- ments of the city, providing captives for sacrifice. Indeed, in the Aztec wars the boundary between ritual and economic significance is ill-defined. By reason of its insular position Tenochtitlan, like Venice, constituted an almost impregnable fortress. Undisturbed and in all secrecy, the Aztecs in the New World could assemble their forces for fresh predatory forays, while Venice, in the Old World, enabled her merchants to accumulate their goods without fear of attack by hostile neighbours. A small garrison guarding the three approach

Calendar glyphs,
Codex Laud. Aztec.

Cipactli (Crocodile)	Coatl (Snake)	Atl (Water)	Acatl (Reed)	Ollin (Movement)
Ehecatl (Wind)	Miquiztli (Death)	Itzcuintli (Dog)	Ocelotl (Ocelot)	Tecpatl (Flint)
Calli (House)	Mazatl (Deer)	Ozomatli (Monkey)	Cuauhtli (Eagle)	Quiahuitl (Rain)
Cuetzpallin (Lizard)	Tochtli (Rabbit)	Malinalli (Grass)	Cozcacuauhtli (Vulture)	Xochitl (Flower)

routes was sufficient defence for Tenochtitlan. Not until 1521 did the city fall, when Cortés, pitting against the Aztecs his superior strategic and technological knowledge, was able to approach from the direction of the lake with the aid of boats.

The writings of the conquistadors express indignation at the horrors of human sacrifice, but also admiration of the city's great market-place. Impressed by the abundance of exotic wealth, Cortés wrote to his king, Charles V:

> The city has many squares where markets are held, and trading is carried on. There is one square, twice as large as that of Salamanca, all surrounded by arcades, where there are daily more than sixty thousand souls, buying and selling, and where are found all the kinds of merchandise produced in these countries, including food products, jewels of gold and silver, lead, brass, copper, zinc, stone, bones, shells, and feathers. Stones are sold, hewn and unhewn, adobe bricks, wood, both in the rough and manufactured in various ways. There is a street for game, where they sell every sort of bird, such as turkeys, wild chickens, partridges, quails, wild ducks, flycatchers, widgeons, turtle-doves, pigeons, reed-birds, parrots, owls, eaglets, owlets, falcons, sparrow-hawks and kestrels, and they sell the skins of some of these birds of prey with their feathers, heads, beaks, and claws. They sell rabbits, hares, and small dogs which they castrate, and raise for the purpose of eating. There is a street set apart for the sale of herbs, where can be found every sort of root and medical herb which grows in the country. There are houses like apothecary shops, where prepared medicines are sold, as well as liquids, ointments, and plasters. There are places like our barber's shops. . . . There are houses where they supply food and drink for payment. . . . They sell bees' honey and wax, and honey made of corn stalks, which is as sweet and syrup-like as that of sugar, also honey from a plant called maguey, which is better than most. . . . They also sell skeins of different kinds of spun cotton, in all colours, so that it seems quite like one of the silk markets of Granada, although it is on a greater scale; also as many different colours for painters as can be found in Spain and of as excellent hues. They sell deer skins with all the hair tanned on them, and of different colours, much earthenware, exceedingly good, many sorts of pots, large and small, pitchers, large

tiles, and infinite variety of vases, all of very singular clay, and most of them glazed and painted. They sell maize, both in the grain and made into bread . . . pies of birds, and fish, also much fish, fresh and salted . . . Finally besides those things I have mentioned, they sell in the city markets everything else which is found in the whole country and which, on account of the profusion and number, does not occur to my memory. . . . Each kind of merchandise is sold in its respective street, and they do not mix their kinds of merchandise of any species; thus they preserve perfect order. Everything is sold by a kind of measure, and, until now, we have not seen anything sold by weight. There is in this square a very large building, like a Court of Justice, where there are always ten or twelve persons, sitting as judges, and delivering their decisions upon all cases which arise in the markets. There are other persons in the same square who go about continually among the people, observing what is sold, and the measures used in selling, and they have been seen to break some which were false . . . and considering that these people were barbarous, so cut off from the knowledge of God, and other civilized peoples, it is admirable to see to what they attained in every respect.

The geographical postion of the Aztec city was favourable in many respects. The complex canal system within the island provided a means of transport for men and merchandise that was unparallelled in pre-Hispanic America, where neither wheel nor draught animal was known. However the city must doubtless have owed its exceptionally rapid rise to the balanced distribution of peasants, traders, and warriors, as well as to the adaptability of its inhabitants, always a characteristic of persecuted minorities and exemplified in the Old World by the Jews. Another, more fundamental reason for Tenochtitlan's rapid flowering is to be found in the energy of its leaders who, unlike those of long-settled tribes, were unencumbered by inherited tradition and borrowed no more than what they needed from earlier cultures. The growth of the city and the increase in population soon gave rise to a class structure with its correspondingly differentiated requirements. Religion, as well as a propensity to display, encouraged specialization among artisans and craftsmen, merchants and peasants. In the *Codex Florentino*, Sahagún tells of the hundred different classes, ranging from prostitutes, by way of merchants – about whom the friar writes a whole book – to singers, writers, and scholars.

There can be no doubt that the merchants' peaceful contacts with other tribes were quite as important to this urban culture as were the bloody exploits of the Aztec warriors; but it was the warriors who brought back with them not only new ideas, gods, and treasure, but labour for the construction of many miles of causeways and aqueducts, for the making of the *chinampas,* and for the erection of temples and palaces. Certainly not all of the many thousands of slaves who were brought to the capital as booty can have been sacrificed on the steps of the pyramids. It is known that craftsmen of exceptional ability were compelled to make their unwilling way to Tenochtitlan from La Mixteca Alta and other parts of the land.

The marshy island became a network of geometrically laid out waterways and stretches of land. A length of almost two miles and an area of nearly 2,500 acres – by comparison

Rome's area within the Aurelian wall measured rather under 3,500 acres – represented its extreme limits. Varying estimates by earlier chroniclers put the number of houses at between 60,000 and 120,000. According to Torquemada, from four to ten persons lived in each dwelling. Taking an average of seven people to a house, and a figure half way between the upper and lower estimated totals of houses, we arrive at a population somewhere between 560,000 and 700,000 at the beginning of the sixteenth century. This is the view taken by Jacques Soustelle, although other scholars are inclined to think it exaggerated, for this would mean that Tenochtitlan was by far the largest city in the world. But given only the usual estimate of 300,000 inhabitants we would be hard put to it to find a city of comparable size in medieval Europe.

For a description of the metropolis we must rely on the conquerors' eye-witness accounts, since the old city of Tenochtitlan now lies beneath the present capital, a city of five and a half million people. Scientific excavation on systematic lines, let alone a reconstruction, is therefore out of the question. Yet the accounts we possess give a clearer picture than do the descriptions of many German cities of the Carolingian period. Moctezuma himself took the intruder Cortés by the hand, conducting him and his captains, among them, of course, Bernal Díaz, up the steps of the highest temple in order to show them Tenochtitlan and the surrounding district from the top.

> We saw . . . his great city and all the other cities standing in the water . . . the three causeways . . . the causeway of Iztapalapa by which we had entered four days before, and that of Tacuba [Tlacopan] along which we were afterwards to flee on the night of our great defeat, when the new prince, Cuitlahuac, drove us out of the city, . . . and that of Tepeaquilla.

Cortés wrote in his second report to Charles V:

> From the mainland to the city is a distance of two leagues, from any side from which you enter. It has four approaches by means of artificial causeways, two cavalry lances in width . . . Its streets (I speak of the principal ones) are very broad and straight; some of these, and all the others, are one half land, and the other half water on which they go about in canoes. All the streets have openings at regular intervals, to let the water flow from one to the other, and at all of these openings, some of which are very broad, there are bridges, very large, strong, and well constructed, so that, over many, ten horsemen can ride abreast. . . .
>
> There are many large and handsome houses in this city, and the reason for this is that all the lords of the country, vassals of Montezuma, inhabit their houses in the city a certain part of the year; moreover there are many rich citizens, who likewise have very good houses. Besides having very good and large dwelling places, all these people have very beautiful flower gardens of divers kinds, as well in the upper as in the lower dwellings.
>
> Along one of the causeways which lead to the city, there are two conduits of masonry . . . through one of which a volume of very good fresh water, the bulk of a man's body, flows into the heart of the city . . . The other which is empty brings the water, when they wish to clean the first conduit. . . . At the different entrances to the

city, and wherever the canoes are unloaded, which is where the greatest quantity of provisions enter the city, there are guards, in huts to collect a *certum quid* of everything that comes in. I do not know whether this goes to the sovereign, or to the city. . . .

The people of this city had better manners . . . than those of . . . other . . . cities, for the reason that the sovereign, Montezuma, always resided there . . . so better manners prevailed. . . . I will not say more than that, in the service and manners of its people, their fashion of living was almost the same as in Spain. . . . This great city contains many mosques, or houses for idols, very beautiful edifices situated in the different precincts of it; in the principal ones of which are the religious orders of their sect, for whom, besides the houses in which they keeep their idols, there are very good habitations provided. All these priests dress in black, and never cut or comb their hair from the time they enter the religious order until they leave it; and the sons of all the principal families, both of chiefs as well as noble citizens, are in these religious orders and habits from the age of seven or eight years till they are taken away for the purpose of marriage. This happens more frequently with the first-born. . . . They have no access to women, nor are any allowed to enter the religious houses; they abstain from eating certain dishes, and more so at certain times of the year than at others. Amongst these mosques there is one principal one . . . so large that within its circuit, which is surrounded by a high wall, a village of five hundred houses could easily be built. . . . There are as many as forty very high and well-built towers. . . .

When the Aztecs arrived on the island, 'poor and modest was the house that they raised to Huitzilopochtli. It was also small, for where in this alien place between reeds and rushes could they have found stone and wood for building?' When the Spaniards arrived the principal temple was higher than the cathedral at Seville. It had the shape of a square pyramid. At the very top on a wide platform reached by a broad external flight of steps, stood two temples in the shape of towers constructed of burnished stone and carved boards. 'Figures of idols, like giants', were enthroned there. Each of the two temples was dedicated to a different god; one to Huitzilopochtli, the war god of the Aztecs, the other to the ancient god of vegetation, Tlaloc. Some 120 steps led to this sanctuary. Two high priests, 'equal in standing and honour', formed the supreme authority of the Aztec religious life. This was an embodiment of the dualism permeating the old Indian conception of religion. Huitzilopochtli, the tribal god and warrior, was a survival of the nomads' old hunting gods, while Tlaloc, the fertility god, was a deity of the sedentary cultivators.

In this fast-growing culture, warriors and peasants formed the backbone of church and state. The priests had to remain celibate, not so the warriors. A class of girls (the *auianime*) acted as unpaid companions to the unmarried soldiery. Furthermore, land and riches were the reward for bravery and success. The privilege of wearing distinctive dress, a special place on the occasion of sacred rites, and, not least, the prospect of a better afterlife for those slain on the field of battle, were an attraction to ambitious members of the lower classes, for whom the warrior caste represented the sole means of social betterment outside the priestly profession. The reason for these exceptional favours lay in the numerous wars and the tremendous demands they made on manpower.

With the end of their nomadic existence and the rapid cultural advance during which the Aztecs, within a few generations, passed through several major phases of human development, this people's social structure underwent a fundamental change. When exactly it was that compulsory universal education came about is unknown, but that it did so is, for that period, indeed a truly remarkable fact. Whereas in medieval Europe the schooling of children was an élite prerogative, every child in Aztec society, irrespective of its birth, underwent a formal education. As with the Inca, responsibility for a child's education was assumed by the state, which took great pains to promote its culture and to mould useful citizens

The *Codex Mendoza* gives a graphic illustration of the birth, naming, and education of children. Immediately following its birth the baby was washed and swaddled by the midwife. The day of birth could be either auspicious or inauspicious. On that day the parents interviewed a priest who consulted the *tonalamatl*, the book of fate. If the day was inauspicious the naming, which usually took place on the fourth day, would be postponed. As with Catholics, not only the day of birth, but also the day on which the child received its name, was a ceremonial occasion. On his wife's confinement the father lit a fire in honour of the fire god which was not extinguished until the naming ceremony. Invited guests cast food and pulque on the flames in order that the god might look favourably on the child. If the baby was a boy his father would presently show him toy weapons; if a girl, spindle and weaving equipment would be displayed by the mother.

Great care was taken by the parents on the occasion of the naming ceremony. Boys were customarily named after the day of their birth, Eight Deer, for example, or Thirteen Serpent, or Four Flower. Many boys were given an alternative name, that of a famous ancestor or a venerated animal. Girl's names were usually those of flowers, stars or birds.

Up to about their third year children were breast-fed and carried about on their mother's backs, a custom that has remained unchanged to this day among rural Indians. For the first ten years parents were responsible for their children's education; after weaning the father instructed the sons and the mother took over the daughters. The *Codex Mendoza* gives a precise inventory of food rations for the various age-groups as well as exact information

Body stamp, squirrel. Puebla

about the children's activities. Three year-olds received half a tortilla (maize cake) each day, those between four and five, one, for by then the latter had to carry out minor tasks about the house. The daily ration for children between six and twelve was one and a half tortillas. Girls learnt from their mothers how to manipulate the spindle and to perform all kinds of housework; boys received instruction in fishing and hunting from their fathers.

This account reflects Aztec ideas about child psychology. Education was devoted primarily to practical and domestic subjects, and it would appear that ill-behaved children were not spared punishment. Pictures show parents pricking their children with a maguey spine or making them breathe the foul smoke of a fire. In really bad cases the child was apparently exposed overnight, bound, naked, and alone. These punishments, however, were probably very much the exception; present-day Mexican Indians are so fond of children that such harshness is difficult to imagine. Nevertheless, Aztec education, even of the very young, aimed at preparing them early for all life's unpleasantnesses.

At twelve, the young Aztec received his full ration of two tortillas, and at about fifteen (we have this from the *Codex Mendoza,* but other chroniclers speak of a lower age) he was entrusted by his parents to a state school. Depending on temperament and character, he entered one of two types: the *telpuchcalli,* or house of youth, a sort of elementary school, and the *calmecac,* roughly comparable to the monastic schools of medieval Europe. The *calmecac* was normally open only to the children of the upper classes, though there were exceptions that proved the rule, for we know of high priests who had risen to their office 'without regard to their origin', and who must undoubtedly have learnt in a *calmecac* what was necessary for their functions. By contrast with the secondary schools, which were under the direction of seasoned warriors, education in the monastic schools was very severe and made great claims on the pupils, although it held the promise of high office in church and state.

Even in the school system there is evidence of the dualism that is the stamp of early Mexican religion and its ideology, namely the conflict of Quetzalcoatl and Tezcatlipoca. Children in the *calmecac* were dedicated to Quetzalcoatl, those in the *telpuchcalli* to Tezcatlipoca. The young Mexican was already exposed to this conflicting outlook – on the one hand knowledge and self-discipline, on the other, adventure, war, and power. While strict fasting, self-mortification, and abstinence were essential features of the religious schools, the young warriors of the *telpuchcalli* beguiled themselves after sunset with 'song and dance in the company of young women', the *auianime* who lightened their existence. (Sahagún's indignation at life in a *telpuchcalli* is understandable. 'They do not lead a respectable life, they entertain courtesans, speak wantonly and ironically withal, and express themselves presumptuously and arrogantly.') Again, the educational contrast is explicable in terms of the blend of ancient Mexico's disparate cultural elements. The *calmecac* represented the spiritual heritage of the sedentary Toltecs, whereas the *telpuchcalli* embodied the warlike qualities of the nomads.

The complicated adult social structure resembled a stepped pyramid with many platforms. At the top was the *tlatoani*, 'he who speaks', who had unlimited administrative and judicial powers.[41] We have already heard eye-witness accounts of the Aztec rulers' magnificence during the sixteenth century, so we shall turn our attention to the class of society immediately below them.

At the time of their arrival in the Valley, the Aztecs' social structure was still little different from that of the other nomadic peoples of the continent. The tribe was led by a chief who also held the office of chief priest. The people were divided into different kinship groups or clans, each forming an entity that was both military and economic. The land was the collective property of these groups, allocated by the supreme chief, and could not be disposed of. Even at the height of the Aztec culture, when the nomads had developed into successful builders of cities, the land was still allocated in this way. At the beginning of the sixteenth century, Tenochtitlan consisted of twenty such clans, the correct term for which was *calpulli* ('great house'). The Spaniards incorrectly used the word *barrio* (city quarter) to translate *calpulli*. Four high officials each governed five of the twenty *calpulli*—a quadripartite division recalling that of the Inca empire. These high dignitaries, all of them members of the reigning dynasty, were answerable only to the *tlatoani*. The freely elected leader of each *calpulli* (*calpullec* or *chinancalles*) exercised limited judicial power within his district and represented the interests of the community in regard to the state. Every *calpulli* had its own *capulteotl* or clan god.

The Aztecs' abandonment of the nomadic life, on the one hand, and their increasingly expansionist policy on the other, as well as the multiplicity both of their own gods and of those introduced by subjected tribes, all involved both church and state in an abundance of administrative tasks. Thus the second platform of the social pyramid consisted of senior military officers, high priests, and paid state officials. After Itzcoatl's victory over Azcapotzalco, warriors and state officials who had distinguished themselves were rewarded with land and other worldly goods, as well as exemption from taxes. In contrast to European nobility, heirs were permitted to enter upon their inheritance only after they had satisfied the ruler that they were worthy of it. Such a procedure ensured that only those had any say in politics who, as the recipients of lavish gifts, were committed to the crown, and hence were no longer able to adopt an objective attitude to their ruler. Whereas Itzcoatl and Moctezuma I had still had to take into account the people's representatives, their successors attached increasing importance to an élite enfeoffed by the crown, and in so doing largely disabled popular representation. After this betrayal of the citizens' right to democratic discussion, all decisions affecting war and peace and other important matters of state fell within the province of the ruler and his henchmen. Moctezuma II could say to his advisers, less than a generation later: 'We are doing nothing. My desire is to attack the people of Huexotcingo, our neighbours and deadly enemies.' So, at any rate, Tezozomoc reports (II, 130); and it is not difficult to imagine how soldiers, whose profession was war, would have responded to such a request. The Aztecs were compelled to wage wars because their gods were in continual need of human sacrifice, and also because the whole economic system was dependent on the payment of tribute by other peoples. The state would never have been able to satisfy the demands of the gods, and of the élite, by the export of its goods and produce. The numerous wars which, in the first instance, had served to advance the military and official élite, as well as the power of the crown, were now necessary to support and maintain them.

At the beginning of the sixteenth century the Aztecs had a hereditary aristocracy in their ruling family (Aztec: *tlazopilli* = precious son) and a professional élite (Aztec: *quauhpilli* = son of the eagle, the eagle being the emblem of the most powerful order of warriors). The remaining aristocrats bore the identification *pilli* (son of someone), an exact equivalent of the Spanish *hidalgo*.

In the later phase of the culture the authority of the *calpullec* (head of the *calpulli*) declined very appreciably in contrast to that of the nobility who were favoured by the crown. The *calpullec* could be regarded as a member of the aristocracy only in the broadest sense.

> At the time of the Spanish invasion, the nobility was in a state of transition from a professional élite into a hereditary aristocracy. Its power was very great but in no way comparable with that of the Old World nobility in late antiquity or the late Middle Ages. As yet, it did not possess the greater part of the land; it did not form a self-contained class, and the people still wielded some, if not very much, influence (Friedrich Katz).[42]

There is some disagreement over the extent of the nobility's political influence. The difficulties in forming a clear idea of this élite are due primarily to the old chronicles, for in hardly any other field are there so many contradictions as those we encounter in the descriptions of the nobility. Privileges such as certain forms of dress and jewellery, better constructed houses, preferential education for children, and, by no means least, private property, all indicate a development similar to that in the Old World. Had the process continued for a few more generations, the similarities would, perhaps, have been even more striking.

The merchant venturers *(pochteca)*, who travelled abroad exchanging home goods for foreign produce, formed a separate class. They had their own powers of jurisdiction, their own gods and temples, and lived together in a special quarter of the city. Entry to this class was either hereditary or by permission of the ruler. In addition to their mercantile activities, these much-travelled individuals were entrusted with the task of assessing possibilities for future predatory wars; because of their bravery they were honoured almost as highly as the warriors. In Aztec society they were the only ones of whom it was said that they strove more for riches than for esteem. But when a *pochtecatl* acquired wealth he acquired esteem, and was not infrequently able to marry his daughter into a noble family. Injury, death or robbery suffered by Aztec merchants on foreign soil are a recurrent theme in Mexican history and were, as often as not, the occasion for launching an offensive war. The chronicler

Body stamp, owl.
Valley of Mexico

Sahagún devoted a whole book of the *Codex Florentino* to the merchants. It should also be mentioned that other forms of trade were conducted by the producers, middlemen being otherwise unknown to the Aztecs.

After the merchants came the artisans and craftsmen *(tolteca)*, whose standing was above that of the plebeians. The class owed its existence to the rapid growth of the city, and thus of specialization. It attracted men with special aptitudes who had had their fill of work on the land. Potters, weavers, goldsmiths, featherworkers, sculptors, and painters, whose occupations in earlier cultures had belonged to the sphere of priests and their novices, formed a secular class in the urban metropolis. We shall consider the ethos of the craftsmen later on. As in the case of the merchants, son usually succeeded father in the same calling, although no one was permitted to practise a trade who had not been examined and found competent. Painters, the 'scribes' who executed the pictographic manuscripts, enjoyed exemption from taxes.

Perhaps the most numerous class in the urban population was that of the plebeians *(maceualtin)*. The individual *maceualli* enjoyed all the rights of citizenship, including education, an inalienable share in the land of his *calpulli,* and a voice in the election of the *calpullec;* he was liable for taxes, for labour on public works, and for service in the army, in which promotion was (at least in theory) open to merit.

The villein or landless peasant *(tlalmaitl,* 'hand of the earth') was in a very different position. He was a sharecropper, liable to his landlord for rent (paid in kind) and for domestic service, and to the state for military service. The presence of villeins in Mexico is difficult to explain, for every member of society was entitled to his own piece of arable land under the control of the *calpulli.* Perhaps they were refugees from other tribes, or else the country's aboriginal inhabitants, whom the Aztecs had robbed of their land, but who had been tolerated as day labourers. The *tlalmaitl* was not a citizen in the accepted sense of the word, since he paid no taxes and was not subject to civil or criminal law.

On the lowest social step we find the *tlatlacotin* (singular *tlacotli*), whom the Spaniards, for want of a better word, described shortly as slaves. They were the property of their master, 'but they were treated like his own children', and could not, except in certain cases, be resold

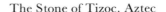

without their own consent. A work-shy *tlacotli*, for example, had to be warned three times that he would be sold. If he was then sold, and subsequently resold twice, the fourth owner had the right to sacrifice him to the gods. Slaves in this category were particularly sought after by the merchants, who, unlike the warriors, had no opportunity to capture prisoners for the altars of the gods. Another alternative was to buy recalcitrant *tlatlacotin* as companions for the dead; the living looked on them as servants of the departed, regardless of their work-shy propensities. Immediately after the death of a highly placed personage, it was the custom to kill a slave to escort him on his way. Further sacrifices took place four or five days later on the occasion of the burial.

By contrast, an industrious slave enjoyed privileges. He could marry a free woman and, even if both parents were slaves, his children were free-born. He was permitted to accumulate private wealth, and even to have his own slaves. Freedom lay in store after the death of his owner, and sometimes came even sooner if the ruler declared an amnesty. (The successful ruler Itzcoatl is said to have been the issue of a union between Acamapichtli and a slave woman.) Another privilege was the opportunity of buying his freedom or of substituting another member of his family. Even for a slave who was being sold because of misconduct there was hope of freedom should he succeed in leaving the market and stepping on human excrement. In this event certain officials cleansed the fugitive and declared him free; his cleansing meant that the besmirched slave had thereby become a 'clean person'. Since anyone who tried to stop a fugitive, apart of course from his owner, was himself made a slave, everyone made way for a fleeing *tlacotli*, thus abetting his bid for freedom. Another possibility was to seek sanctuary in the ruler's palace.

The *tlatlacotin* were not subject to taxation, forced labour or military service. Their lot could have been worse, for they always had a roof above their heads and were not responsible for their own upkeep. 'The owner strictly forbade all members of the family to harm a slave. It is even said that when someone chastises a *tlacotli* he calls down upon himself illness, poverty, and misfortune, and himself deserves to become a slave because he has maltreated a son of Tezcatlipoca, the patron of slaves. . . .' Designated 'slaves' by the Europeans, the *tlatlacotin* had little in common with the slaves of ancient Rome and Islam;

their lot was in no way comparable to the hopeless existence of slaves in Roman society, where life or death was at the whim of their masters.

In spite of frequent manumissions, the numbers of *tlatlacotin* at the beginning of the sixteenth century were still considerable. The many tributary obligations of the conquered lands, as well as the comparatively rapid transition from a nomadic people to a city-state skilled in warfare, brought prosperity to some, poverty to others. To the question of the identity of the *tlatlacotin*, since all were born free, there are a variety of answers.

Captured warriors *(uauntin)* formed a special group; they were not accounted slaves of men, belonging rather to the gods to whom their hearts were sacrificed. The employment of captured members of the warrior class on manual work for the community was evidently regarded as sacrilege against the gods, no doubt also as a serious affront to the warriors themselves, who held it an honour to meet their death by sacrifice. For Europeans, the practice of human sacrifice has always seemed vile and barbaric, but the Mexicans saw it in religious terms as a highly desirable form of death. The victims looked forward to a kind of paradise; like those killed in battle, the sacrificed warriors entered the eastern sky, the seat of the sun god. Each day they accompanied him to his zenith, becoming at noon butterflies or birds and returning to earth where they sipped sweet honey from the flowers. At his zenith the sun god received a new escort, consisting of women who had died in childbirth. On departing from this life, so the Aztecs believed, they were classed with the warriors, and it was their honour to accompany the sun god until the end of the day, when he made his entry into the underworld.

But the *tlatlacotin* were of much inferior standing. They became slaves either through being sold by their families in times of need or else by selling themselves. Sahagún reports that in 1454, the year of famine, whole families of nobles were actually forced to sell themselves to other peoples or city-states. But cases of slave raiding have also been reported. The best known concerns Doña Marina, Cortés' interpreter and lover. Stolen as a child – not, be it noted, in the Aztec sphere of influence – she was sold in the market as a slave and later presented by her owner to Cortés.

The main source of slaves was the institution of penal servitude. Since prisons had no part in the Aztec penal code – in many respects exemplary, and doubtless coloured by the intellectual influence of Texcoco, the neighbouring city – a man found guilty was sentenced to make good the damage he had done. The concept of reparation, whatever shape it might take, was at the root of every punishment imposed upon a wrong-doer. Such restitution was obligatory upon all who had failed to pay their taxes, had been unable to repay their debts or had defaulted on bets lost at a ball game. Thieves and debtors were made to serve as the slaves of those from whom they had stolen or borrowed until such time as they had, by their labours, made good the damage. More serious offences, such as treason, sacrilege and murder, carried the death penalty; but if, for instance, a murdered man's widow forgave the perpetrator, sentence could be commuted to one of slavery for life.

Finally, the carefree life of the *tlatlacotin* also attracted those who disliked responsibilities and obligations or those, such as superannuated courtesans, who saw few prospects of making a living within free society and preferred instead the secure, legally protected existence of the *tlacotli*.

Shortly before the Conquest we find a people at once cultivated and self-controlled, whom, during the fourteenth and fifteenth centuries, we have seen barbaric, unscrupulous, and impulsive. The ideal of the headstrong, brutal warrior gave way to that of the benevolent man of sensibility. This change is unthinkable without the influence of Texcoco, the allied city. In jurisprudence, the arts, architecture, above all in philosophy, great achievements had placed Aztec culture on an equal footing with the great civilizations of the Old World.

> Remember, lord, that henceforth thy foot is on a high ridge, a narrow path, with, on either side, a deep abyss. . . . Be moderate in the exercise of thy power, bare neither tooth nor claw . . . thy people stands in the shadow of thy protection. Thy heart must now acquire the circumspection of old age. Do not deliver thyself up to women. Do not believe, lord, that the mat and the head-band of the kings are there only for pleasure and relaxation; on the contrary they bring only work, sorrow and care.

These and similar injunctions were conveyed to the young Moctezuma by the elders. Besides the ruler, the sons of other highly placed personages were also the objects of wise precepts. Friar Olmos' collected rules of behaviour rather give the impression of an Aztec book of étiquette:

> *Hurl not yourself at women like a dog at his food.*
> *Speak not too hastily, nor become too heated . . .*
> *Adopt measured tones, neither too high nor too deep.*
> *Your mode of expression should be gentle and serene.*
> *If you see or hear something,*
> *especially something that is evil,*
> *take no note of it and hold your peace.*
> *Let not men call you twice, answer directly the first time.*
>
> *Go calmly about the streets,*
> *neither too fast nor too slow . . .*
> *Let not your head sink forward,*
> *nor incline to one side.*

Body stamp. Tenochtitlan

Never stare to right or left,
lest men say: you are foolish,
uneducated, and ill-bred.

At table, be slow and restrained in your eating,
take moderate bites,
avoid a full-stuffed mouth,
and do not swallow food as does a dog.
Do not crumble the cake,
nor bend greedily over your plate,
eat calmly, that others may not laugh at you.

Wash hands and mouth before the meal,
and do the same after eating . . .
Grimace not during the meal,
eat silently and with care . . .
Avoid sucking-noises when drinking,
you are not a little dog. . . .
Cough not and do not spit
and take care
lest you bespatter your neighbour's clothes.

The above and other injunctions, the 'precepts of the elders' *(huehuetlatolli)*, are illustrative of the efforts of these 'parvenus' – as H. D. Disselhoff so appropriately described the Aztecs – to reach a higher cultural level. They reveal to us a culture that grew rapidly and then, while still in its first flowering, unhappily met its end. While good manners, particularly towards strangers and old people, have survived to this day among the rural Indians, the very considerable talents of the anonymous artists and master builders disappeared with the eradication of the native religion. (Throughout the entire continent, there is hardly one original work by an identified Indian artist dating from the Spanish colonial period.

It was not until the present century that a pure-blooded Indian painter from Mexico, Rufino Tamayo, gained an international reputation.)

During the fifteenth and sixteenth centuries, the art of the Aztecs, like their religion, was a jumble of many, often highly contradictory, forms and ideas derived from earlier cultures and from foreign peoples who, at one time or another, whether simultaneously or in succession, had settled on Mexican soil. Thus, there is no pure Aztec art. Under Moctezuma II thirty provinces were made tributary to Tenochtitlan. The captives, merchants, and artists brought not only new ideas and foreign gods but in some cases, too, the ability to translate their metaphysical experience into pictures. In the course of history both the power of rulers and the influence of peoples waxed and waned; power and influence were seldom of long duration. What has survived as 'Aztec art' did not acquire its individual stamp until the years leading up to the Conquest, and even then it is not certain that it was the work of the Aztecs themselves. To the north-west there lived the Matlatzinca and Otomi, who spoke a different language, as well as a number of Nahuatl speaking tribes; in the south-east were the Mixtecs and Zapotecs with their long artistic tradition, and on the Gulf coast the Huaxtecs and Totonacs. Even the tribes in the immediate neighbourhood of the Aztecs, whether subject or independent, remained not only distinct but hostile. Nevertheless it was ambitious Tenochtitlan that was, so to speak, the melting-pot where the various influences combined. Tula would be inconceivable without Teotihuacan, as would Mexico-Tenochtitlan without Tula.

When the Aztecs arrived in the highlands they brought with them exiguous carved figures in volcanic rock, with an archaic aspect undoubtedly related to the Tarascan culture of the north-west. Even the great temple in Tenochtitlan, that was not started until 1483, *pl. 203* was no more than a copy on a larger scale of the Chichimec sanctuary at Tenayuca. For the Aztecs adopted anything they came across. In its main features their art may be traced back to a happy combination of the severely composed patterns of the Toltecs and the formalistic, highly pictorial style of the Mixteca-Puebla region. Other influences, too, such as those of the Totonacs and Huaxtecs were gratefully absorbed. Even the Olmec preference for hard stone seemed to have been reborn.

When speaking of Aztec art, it must never be forgotten that much less of it has survived than of the art of preceding cultures, which lay undisturbed in graves and in abandoned cities. Aztec gold almost invariably found its way to the Spaniards' melting-pots; all but a few of the pictographic manuscripts were consumed by the flames of the Inquisition; time and the damp climate destroyed the rich featherwork and textiles; buildings, mural paintings, and countless sculptures succumbed to the fury of the invaders; and in accordance with the Mexicans' own religious custom, the pottery was destroyed at the end of each cycle of 52 years. Much of the poetry, too, which existed only in oral tradition, fell into oblivion, for the new overlords had different ways of thought.

Surprisingly, art was, with very few exceptions, devoted wholly to religion, in spite of the rise of the Aztec court and its ruling houses and nobility. Statues of the gods embellished the Aztec ruler's palace. The few secular monuments all display religious symbols, an example being the Stone of Tizoc, whose only purpose was to proclaim this ruler's warlike renown. The massive stone is encircled by a relief depicting his victory over fifteen chieftains who are marked with the name glyphs of their cities. This historical monument wholly contradicts early written tradition which fails to credit Tizoc with any of the Aztec military virtues.

If we are to describe the conception and general framework of Aztec art, we could take no better or more eloquent example than the statue, excavated in Mexico City, of the earth goddess Coatlicue. 'Our lady of the serpent skirt', the primeval symbol of the duality of all human existence, is the mother of all things as she is also their destroyer. She embodies the earth that both gives and takes life. As the mother of Huitzilopochtli she confronts the heavens who are the father, the male part. She is the monster that in the evening devours the sun and is delivered of him again in the morning. Coatlicue is in direct antithesis to the god of death and the underworld. This andesite sculpture, eight feet high, represents no earthly being but the embodiment of an idea. The centre, a female torso with pendulous breasts, is still human but is insignificant compared with the surrounding luxuriance of animal, not to say bestial, forms. From the hips downwards the body is concealed by a skirt of entwined serpents. A pectoral ornament in the form of a skull is suspended at the level of the navel from a necklace strung with human hands and hearts. The deformed arms are shaped like the jaws of a snake that is ready to strike, the feet are jaguar paws. The head consists of two interconnected, symmetrically arranged snakes' heads with forked, protruding tongues that merge together. Eduard Seler sees the two snakes' heads as a symbol of two torrents of blood flowing from the goddess's decapitated body. He also refers to another representation, *pl. 207* more conservative in conception, depicting Coatlicue with a skull in place of a head. The curious idea of portraying a decapitated earth goddess he believes to derive from an Aztec ritual whereby, on the occasion of feasts in honour of the goddess, a woman in her image was beheaded and subsequently flayed. Flaying, perhaps on the analogy of a snake renewing *pl. 205* its skin, was the symbol of nature's rejuvenation. The vegetation god Xipe Totec, the god of spring, is always portrayed wearing the skin of a flayed sacrificial victim.

The back of the powerful sculpture of Coatlicue is very similar to the front. From the belt, which appears to be fastened with a skull, depend plaited thongs adorned with snail shells. This is the 'stellar loincloth' of the earth goddesses. The underside of the figure displays in carved relief a deity with outspread arms and legs to which four skulls are attached; the hands contain two infants' heads. Opinions differ as to this figure, which wears a mask similar to that of the rain god. Some see it as a representation of the death god, others as symbolic of a toad, which would undoubtedly relate it to Tlaloc, the rain god. Which explanation is correct is of little significance. The essential thing is that here, and in other monumental sculptures, the artist created something that would never be seen by the beholder. Had he failed to include this essential part of his message, his prayer in stone would have lost its magic powers. Almost nowhere else is the difference between European and Indian art so clearly discernible. It was not the Mexican's concern to please, or to reveal everything to the living; what mattered to him was to translate an idea in its entirety into the reality of visual art (see p. 107).

From the point of view of formal art, this large-scale sculpture is remarkable only because of its monumentality and symmetrical composition. The air of sacred solemnity

Body stamp. Tenochtitlan

conveys the controlled but nevertheless immense strength of the forces of nature. The sculpture conjures up, as it were, all the daemonic and inexplicable forces; it is composed in as fantastic a manner as possible, having recourse to that mysterious yet earthly creature, the snake, as a unifying element. A diagrammatic drawing has been deliberately chosen here, rather than a photograph, in order to show more clearly the many animal and daemonic forms. As Picasso, in his *Guernica*, refrained from endowing war with the attributes of reality, so here the artist has made no attempt to portray the deity as a real being. In his detail the unknown master has observed a meticulous exactitude which, while acknowledging the natural model, reproduces it in stylized form. The work as a whole is transcendental; it belongs to the world of the gods. The only explanation of this fantastic image is to be found in a myth to the effect that on every joint the earth goddess has eyes, and mouths with which she can bite. Sometimes she cries out in the night for human sacrifice, and will not desist, or be fruitful, until men have fulfilled her wish.

> What distinguishes this Aztec masterpiece, Coatlicue, from the Venus de Milo, is not merely the way it is represented but rather the differing concept held by Aztecs and Greeks of the nature of a deity. Because the metaphysical experience which is given form is so wholly other, the works that are created derive artistically from a totally different conception (Paul Westheim).[43]

The classical Greeks discovered the divine proportions in man and adopted him as their ·mean. Their heroes became gods, and as gods they remained heroes, human passions, even human failings being attributed to them. The tragic inevitability of man's fate in the universe was of no more than secondary importance to Greek art and religion, whereas with the Aztecs it permeated their whole thinking. In the Aztec view, man as the servant of the gods could expect little from life. A new-born child was greeted with the words: 'You will learn to know and to taste sorrow, to see misfortune and disgust. Your lot will be one of grief and misery. Where there is pain, where it is wretched.'

A warrior's personal success was certainly desirable, but it was of comparative insignificance. Of primary importance was the service of the gods.

So that the sun can give light to the earth, he must feed on human hearts and drink blood. Hence wars must be waged, for by these alone can blood and hearts be obtained. Since the gods wished this to be so, they created war.[44]

This is the message of an Aztec account of creation. According to the Aztec conception earthly events were only the reflection of heavenly ones. Day after day they saw in the heavens the exemplar for their actions, the perpetual war between stars, moon, and sun.

In Mexico there is no Homer to give a full account of the divine hierarchy. Nevertheless the records of the Franciscan Sahagún help us to identify most of the gods and to isolate in some degree their symbolic content. Both his and other reports have made many of the Aztec statues of the gods, alien as they are, at least partially comprehensible. Such written confirmation is indispensable, for in hardly any other culture, with the exception, perhaps, of India, are religion and art so completely blended. When we wish to speak of major Aztec works, we are compelled each time to refer to their gods. All their religious ideas, their constant desire to achieve a balanced relation between visible and invisible, are comprised in these sculptures of the late period. Besides the dehumanized Coatlicue, the mother of the gods, we find among the major works portraits of the sun god, Tonatiuh, who bears on his back the calendric sign *Nahui Ollin* (4 Motion). He appears to be one of the few gods with the amiable, likeable features of a young warrior. His person is identified with the live-giving sun. By contrast, Xolotl, the god of death, appears in the form of a skeleton. We encounter, too, Tonacatecuhtli, the bearded creator god, in the guise of an old man clothed in a tortoise-shell. Tlaloc's countenance comprises various components: snakes' bodies, human features, and abstract ornamentation. The goddess Itzpapalotl ('obsidian knife butterfly') has a hole in her breast from which protrudes a flower. The sculptors often translated Quetzalcoatl ('feathered serpent') literally into stone, depicting him as an erect snake covered with feathers. In his capacity as the wind god Ehecatl he is depicted life-size and in human form in a statue at Calixtlahuaca; only his mask, in the form of a bird's beak, proclaims him the god who speeds through the air. On the other hand Xochipilli ('flower prince'), *pl. 193* the god of pleasure and music, wears an impenetrable mask that conceals his true face; his body is tattooed with flowers and blossom. His swarthy counterpart is Ixtlilton ('little *pl. 209* black face'), the god of dance wearing nothing but a loincloth, his arms propped on his knees; his is one of the most human forms in the Aztec pantheon.

In many of these Aztec sculptures of the gods the most varied forms blend in a spiritual whole. The sculptor sought the superhuman rather than the human, so that many works became visible images of the powers of nature. Again and again he endeavoured to give expression to imaginary things; thus the poetic often stands immediately next to the brutal, the pure next to the repellent. The Maya culture's esoteric and delicately structured formal language was foreign to the Aztecs whose sculptures are distinguished by the vitality of former barbarians with no tradition of their own to look back on. Virtually all the Aztec masterpieces known to us came into being under the last three independent rulers. By its dynamism, and frequently its monumentality, the sculpture demonstrates its creators' pride, or at least the pride of those who commissioned it, of the 'chosen people', the nourishers of the gods. At the same time it reflects their fear of these same gods.

Painter, *Codex Mendoza*

It was not fortuitous that the Aztecs should have neglected clay, a medium much in favour elsewhere in Mexico. Hard stone was their favourite material, for against this they *pl. 214* could measure their strength. Not even the brittle rock-crystal and obsidian deterred the sculptors who, with their stone implements, fashioned from them the most fantastic sculptures. It is this preference which partly distinguishes them as the cultural heirs of La Venta, for in the intervening fifteen hundred years no other Mexican people had succeeded like the Aztecs in imparting life to stone. Innumerable monuments were produced regardless of time and technical difficulties; many lie buried beneath the present-day capital of the republic. The aesthetic philosophy of the artists is in direct antithesis to the people's fatalistic conception of life.

The artist[45] is an educated man,
skilled is he.
Sensible, resourceful, clever, and reticent;
all these must the good artist be.
The true artist
works with glad heart,
patiently and without haste,
with care he goes about his work,
creates it with skill,
builds it up, devises its shape.
He gives order to his matter,
makes all into a whole
harmoniously.
The bad artist,
careless and sanctimonious is he,
mocks men,
deceives people.
He is a thief.
The mason,

who uses a chisel,
who moves and guides it,
with tenacity, power, and energy,
a mason is he and
a good master builder too.
The true sculptor,
upright, prudent, discreet is he,
temperate and successful.
He has deft hands,
capable are his fingers.
He works in the style of Tula.
He brings and breaks the stone,
chisels and polishes it. . . .
He makes every possible thing,
builds a house,
plans and designs it,
draws the plans,
produces the house. . . .

The foregoing, gleaned by Sahagún from his Aztec informants, shows that there was little distinction between sculptors and master builders. Monumental sculpture and architecture formed a unity: the purpose of one was to enhance the effect of the other. The sculptures sprang from the same feeling for discipline and symmetry as did the temples and pyramids, and complemented their austere architecture. Unfortunately we can no longer experience the portraits of the gods in their context. The broad-planed but nevertheless restive modelling of the Aztec sculptures must have imparted tension to the inert mass of the buildings. Both in Tula and in Tenochtitlan it was from the play of light and shade, the ambiance of many-coloured temples and 'heavenly mountains' (pyramids) that the figures of the gods derived their tremendous expressiveness. This play of light and shade alone emphasized the substantiality and multiplicity of the details, and, too, the emblematic representation of the divine attributes of a strange conceptual world. Brilliant colour combined with the rough texture of volcanic rock enhanced the effect of magic, mystical art. Aztec monumental sculpture is hardly imaginable in marble. Even today, it is still possible to sense this formal strength *pls 199, 201, 204* and to experience something of the unique aesthetic which underlies Aztec temple sculpture.

Besides architectonic sculpture we find many naturalistic creations of rare sensibility *pls 206, 208–9* and great simplicity, depicting men and animals. There is no sign of laughter in the men's faces, which are impassive and contemptuous of pain. The bodies, however, are occasionally shown in action. Here again, the art is a clear expression of the environment and the ideas and customs of the people. In contrast to the menacing attitude of the many realistic carvings of coiled snakes, without doubt a magic symbol, there is the passive fatalism of the Indian. The natural model was simplified in accordance with the subject matter, although important details were not omitted; the snakes' vertebrae, for example, are fashioned in the minutest detail. Thus, curiously enough, these stone animals are alive, whereas the men's faces are

expressionless masks. The explanation for this cannot possibly lie in a lack of sculptural ability; we are forced to suppose that there was a religious prohibition against the depiction in sculpture of everyday or even cheerful subjects. The only exceptions were earthen rattles and children's toys, which could not be regarded as art.

The crisis that came about in Aztec pottery had already begun at the time of the late Teotihuacan culture. Leading up to it was the growth of population in the large centres, and the point of crisis was reached when ceramic art went over to mass production. Hundreds, even thousands, of small votive figurines were produced from the same moulds. Nevertheless, even during the period of urban quantity production, there still appeared articles of the highest quality (although these are rightly attributed to the Mixtecs, or else to strong Mixtec influence). The pottery – vases, plates, bowls, and incense burners – peculiar to this best-known culture of ancient Mexico, is usually decorated with small geometric or plant designs. The delicate brush strokes, and particularly the lack of vigour of the whole decoration, are strongly reminiscent of the ornamentation of Inca pottery. Under the militaristic régime of the Peruvian monarchs and of the Aztec rulers alike, the ceramic skills of preceding cultures languished. Pottery seems to have been the province of part-time craftsmen, not full-time professionals; and urban or military life deprived the occasional artist of leisure and inspiration. The contrast between the decline of pottery and the comparatively high quality of work by professional artists in the fields of sculpture, metal work, and architecture would seem to prove this point.

None of Tenochtitlan's frescoes remains. The few surviving fragments of this period are far outclassed by the marvellous mural paintings of Teotihuacan, and are of little artistic importance. A similar deterioration in quality compared with their Mixtec predecessors is apparent in Aztec pictrographic script. The transition from ideograms to phonograms, where each image represents a syllable, had already started with the Aztecs' use of rebus glyphs for names and places. Further development, was, however, thwarted by the arrival of the Spaniards with their Roman script.

Nahuatl, the language of the Aztecs, is a beautiful, sonorous tongue. By virtue of its grammar and its rich store of verbs the language affords innumerable possibilities for abstract expression. Sometimes a single word will suffice to convey a whole concept which, in translation, could be interpreted only approximately and by the use of several words. It is a language capable of expressing the finest nuances of thought. With only a few minor variations, Nahuatl as the Aztecs spoke it is still the language of nearly half a million Mexican Indians in the highlands and in the valleys of the south. Along with the Quechua of the Inca and the languages of the Maya peoples, Nahuatl was a fully-fledged literary language in pre-Hispanic America.

Historical accounts, hymns to the gods, dirges and war songs, myths, and the art of dialogue were all part of the curriculum in the priestly schools.[46] It was beyond the power of pictographic writing to capture the poetic inspiration of this medium. Well-known works such as those of the poet prince Nezahualcoyotl (1418–72), king of Texcoco, were passed down orally from generation to generation. Although the poems were still remembered by the natives during the first century of colonial rule, no more than a few far-sighted men paid any attention to this valuable cultural heritage, with the consequence that a large part of early Mexican poetry was lost in oblivion. What remains is the material which was set down in Nahuatl, using the Roman alphabet, by Sahagún and a few other scholars.

Even historical accounts and creation legends, that in the literate Old World would have been set down in prose, were, in the New World, put into verse so that they could be learnt more easily. One form of poetic technique consists in the juxtaposition of two distinct terms which tacitly express a third. This method is not unlike the montage technique of the great Russian masters of the silent cinema, who were less concerned with narrative than with the evocation of specific associations by a juxtaposition of shots. 'Grief' is expressed by saying 'sorrow increases, tears run' *(choquitzli moteca ixayotl pixahui)*. 'My hand, my foot' is the figure of speech used to denote 'my body'. Other examples are: 'jade stone, quetzal feathers', meaning 'precious, riches, beauty'; 'his word, his breath', meaning 'his speech'; 'water and hill', meaning 'settlement'; 'spear and lance' or 'water and fire', meaning 'war'; 'mat and stool', meaning 'authority or dignity'; 'clouds and mist', meaning 'the mystery of the unknown'; 'skirt and blouse', meaning 'woman'; 'night and wind', meaning 'unseen gods'; 'flower and song', meaning 'poetry'. Rhythmically arranged repetition enhances the effect of this verse. Much of the pristine beauty was lost after the poetry had been written down: when, that is, it became literature. Nevertheless sufficient of its substance has survived to give us an insight into its spiritual world and to show that the gifts of the Aztec poets were in no way inferior to those of the sculptors.[47]

> *Colours I know,*
> *I mingle the flowers,*
> *Fair as a necklace,*
> *our songs, our singing.*[48]
> *Nought else but flowers*
> *now surrounds us,*
> *nought else but song*
> *beguiles our cares.*[49]

Thus the poets praised the songs they sang 'to delight the princes'.

Dancer, *Codex Borgia*

Who am I
that do forever fly?
now here, now there,
I alight,
the singer of the flowers am I
the butterfly of song.[50]

The tone of optimism in these lines is deceptive. In the songs, many of which are very long, the poet is divided, one of his selves contradicting the other.[51] Grief and melancholy prevail over joy in life. In his dialogue with himself the poet repeatedly turns to the vanity of man's existence. Thus death is never far off in this poetic world of birds, flowers and butterflies. Life is seen as something transient, something merely borrowed.

We shall all fade away,
so be of joyful heart.
I,
Nezahualcoyotl, asked:
on this earth
do we live not in reality
but only in this manner?

And the same poet answers:

Everywhere upon this earth
is woe.
Green precious stones there are,
but they shatter,
gold also splits,
and quetzal feathers break.
Everywhere upon this earth
is woe.[52]

Other poets, too, besides King Nezahualcoyotl, express similar thoughts about the meaning of life.

> *We can only sleep,*
> *only dream,*
> *it is not true, no,*
> *it is not the truth*
> *that we came*
> *to live forever on this earth.*
> *For the grass of spring*
> *our hearts are destined,*
> *they will grow green again,*
> *will open their petals;*
> *for we are as a rose-tree*
> *that blossoms*
> *then withers away.*[53]

Although the poet's vocabulary was far from rich, he was nevertheless able to formulate thoughts and sentiments that belong to man's deepest emotions. Beside *angst* about existence and death, we find gratitude to his gods and love of his rulers. Whoever seeks the poet's private loves and experiences will do so in vain, for poetry, like sculpture, was a sacred art, and, with rare exceptions, was devoted to the service of religion and its earthly representatives. This lyric poetry, if we may use a comparatively modern expression for songs of such an alien and ancient type, tells of might confronted by the inevitable. It speaks with many tongues, and the frequently abstract imagery as well as the apparently contradictory trains of thought endow it with a peculiar charm. To the uninitiated the accumulation of unfamiliar symbols, however, is a hindrance to clear understanding, for everything is indirect and ambiguous, expressed in images aimed at the listeners' senses and evoking his emotions by means of colour and metaphor. It is a poetry permeated as much by the scent of flowers as by the smell of death. Luxuriant blooms at the water's edge, the symbols of fallen warriors in the realm of the rain god, contrast with the dry dust of the battlefield. Admonition and consolation, joy and sorrow, thesis and antithesis, all these alternate in the songs.

The Aztecs were a people of warriors; it is not surprising that war, waged continuously to gain supremacy in the Valley, should have had such an important place in their poetry, where it is recounted with a rousing rhythm. The singers' thoughts take form like sculpture. Nothing is glamourized; the poet merely accepts and describes war as inevitable. The warrior is not an ideal or an example to be emulated, as he is in much Old World literature, but is related above all to the rank and dignity of his caste. Similarly, the status of the chiefs and priests, who were the intermediaries between the divine powers and the people, was not assessed in terms of individual prestige but was the badge of their prescribed, inalienable role in life.

In Aztec poetry war is compared to burnt food, whose pungent smell nevertheless whets the appetite. Death on the battlefield was regarded, not so much as something essentially desirable, but rather as the lesser of two evils, entailing as it did a glimmer of hope.

> *There spreads the thrill of war.*
> *Of the eagle and the jaguar warriors,*
> *some blossom,*
> *others wither away.*
> *How many have perished?*
> *But how many will live on*
> *with thee, o god,*
> *in thy company.*

Some lines later the singer tells of the warriors' preparations:

> *O strike up*
> *your flower-decked skin drums*
> *your flower-decked dancing-rattles.*
> *Hither you have come,*
> *the 'place of flowers' stands ready,*
> *and fair*
> *begins the song.*

A few lines further on the singer discusses war:

> *Across the fields there flares and flickers*
> *the fire of war,*
> *effacing*
> *overnight*
> *honour and renown [of a people],*
> *smothering them in its dust.*
>
> *Yet never will war's flowers wither,*
> *they will spread at the edge of the water.*
> *The brilliant blooms of the jaguar warriors,*
> *those armed with shields,*

Body stamp, numeral 13. Valley of Mexico

will overnight
be laid out in the dust.
Heroes like jaguars
lie fallen,
like raindrops,
scattered over the field.[54]

The Aztec poets did not speak in a void. In order to understand their enormous emotional impact on the masses we must imagine ourselves in the environment where this poetry grew up and had its being: the pyramids thrusting skywards with their temples and steeply rising steps; the awesomely imposing dignitaries in their rich, many-coloured garments; a great throng below, the 'extras' in this divine drama, forming a devout assembly in the squares: all these were the setting. Primeval notes from earthen trumpets and large conch-shells, and the rhythmic, dull beat of wooden gongs and skin-headed drums, accompanied the partly danced, partly acted, recitations of the singers. Poetry became drama, frequently the bloody drama of the rites demanded by the gods. Continued repetition of phonetic and rhythmic word formations, imitative of beasts or daemons (which appear only once in the quotation which follows), acted like a drug on the huge audience. This was not their own language they were hearing but that of their gods. Many of the words – like those in a Catholic Mass – were incomprehensible, but they left a deep impression.

Night.
Dust clouds
and swirls upwards.
Happy is he
the one
'by whom man lives'.
Bright lie the shields
and the scattered flowers.
Terror spreads.

The world quakes,
here,
on the ground, the place
of those dedicated to flowery death.

Where there is war
where it touches the soil
there
swirls the dust,
winding
turning
like a spindle.
He who awaits
a flowery death,
one of the nobles,
o masters,
a true Chichimec.

My heart knows no fear
out on the field of battle,
since I long
for death;
death by a stone knife.
The heart,
like all our hearts,
like mine as well
wants death in war.
Now hear:
out there in the war
I long for death;
death in war
by a stone knife
is my heart's desire.
The swirling dust
surrounds thy feet
o Lord by whom we live.
The eagle and the jaguar are thine,
and thine is the fire of war,
the glowing fire
of the nobles.

Let us now rejoice,
You, our friends.
Enjoy your pleasures,

Body stamp, numeral 13. Valley of Mexico

you nobles,
the place of battle awaits you.
Take the flower-decked shields,
kindle
the torch of war.[54]

The ceremonial splendour that accompanied the songs of war and heroism was surpassed by the ceremonies in honour of the vegetation and tribal deities; The rhythm of the supplicatory songs and hymns to the gods resembled human heart-beats; it began quietly, gradually growing louder and quicker until it excluded everything else. The late winter ceremony in honour of the vegetation god Xipe Totec ('our lord, the flayed one'), fell shortly before the sowing. This was *Tlacaxipeualiztli*, the feast of the 'boning of men'. Prisoners were tied to a wooden scaffold with their arms outstretched and were killed with spears. (According to Eduard Seler their blood falling to the ground symbolized the fertilization of the earth). Next the priest put on the flayed victim's skin, so displaying before the people the earth's new garment. The following invocation to the 'defeater of winter' concerns this ceremony:

Thou, drinker of the night
why dost thou stay to be asked?
Put on thy mask,
draw on the golden garment,
place it upon thee.

O my god,
thy precious stone water [blood]
has flowed
and
the great cypresses
have become
a quetzal.

The fire serpent
has given way to the quetzal-feathered serpent.
The fire serpent
at last has set me free.
Perhaps it will vanish,
perhaps
it will not reappear,
and I,
the young corn plant,
shall
not perhaps
have to perish.

As green precious stone
is my heart.
As gold
I have yet to see it.
And it will be good
if my end
will be such
when it ripens,
when the chieftain of war
is born
[as I can proclaim.]

O my god,
let some ripen,
let there be overabundance.
Men look toward thy mountain,
men look to thee,
and all beseech thee.
And happy
I shall be
when something ripens,
[when I can proclaim,]
the chieftain of war is born.[55]

Another hymn is dedicated to the goddess Tlazolteotl. As the earth deity she was held to have a great influence on the growth of plants, and the following is a song that was sung every eighth year on the occasion of the ceremony of 'eating the unseasoned bread':[56]

The flower, my heart, has opened,
[and] he, the lord of midnight [is there],
Oya, ovayaya.
Our mother is come,

the goddess, she has come,
Tlazolteotl, oya ovayaya.

The corn god is born
in the house of the descent,
in the place where the flowers blow,
he who is called One Flower.
Oya, ovayaya.

The corn god is born
in the land of mist and rain,
where live the unborn children,
where fish of jade are caught.
Oya, ovayaya.

Day breaks, the darkness pales,
the Quechol birds [taste] the flowers,
in the land where the flowers bloom.
Oya, ovayaya.[57]

Perhaps it was only the poets who foresaw the disaster of the Conquest. The *cantos tristes* express, indeed endorse and promote, a fatalism that must have drawn this people of warriors and peasants compulsively into the hands of their destroyers who, in different circumstances, might not necessarily have acted like butchers. Better than any other sources, the 'sad songs' explain Moctezuma's irresolution in the face of a handful of Spaniards, and it is the mentality of this civilization, rather than the conquistadors' annals, that makes its eventual fall easier to understand.

With tears and flowers of grief
I, the poet,
compose my song.
I think
of those
who broken and shattered lie
in the realm of the dead.

They came,
lords and rulers
to be on earth.
Like limp quetzal feathers,
like shattered precious stone,
now do the nobles grow pale. . . .[58]

We do not know whether these songs are the work of the same poets who composed the rousing martial and liturgical poetry; but it would seem most improbable, since here even death in war, 'flowery death', arouses no enthusiasm. All is resignation, suffering as a way

of life. In the *cantos tristes*, of which a comparatively large number survive, we see another side of this gifted people who have so often been execrated and dismissed as barbarians by Europeans on account of their bloody sacrifices. Their love of beauty and affection for nature, as well as their unfortunate fatalism that was so often a bar to progress, live on in the revolutionary and folk songs of the modern republic.

Like the goldsmiths, featherworkers, sculptors and architects who belonged to this society, the poets, too, were specialists. In Moctezuma II's time the place of assembly for all the professional dancers and singers of Tenochtitlan and her sister city, Tlatelolco, was the 'house of the cloud serpent' in the ruler's palace. There they awaited their masters' instructions; and in this hierarchical society there can be no doubt that, should they strike up a song, it would not be out of tune with the views of their rulers and patrons.

> *Like quetzal feathers,*
> *like jade stone,*
> *so is a fair song dear to me,*
> *and its flowers precious.*
> *You, nobles,*
> *you, young brothers,*
> *be joyful,*
> *since no man*
> *will dwell forever on this earth.*
>
> *I, too,*
> *will with my lovely*
> *songs and flowers*
> *pass away.*
> *Think of it,*
> *you nobles,*
> *young brothers.*

I weep
and strew the flowers.
Thou, like me,
wilt go away
to the land of riddles,
and I shall take my flowers.
So be happy now
that thou livest
and hearest my song.

I, the singer,
I must weep.
Never will it be
a song of a land of pleasure,
for the pretty flowers will be borne
to the land of the dead.
Thither
have they turned.

To be wound
in the shroud of the dead,
that is the fortune
that blossoms for you,
you nobles.
Never will my song
come easily to me.[59]

A language so fully evolved certainly could not have come into being in a short space of time. Like the visual arts, Aztec poetry must without doubt have been based on earlier cultures.

Prophetic to a degree unknown to us in any other bygone culture, Aztec poetry forecast the ominous events to come. On 8 November 1519 the Spaniards entered Tenochtitlan as gods and were treated as friends; on 30 June 1520, the *noche triste*, they were driven like devils from the city. But the riches that the conquerors had seen gave them no peace. Reinforced by fresh troops and by auxiliaries from tribes hostile to the Aztecs, and aided by their technical superiority, they began the siege of the Aztec capital. Cortés writes of the seventy-five days (Bernal Díaz speaks of ninety-three) that elapsed before the young Aztec ruler Cuauhtemoc was captured. Cortés' promise not to hold the latter's courage against him and to permit him to remain on the throne was more in keeping with the *cortesía* of the time than it was with the historical circumstances, for a few years later the conqueror of Mexico used the flimsiest of pretexts to hang the last Aztec ruler. After her husband's death, Cuauhtemoc's young and pretty wife, Moctezuma's youngest sister, gave her hand in marriage to three Spanish noblemen in succession.[60] Thus the reviled blood of the Aztecs became mingled with that of some of Spain's most distinguished families.

Body stamp, skulls and
spear points. Tenochtitlan

But to return to Tenochtitlan. With the capture of the highest Indian dignitary on
13 August 1521 the people's resistance was broken. A great silence descended on the once
magnificent city.

The spears lie broken on the streets.
Our hair is torn.
Gone are the roofs of our houses,
*   their walls red with blood.*
Worms crawl across the streets and squares,
*   brains cling to walls.*
Red are the waters,
*   lurid as tan-bark,*
*   and when we drink*
*   the water tastes of tears.*

We beat upon the walls of clay,
*   our heritage a much-rent net.*
The shields
*   could give us no safety.*
Roots have we eaten,
*   chewed water-weed.*
With dust and rubble
*   we stilled our hunger,*
*   with lizards, rats, and worms.*
If we saw meat
*   we ate it almost raw,*
*   seized it impatiently,*
*   swallowed it.*

Gold, jade, precious raiment,
quetzal feathers,
everything once of value
has become nothing.[61]

Thus a nameless Indian poet described the plight of those besieged. Bernal Díaz, who boasted of having taken part in 119 battles in the New World, tells how conditions in the city were so bad that after its capture they returned to their camp. In his unmistakable manner he describes the scene:

> Now to speak of the dead bodies and heads that were in the houses where Guatemoc [Cuauhtemoc] had taken refuge. I solemnly swear that all the houses and stockades in the lake were full of heads and corpses. I do not know how to describe it but it was the same in the streets and courts of Tlatelolco. We could not walk without treading on the bodies and heads of dead Indians. I have read about the destruction of Jerusalem, but I do not think the mortality was greater there than here... where most of the warriors who had crowded in from all the provinces and subject towns had died. As I have said, the dry land and the stockades were piled with corpses ... even Cortés was ill from the odours which assailed his nostrils. ... [Because of the conditions Cuauhtemoc asked Cortés for permission to evacuate the city's survivors.] For three whole days and nights they never ceased streaming out and all three causeways were crowded with men, women, and children so thin, sallow, dirty, and stinking that it was pitiful to see them. Once the city was free from them Cortés went out to inspect it. We found the houses full of corpses. ... The city looked as if it had been ploughed up. The roots of any edible greenery had been dug out, boiled, and eaten, and they had even cooked the bark of some of the trees. There was no fresh water to be found; all of it was brackish. I must also remark that the Mexicans did not eat the flesh of their own people, only that of our men and our Tlascalan allies whom they had captured. ... In truth few people on this earth can have suffered such hunger and thirst or have been exposed to such misery by war.

The inhuman story of the destruction of the Aztec capital, and with it the flourishing cultures of Mexico, has an all too human ending.

> After the banquet [a consignment of pigs and wine had arrived from overseas], when they had cleared away the tables, such ladies as were present went out to dance with the gallants who were weighted with their cotton armour and it seemed to me to be a thing to be laughed at. They were ladies whom I will not here describe for there were no others in camp. ... There was much disorder, and it would have been better not to have given that banquet on account of many things which happened at it which were not creditable. ...

3

4

5

6

7

8

7 Vessel in the form of an owl. Tlatilco
8 Vessel in the form of a bird. Tlatilco style
9 Part of the pyramid of Cuicuilco

9

10

11

12

10 Clay fragment of a female figure. Malinalco
11 Female figure. Aguascalientes
12 Statuettes of 'dancing girls'. Tlatilco
13 Fragment of a Preclassic figure. Morelos
14 Miniature mask. Tlatilco
15 Vessel in the form of a fat man. Tlatilco
16 Large hollow figure of a baby. Tlatilco
17 Small jadeite head. Tenango del Valle, La Venta culture

13

14 15

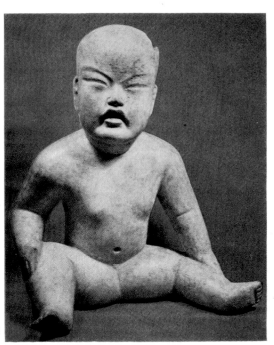

16 17

18 Jade standing figure. Ocozocoautla, La Venta culture
19 Basalt colossal head. La Venta
20 Fragment of figure in dark green stone. La Venta culture

19 20

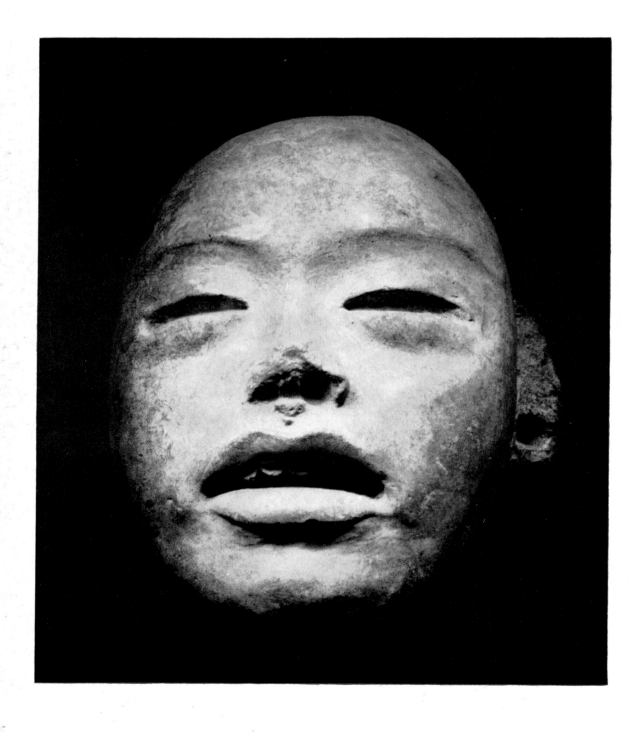

23

23 Stone with relief of a messenger. La Venta
24 'Altar B' with relief of priests and dwarfish figures. La Venta
25 'Altar' with relief of warriors. Tazumal, El Salvador, La Venta culture

24

25

26

26 Figure of a kneeling man. Honduras, La Venta culture
27 Fragment of jade plaque. Olinala, La Venta culture
28 Ceremonial axe. La Mixteca Alta, La Venta culture

27

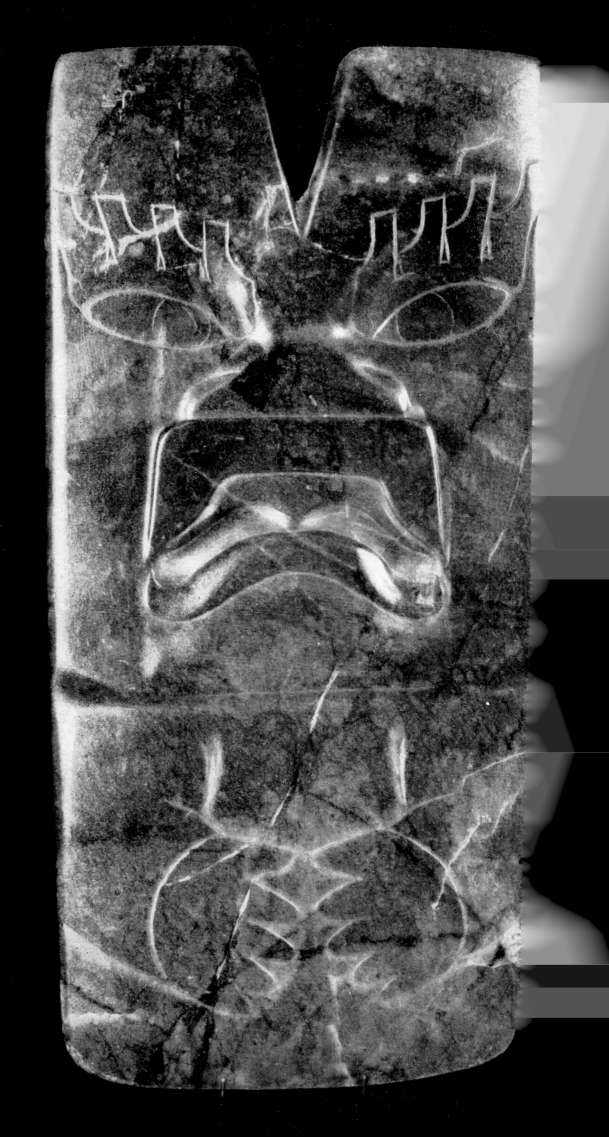

28

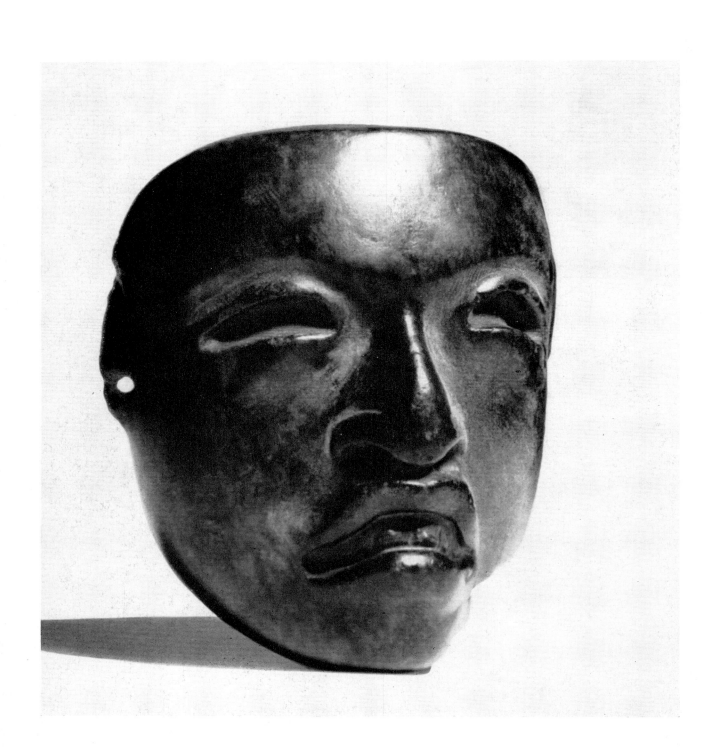

29 Mask. Southern Vera Cruz, La Venta culture
30 Jade figure of a standing man holding a child. Gulf coast, La Venta culture
31 Seated figure of corpulent dwarf or child. La Venta culture

29 30   31

32

32 Figure of kneeling man, back view. La Venta culture

33 Front view of the same sculpture

33

39   Standing female figure. Chupicuaro
40   Relief of priest or warrior. La Venta

39

40

41 Seated figure of hunchback. North-west coast culture
42 Mother and child. North-west coast culture

41

42

47 Seated female figure.
North-west coast culture

48 Figure of a warrior.
North-west coast culture

49

50

54   Incense-burner in the form of a
daemon. North-west coast culture
55   Vessel in the form of a seated
man. North-west coast culture

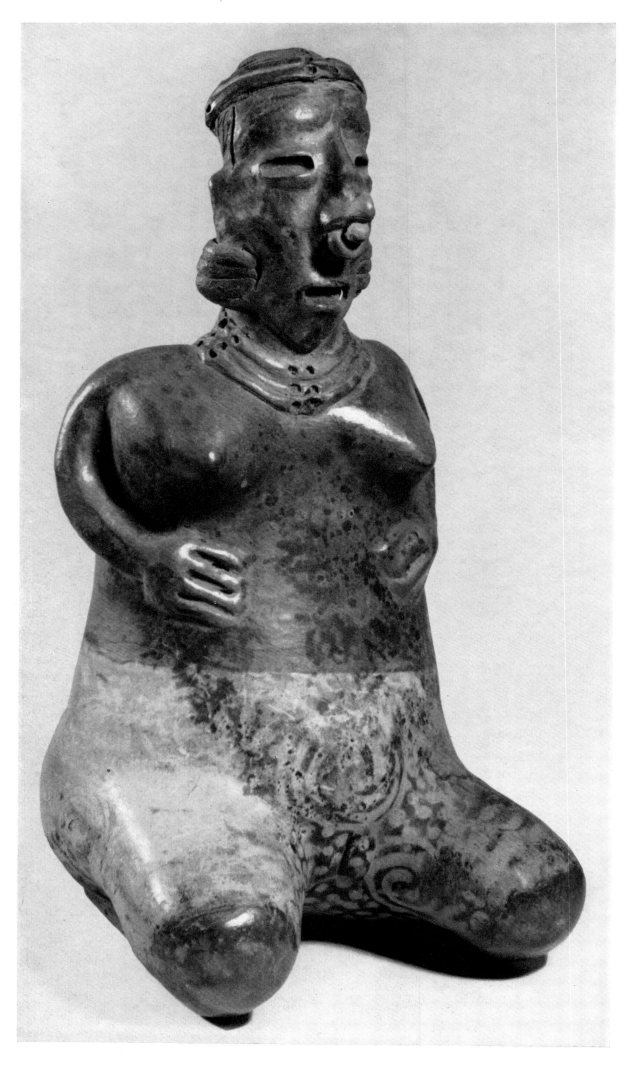

56 Figure of a kneeling
woman.
North-west coast culture

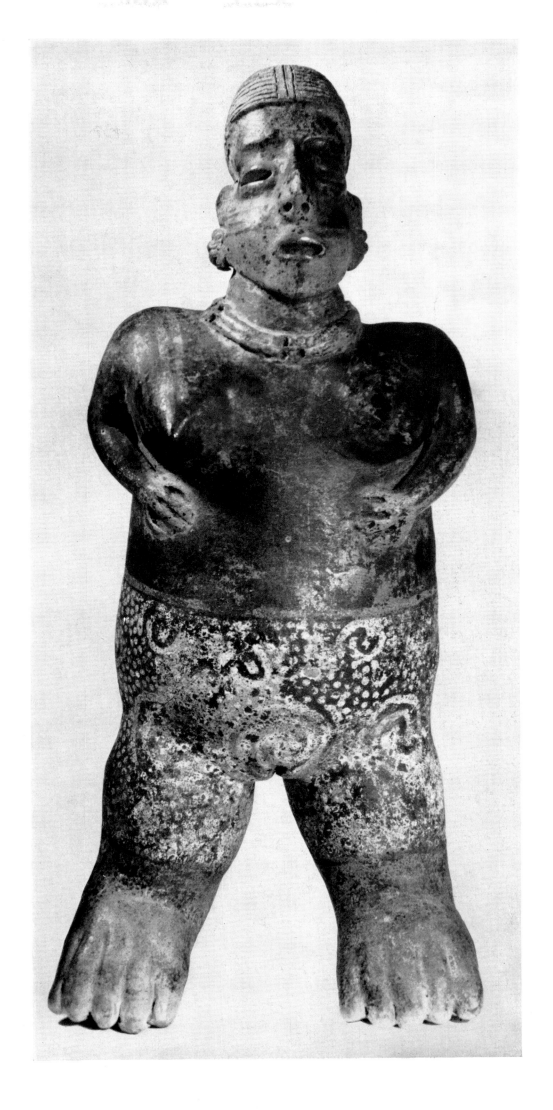

57 Standing female figure.
North-west coast culture

60 Group of people eating. North-west coast
culture

61

60

61 Figure of a warrior. North-west coast culture

62

63   Figure of a hunchbacked child. North-west coast culture

64 Seated figure with bone rattle. North-west coast culture

65

66

68 Mother and child. North-west coast culture
69 Seated figure of a woman. North-west coast culture

74 75

74 Vessel in the form of
a dog scratching itself.
North-west coast culture

75 Vessel in the form of a dog
wearing a human mask.
North-west coast culture

76 Vessel in the form of a sleeping
dog. North-west coast culture

77 Vessel in the form of a dog lying
on its back. North-west coast culture

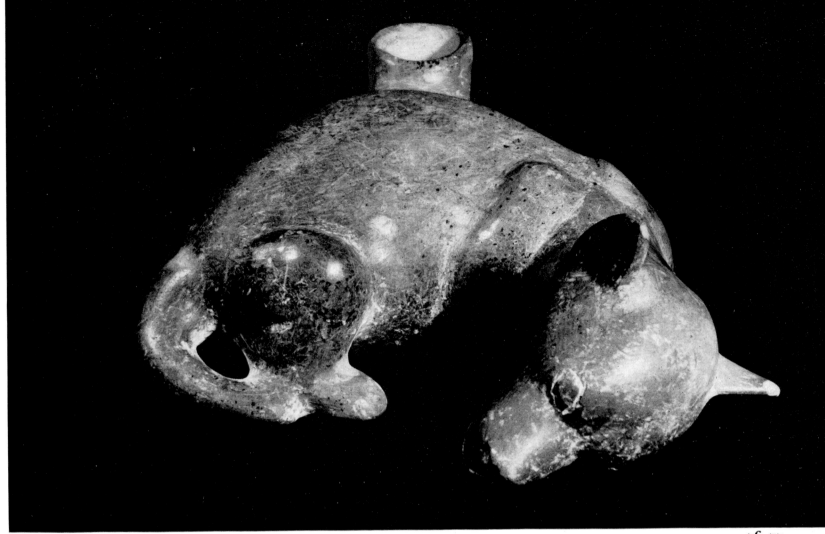

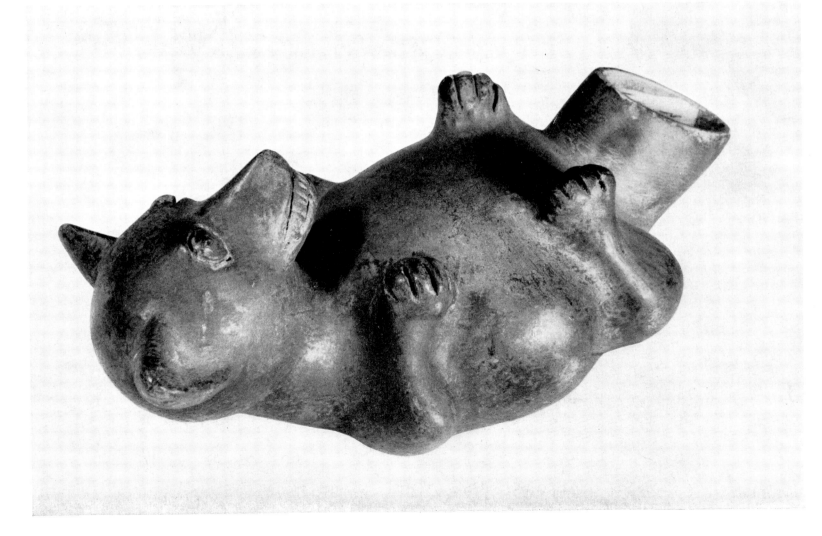

80 Pyramid of the Sun. Teotihuacan
81 Pyramid of the Moon seen from the Pyramid of the Sun. Teotihuacan
82 Detail of west façade, Temple of Quetzalcoatl. Teotihuacan

83 Figure of Xiuhtecuhtli, the
fire god. Teotihuacan culture

83 84

84 Seated figure, probably depicting
the fire god. Teotihuacan culture

85

85   Mural painting depicting a priest. Tepantitla, Teotihuacan

86 Standing figure. Teotihuacan culture   87 Fragment of head. Ahuizotla, Valley of Mexico, Teotihuacan culture

87 88 89

88   Standing figure. Teotihuacan culture
89   Standing figure. Teotihuacan culture

90–92   Three masks. Valley of
Mexico, Teotihuacan culture

90 91 92 93

93   Mask. Guerrero(?), Teotihuacan culture
94   Seated tend standing figures. Valley
of Mexico, Teotihuacan culture
95   Figures of dancers. Teotihuacan

96 Tripod vessel. Valley of Mexico, Teotihuacan culture
97 Tripod vessel with lid. Xolalpan, San Francisco Mazapan,
Teotihuacan culture
98 Mother and child. Teotihuacan

99

100

101

102 Battleaxe in the form of a stylized human figure.
Guerrero, Mescala style

103 Ceremonial axe in the form of a seated figure.
Guerrero, Mescala style

104 Mask with mosaic inlay. Guerrero(?), Teotihuacan culture

102

103

104

107 108

107   Vessel in the form of a head. Valley of Oaxaca, Monte Alban I culture
108   Drinking vessel with incised jaguar's head. Monte Alban I culture

125
126

124

122 123

116

117

118

119

114

112 Urn depicting a musician. San Pedro Martin, Monte Alban III culture
113 Fragment of an altar. Monte Alban IV
114 Stela depicting a speaking priest. Monte Alban IIIb

112

113

109

109 Standing figure with hands pressed against chest. Monte Alban I culture
110 *Danzante*, grotesque figure. Monte Alban I
111 Court of the *Danzantes*. Monte Alban

125 Building of the Columns, Mitla.
Monte Alban V culture
126 Monte Alban, the sacred mountain
of the Zapotecs
127 Jade ornamental pendant. Silacayoapan,
Mixtec culture(?)
128 Gold ornamental pendant. Monte Alban,
Mixtec culture

127

128

129   Bone comb with carved figure. Monte Alban, Mixtec culture

130   Bone flute. Mitla region, Mixtec culture

131   Bone relief. Monte Alban, Mixtec culture

132   Two kneeling warriors, carved from a jaguar bone.
         Monte Alban, Mixtec culture

133   Gold pectoral ornament depicting the death god, Mictlantecuhtli.
         Monte Alban. Mixtec culture

134   Gold mask of the god of spring, Xipe Totec. Monte Alban, Mixtec culture

135   Necklace of gold beads, shell and turquoise. Monte Alban, Mixtec culture

129

130

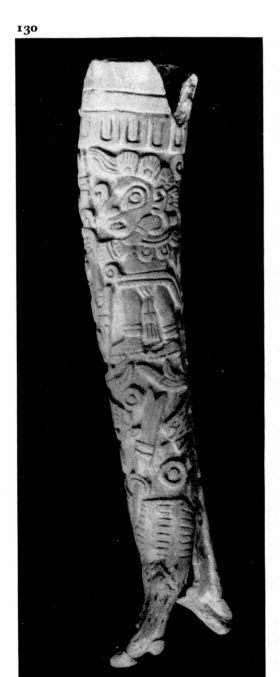

131

132

133

134

135

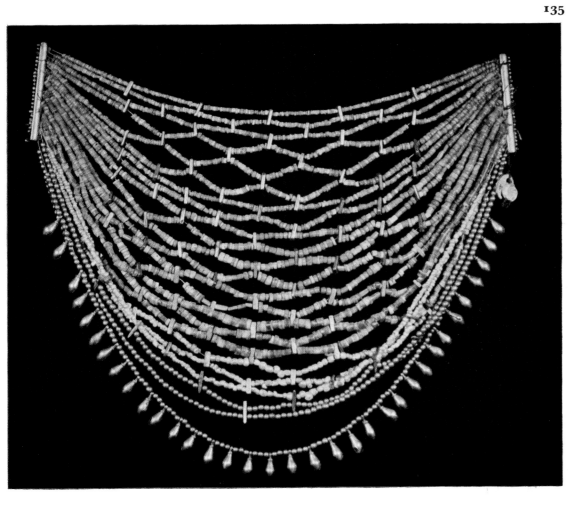

136

136 *Teponaztli*. Mixtec culture
137 *Teponaztli* inlaid with mother-of-pearl and pyrite. Tlaxcala, Mixteca-Puebla culture
138–142 Gold rings and ornamental pendants. Oaxaca, Mixtec culture

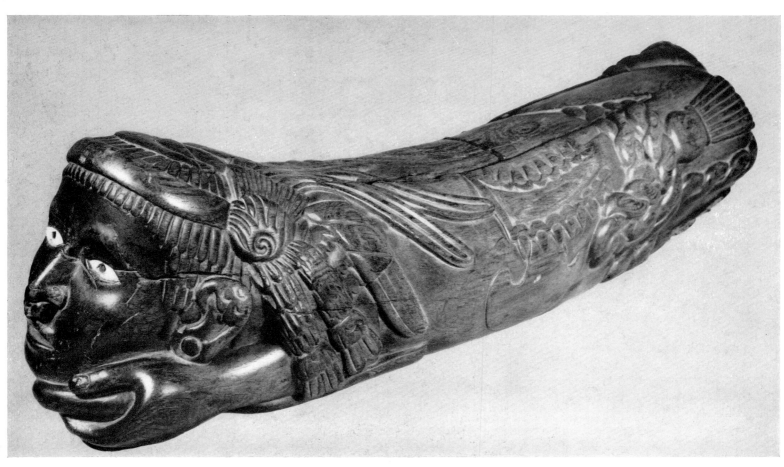

137

138

139

140

141

142

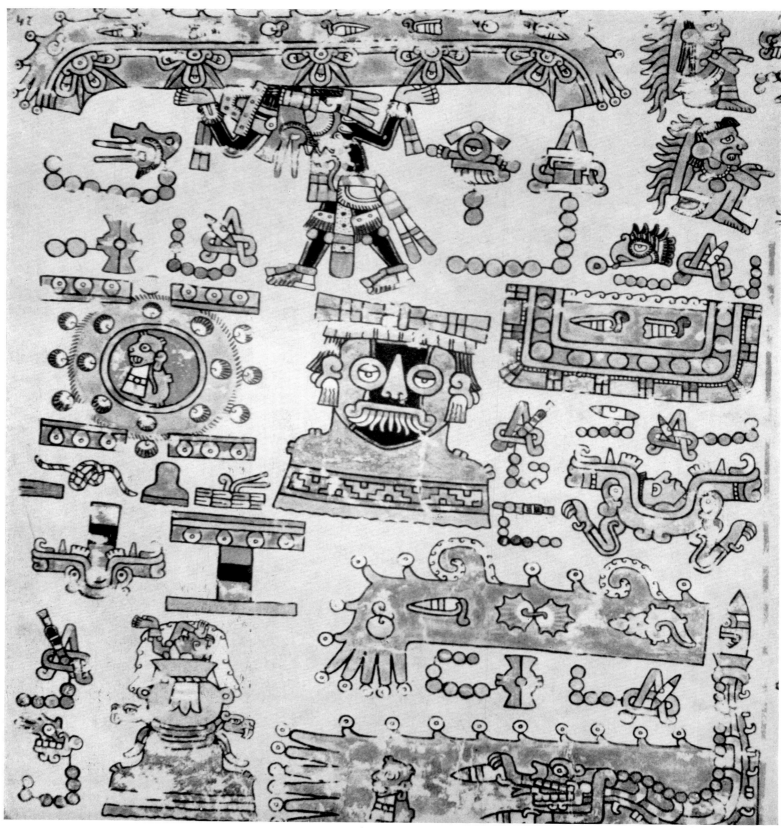

143

143   Page 47 of the *Codex Vindobonensis Mexicanus 1*. Mixtec culture
144   Small figure of the god Xolotl in a dog mask. Mixtec culture
145   Polychrome stirrup-spouted vessel. Mixteca-Puebla culture
146   Polychrome tripod vessel. Nochistlan, Mixtec culture

149 *Palma* in the form of a sacrificial
victim. Coatepec, El Tajin culture
150 *Palma* in the form of a fish's
head. El Tajin culture

151 *Palma* showing a split face, half alive, half dead. El Tajin culture
152 Split face, half alive, half dead. Oaxaca, Monte Alban culture

153 Fragment of *yugo*. El Tajin culture
154 Prone figure. El Tajin culture

155-156 Side and front views of a *yugo*. El Tajin culture
157 *Hacha* with a human figure. El Tajin culture

158

159

160

161

162

158   Standing, smiling figure of the *cabezas sonrientes*
type. Tierra Blanca, El Tajin culture
159   Fragment of head. El Tajin culture
160   Standing human figure. El Tajin culture
161   *Hacha* representing human head. Central Gulf
coast, El Tajin culture
162   *Hacha* representing human head. Grey stone.
Tesecheacan, Vera Cruz. El Tajin culture

163   Human head. Las Remojadas, Vera Cruz, El Tajin culture

164   Human head, fragment of figure. Ignacio de la Llave region, El Tajin culture

165 166 167 168

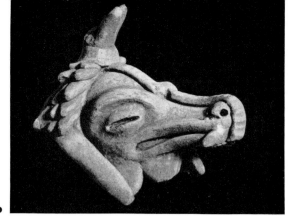

169 170

171 172

173

174

166–175　Ten clay fragments.
El Tajin culture

175

176–177 Two reliefs on the southern ball court, El Tajin
178 Standing figure. El Tajin culture

179–180 Front and back views of a standing figure (Quetzalcoatl?)
San Vincente Tancuayalab, Huaxtec culture

181 Shell pendant with mythological scenes.
Near city of Vera Cruz, Huaxtec culture

182   Figure of a man with the face of a jaguar, grasping a serpent. Huaxtec culture

183 Vessel in the form of a stylized temple. Azcapotzalco
184 Cylinder-shaped vase depicting highly stylized priests or warriors.
Huaxtec culture

185 *Chacmool*. Tula, Hidalgo, Toltec culture
186 Atlantean figure. Tula, Hidalgo, Toltec culture

187, 190   Platform of the pyramid of Xochicalco (Morelos). Full view and detail. Toltec culture (?)
188–189   Adobe frieze. Tula, Hidalgo, Toltec culture

187 188

189 190

193   Figure of Xochipilli, god of the dance
and music. Tamanalco, Aztec culture
194   Circular shield with feather mosaic
design. Aztec culture

195

196

195 Calendar Stone. Tenochtitlan (Mexico City), Aztec culture
196 Circular sacrificial stone. Tenochtitlan (Mexico City), Aztec culture
197 Figure of Coatlicue, goddess of earth and death. Aztec culture
198 *Chacmool*. Toltec culture

197

198

199   Model of the Temple of the Sun, Tenochtitlan.
Tenochtitlan (Mexico City), Aztec culture
200   Pyramid, Tepanzolco. Aztec culture

199
200

201 Model of the Temple of the Sun,
Tenochtitlan, detail of the back.
Tenochtitlan (Mexico City), Aztec culture
202 Round pyramid, Calixtlahuaca.
Aztec culture

201
202

203

204

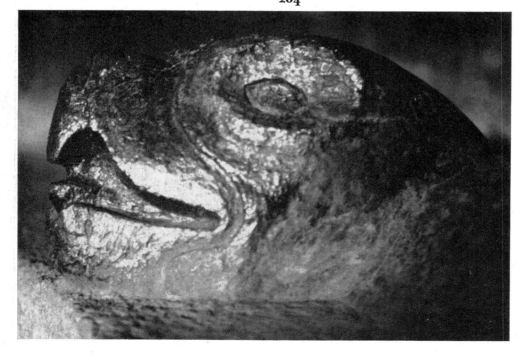

205

206   Detail of unfinished sculpture.
Aztec culture

207 Figure of Coatlicue, goddess of earth
and death. Cozcatlan, Aztec culture

208　Figure of a squatting man. Aztec culture

209 Figure of the god Ixtlilton. Aztec culture

210 Male head, inlaid with shell and pyrite. Tenochtitlan (Mexico City), Aztec culture
211 The earth goddess Tlazolteotl giving birth to the maize god. Aztec culture

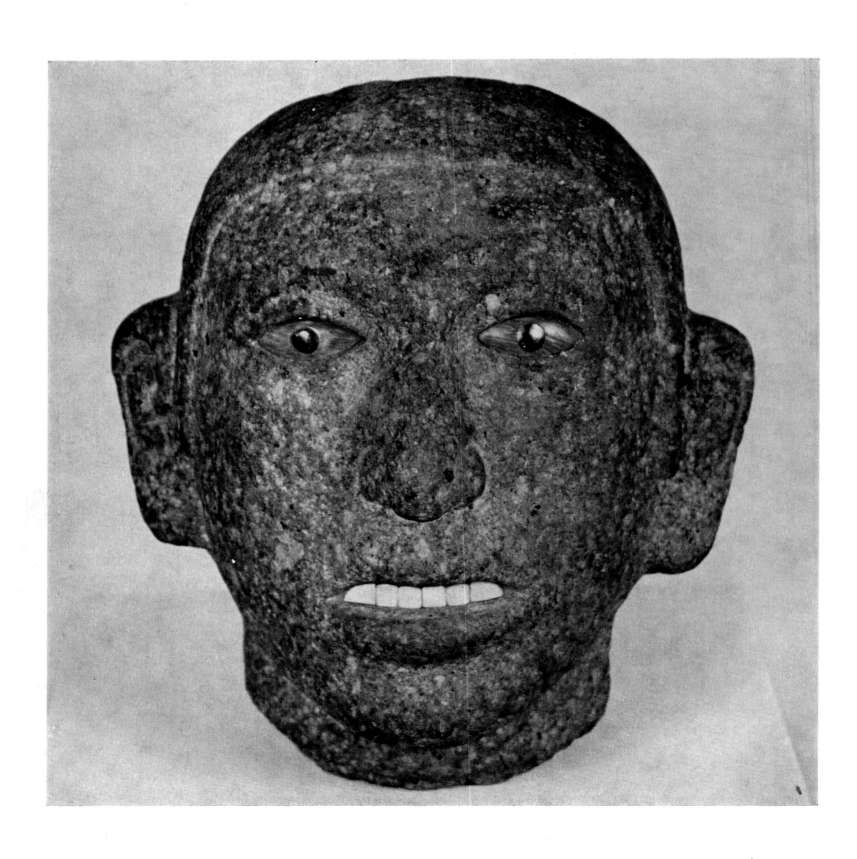

212 Tripod dish. Aztec culture
213 *Quauhxicalli* in the form of a jaguar. Tenochtitlan (Mexico City), Aztec culture
214 Obsidian mask. Aztec culture
215 Page from the *Codex Borbonicus* showing Tezcatlipoca with sacrificial offerings. Aztec culture

212

214

213

los ɡ̃ aquy nacõ
ardin de ſpoteɡ̃

ʒ̃o & ɡ̃mıemes

Rubbing of *Danzante*. Monte Alban

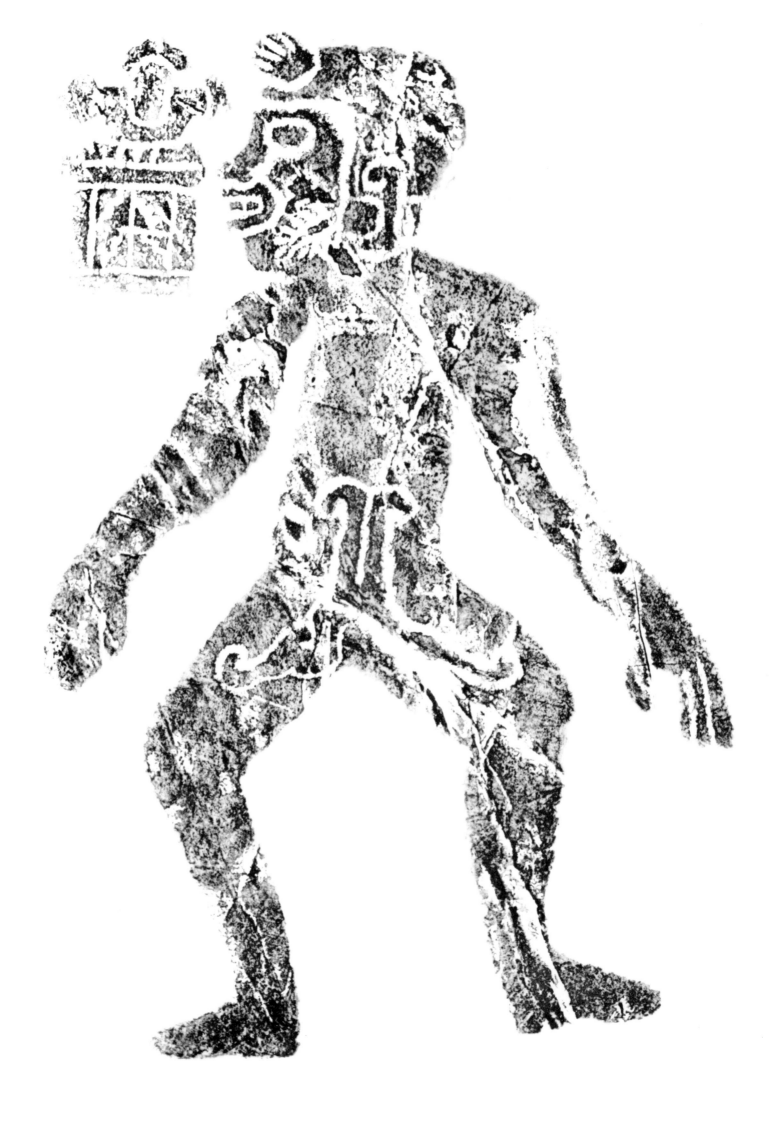

Body stamp, bird. Tenochtitlan

Notes on the text

1   Geographically Mexico is part of North America. Scholars speak of Mesoamerica in order to distinguish the advanced cultures in this region from the agricultural, nomadic and hunting cultures of North America (including, in this context, the north of Mexico).

2   *Popol Vuh*, 'the holy book of the Quiché Indians'. The Quiché, like the Cakchiquel, belong to the Maya family, and live on the high plateau of Guatemala. Records of their creative history are therefore of the highest importance, since they also reflect Mexican trains of thought. Toltec tribes, which emigrated from the much-vaunted city of Tula, brought with them to Maya territory their religious ideas. Since Brasseur de Bourbourg's work, several editions have appeared in a number of languages. In German: *Das Popol Wuh*, translated and edited by Noah Elieser Pohorilles, Leipzig 1913, and by Leonhard Schultze Jena, Berlin 1944. In English: Adrian Recinos, *Popol Vuh: the Sacred Book of the Ancient Quiché Maya*, Norman, Okla. 1950.

3   In terms of volume, the pyramid of Cholula is much larger than the pyramid of Cheops in Egypt.

4   The Mexican calendar involves two interlocking systems. In the first, the so-called 'almanac year', there are twenty day names (where we have seven) and thirteen possible numbers (where we have up to thirty-one). Thus, in the table on p. 95, if the first day is 1 Crocodile, the thirteenth will be 13 House, the fourteenth 1 Eagle, and the twenty-first 8 Crocodile. The date 1 Crocodile does not recur until $13 \times 20 = 260$ days have elapsed. This period, the 'almanac year', is the basis of calendar divination *(cf. pl. 215)*. It enmeshes with the solar or ritual year of 365 days (eighteen twenty-day months plus five intercalated days) in such a way that only four day names out of twenty can begin a new solar year. These are House, Rabbit, Reed and Flint. As the year is named after its first day, any given year name recurs after $4 \times 13 = 52$ years. The beginning of this larger cycle, the Calendar Round, was marked, whenever the year 2 Reed came round, with a ceremony of renewal, the New Fire, which seems to have entailed the addition of a new layer to the temple pyramids. The last New Fire was in 1507. Obviously, a cyclic calendar, with only 52 year names, easily results in chronological errors; Aztec historical codices sometimes have a complete list of years in sequence, in order to avoid such confusions as that between 8 Rabbit (1318) and 8 Rabbit (1370); see note 35, below. The Aztecs possibly coped with the error inherent in the 365-day solar year not by having official leap years but by silently inserting dateless days from time to time.

5   Figures for Mexico are available only from 1532 onwards, and are based on the native population's tribute payments. The estimated Indian population in 1532 was about 16,871,408; in 1568, 2,649,573; in 1608, 1,069,255. (S. F. Cook and Woodrow Borah, *The Indian Population of Central Mexico 1531–1610*. University of California Press, Berkeley 1960.)

6   Almost all the gold reaching the imperial and princely courts of Europa was melted down into bars, since men were blind to the merits of these Indian works of art. One exception was Albrecht Dürer, who wrote in the diary of his journey through the Low Countries: 'I, too, have seen the things men brought to the king from the new golden lands: a whole golden sun a full fathom broad, likewise a whole silver moon, also as large, likewise two chambers full of the armour from the same, likewise of all their weapons, harness, artillery, strange forsooth, likewise curious raiment, bed coverings and all manner of strange things for a multitude of uses more beautiful to see than can be imagined. All these things were precious, men say their worth is one hundred thousand guilders. And never in all my days have I seen such things as did so gladden my heart as these. For

there I have seen things of wonderful artistry and have marvelled at the subtle *ingenia* of the men in foreign lands. And I know not how I shall describe the things I did experience there.'

7   The earliest trace of the continent's original inhabitants is a camp fire discovered in Lewisville, Texas. A C-14 test put its age at 37,000 years. This test, which enables reasonably accurate datings to be made, consists in the measurement of the degeneration of radioactive atoms in a radioactive isotope of carbon known as C-14; 5570 years after the death of an organism, its content of C-14 atoms is reduced by exactly one half.

8   In Mexico some 60 per cent of the population still speak the native languages: Nahuatl 822,000, Otomi 209,000, Zapotec 248,000, Totonac 136,000, Huaxtec 54,000, Mixtec 270,000, Tarascan 44,000, to name only the most important tribes. (The Maya languages are not included in these figures.)

9   At the 1962 International Congress of Americanists in Mexico City it was established that maize was first grown about 5000 BC and harvested in its present form in about 3500 BC.

10 Numerous studies of the Maya exist in English, including: Sylvanus G. Morley, *The Ancient Maya*, 3rd edn, Stanford 1956; J. Eric S. Thompson, *The Rise and Fall of Maya Civilization*, Norman, Okla. 1954; and a concise survey, Michael D. Coe, *The Maya*, London and New York 1966. The author and publishers of the present book are preparing a companion volume in the same format, *Art of the Maya*.

11 The most important centres apart from Tlatilco are El Arbolillo, a small village built beside an arm of the lake, and Zacatenco, a large site which testifies to great advances in agrarian economy; Copilco, near Cuicuilco, was destroyed by volcanic eruption. The dead were usually buried beneath the houses of the living. Offerings took the form of mats, which served as beds during the lifetime of those who had died, tools, pottery and occasionally, a jade bead placed in the mouth. The collective graves that are sometimes found date from this period. Infant mortality was very high and the expectation of life was short.

12 In the so-called batik, or negative, process parts of the vessel were coated with wax and the whole then dipped in pigment. The waxed portion remained 'negative', or free of colour.

13 For a discussion of 'Olmec' culture, see the following chapter.

14 This jadeite sculpture, now in the National Museum in Washington, shows a deity with a protruding tongue. The dating method used in the calendric inscription is that of the Maya, who probably adopted 13 April 313 BC as their starting date. Scholars are agreed as to the calendric hieroglyphs, but not the date from which time was reckoned. Of the two correlations, the author uses that of Goodman-Martinez, Hernandez-Thompson. The other, by Herbert Spinden, puts all dates 260 years earlier.

15 La Venta lay on a small island, surrounded by swamps and marshes, not far from the Tonala river which is still partially subject to the Atlantic tides. According to Philip Drucker ('Some implications of the ceramic complex of La Venta'), the inhabited zone was relatively small; rather, it would seem to have been a religious centre with a small number of regular inhabitants – priests or priest-kings and their assistants, as well as artists.

16 The Nahuatl text of the *Codex Florentino* was recently translated into English by C. E. Dibble and A. J. O. Anderson and published by the University of Utah (*Florentine Codex* ..., Salt Lake City 1957–65). Sahagún himself translated the reports of his Aztec informants, which he issued under the title *Historia General de las Cosas de Nueva España*. The most recent Spanish edition, with copious commentaries by Angel M. Garibay K., appeared in Mexico City in 1956.

17 Burial offerings from the central Gulf coast region show that, in these zones at any rate, the wheel was known. Figurines of jaguars and other beasts standing on four wheels have been found; whether they were toys or sacred objects is not known. The wheel, an invention of such importance to the Old World, would in any case have been of smaller consequence in Mesoamerica, where no draught animals were available.

18 C. A. Burland, in his postscript to *The Aztecs of Mexico*, by George C. Vaillant, German edn, *Die Azteken*, Cologne 1957.

19 The Teotihuacan I period is divided into two phases, Chimalhuacan and the earlier Tzacualli. The artifacts originate mainly from building material in the pyramid of the sun. A C-14 test put their date at 900 BC.

20 Teotihuacan II is also known to archaeologists as 'Miccaotli', the Nahuatl name of the Avenue of the Dead.

21 The water goddess is now in the Museo Nacional, Mexico. When it was transported the sculpture's weight was found to be nearly 23 tons.

22 Francisco de Burgoa: *Palestra historial de virtudes, y exemplares apostólicos*, Mexico City 1670 (Mexico City 1904).

23 E. E. Kisch: *Entdeckungen in Mexiko*, Berlin 1953.

24 According to early Spanish reports they took their name from a chieftain called Cuextecatl.

25 According to another tradition, Huaxteca means 'disc', after the fan-shaped head-dress of palm leaves and feathers worn by the women of quality, and the goddesses, of the region.

26 In connection with the Huaxtecs, reference should be made to the works of Gordon F. Ekholm; see Vaillant's *Aztecs of Mexico*, bibliography.

27 The greatest caution is also necessary in assigning dates, at least until clear-cut evidence is obtained from excavation of the layers in the region.

28 Chupicuaro was the burial site of a Preclassic settlement lying on the Lerma river, some 70 miles north-west of Mexico City.

29 Tezozomoc, *Cronica Mexicana*, ch. 56.

30 Sahagún, *Historia General de las Cosas de Nueva España*.

31 *Ibid*. Tlapallan is the 'land of the red colour', i.e. the land of the dawn.

32 *Codice Chimalpopoca (Anales de Cuauhtitlan y Leyenda de los soles*, Mexico City 1945).

33 According to mythology the Aztecs lived during the fifth age, in the age of the fifth sun. The four preceding suns or worlds ended in cataclysms. The first world was destroyed because the heavens fell on the earth, the second met its end through storms, and the third went up in flames. The fourth world was destroyed by flood, and it is prophesied that the fifth world, the one we live in now, will succumb to an earthquake in the year 4 Motion.

34 *Tira de la Peregrinación México*, Mexico City 1944.

35 The calendar is cyclic (see note 4); the same combination of numeral and symbol is repeated every 52 years. The year 8 Rabbit could be 1318 (the most likely in this case), 1370 or 1422.

36 *Chinampas* were rafts of woven reed or willow, covered with soil and positioned in the lake. These 'floating gardens', producing two or three crops each year, were the only possible solution for the Aztecs who were otherwise very short of arable land. The system has survived up till the present day, at Xochimilco, where the *chinampas* provide vegetables and flowers for the capital.

37 One of the most remarkable treaties in the history of the world was that concluded between the Aztecs of Tenochtitlan and the warriors of Tlaxcala: In the absence of a *casus belli* the warriors of both city states joined battle in the so-called 'flowery war' *(xochiyaoyotl)*, which was not only a display of military virtuosity but also a means of obtaining sacrificial victims for the altars of the gods. The men of Tlaxcala, who tended to come off worst in these very real life-and-death exercises, losing much valuable manpower in the process, joined forces with Cortés against the Aztecs. After the conquest of Mexico, Cortés wrote to his king: '...such was the slaughter

done that day on water and on land, that with prisoners taken they numbered in all more than forty thousand men... Our allies handled the enemy most cruelly, for they would in no wise spare any life, although they were reproved and punished by us' (Third letter to the emperor Charles V).

38 Tlatelolco was almost the same size as Tenochtitlan. Up to the Conquest the market in Tlatelolco was the largest in the country and was described at length by Cortés in his second letter. Hostility between the two neighbours is supposed to have had a trifling cause: While a temple was being built for Huitzilopochtli, both cities competed for the god's favour. The women of Tlatelolco were so carried away by this rivalry that they exposed their bare posteriors as an insult to the people of Tenochtitlan. This is what started the war. (Tezozomoc, XLI–XLII).

39 The last independent ruler of Texcoco (1472–1516) was Nezahualpilli, a son of Nezahualcoyotl, and the husband of a sister of Moctezuma II. If we are to believe the chroniclers Torquemada, Clavigero, and Ixtil-xochitl, this lady bestowed her favours on young men and hence paid very little attention to her husband. In 1498, the husband drew the necessary conclusions and had her put to death. The ruler of Tenochtitlan, Ahuizotl, bitterly resented this act, which although it did not lead to open war, nevertheless gave rise to intrigues that were to weaken Texcoco's influence and to place Tenochtitlan at the head of the alliance of the three cities.

40 Bernal Díaz's allusion to sodomy is uncalled-for, certainly in the case of the Aztecs. According to their law this vice was punished by death.

41 *Tlatoani* (from *tlatoa* = speak) was, according to A. Zurita, also applied to princes of subordinate rank.

42 Friedrich Katz, *Die sozialökonomischen Verhältnisse bei den Azteken im 15. und 16. Jahrhundert. Ethnographisch-Archäologische Forschungen*, III, 2, Berlin 1956.

43 Paul Westheim, 'Das Pantheon des Maises', in *Kunstwerk*, Nov./Dec. 1959.

44 *Historia de los mexicanos por sus Pinturas,* ed. Joaquín García Icazbalceta, *Nueva colección de documentos para la historia de México*, Mexico City 1891.

45 The word *toltecatl* ('Toltec'), which I translate as 'artist', Sahagún translates into Spanish as *mechanico*.

46 One striking example of dialogue that is known to us originates in the early colonial period. A fragment of it, written in Nahuatl, was found in the secret archives of the Vatican in 1925. In these *Colóquios* the Indians seek to defend their ancient gods while the Christians are at pains to present their own view. This was translated by Walter Lehmann and edited after his death by Gerdt Kutscher: *Sterbende Götter und christliche Heilsbotschaft – Wechselreden indianischer Vornehmer und spanischer Glaubensapostel in Mexiko 1524*, Stuttgart 1949.

47 The translation of early Mexican poetry is necessarily attended by problems. A literal translation will convey no more than a limited impression. However, the translator must guard against excessive freedom. With the aid of the original text and of English, Spanish, and German translations, where available, I have attempted to follow a middle course in order to convey something of the flavour of the original.

48 From a Mexican 'epic song' preserved in manuscript in the Biblioteca Nacional in Mexico. The author of these *Cantares Mexicanos*, which are written in Nahuatl in Latin script, is anonymous. According to ancient traditions these 'songs' must have been set down in Latin script between 1536 and 1564. Many of the passages – not quoted here – reveal Christian ideas whose object undoubtedly was to get the work past the censorship of the new masters. A facsimile edition was brought out by Antonio Peñafiel in 1899. Brasseur de Bourbourg had earlier copied out sections which were used by Daniel G. Brinton as the basis for his translation of Aztec texts into English, an attempt at translation that was not a success. Other authors, among them Cecilio Robelo, Walter Lehmann, August Freiherr von Gall and, most recently, Angel M. Garibay K., have applied themselves to these valuable writings. The most thorough work, a literal translation, was carried out by Leonhard Schultze Jena (published posthumously by the Ibero-Amerikanische Bibliothek, Berlin, editor Gerdt Kutscher, Kohlhammer Verlag, Stuttgart 1957).

49 From another typical Mexican song *(Cantares Mexicanos)*.

50 Verse from a 'flower song' *(Cantares Mexicanos)*.

51 Poetry and song are synonymous in Nahuatl. The word for poet, *cuicani*, means 'he who sings'.

52 From a trilogy (A 'Flower song', 'Night song', 'Song of grief') attributed to Nezahualcoyotl. Recorded in the *Cantares Mexicanos*.

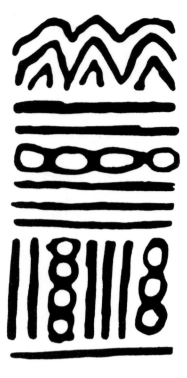

Roller stamp. San Andres Tuxtla

54   A 'war song' from *Cantares Mexicanos* (abridged).

55   Bernardino de Sahagún: 'de los cantares que deziá a hónora de los dioses en los temples y fuera dellos' *(Codex Florentino)*. The 'fire serpent', *xiuhcoatl*, is the earth in winter, and the quetzal-feathered serpent, Quetzalcoatl, is the earth in spring.

56   *atamalli*, a sort of bread made with water but without capsicum pepper, and eaten when fasting.

57   Sahagún, *Codex Florentino*. (I have refrained from giving volume and page numbers because the several editions are all differently numbered. Mistakes could thus easily arise.)

58   'Yet another song sung by a ruler in memory of rulers', *Cantares Mexicanos*.

59   'Elegy', abbreviated extract, *Cantares Mexicanos*.

60   Prescott, *History of the Conquest of Mexico*.

61   'Relación de la Conquista (1528) por informantes anónimos de Tlatelolco' in the Bibliothèque Nationale, Paris under the title *Unos anales históricos de la nación mexicana*. This is probably the earliest document describing the Conquest from the Indian viewpoint. (A Spanish translation by Angel M. Garibay K., edited by Miguel León Portilla, has appeared in Mexico under the title *Visión de los Vencidos*. There is a German edition, *Rückkehr der Götter*, Cologne and Opladen 1962, Leipzig 1964).

Body stamp. Tepoztlan

Notes on the illustrations

Numbered figures
(see pp. 14–15, 18–19)

1   Colossal head from La Venta. La Venta culture, *c.* 500 BC – AD 200.
Height 8 ft.
Park Museum, Villa Hermosa, Tabasco.

2   Maya Indian, about twelve years old, from Uxmal (Yucatan). Eyes and mouth bear a striking resemblance to those of the colossal heads of the La Venta culture, carved some 2,000 years ago.

3   The ball court at Chichen Itza, which differs from similar courts of the Classic Maya culture in having elements of the Toltec style.
Postclassic period, Maya-Toltec culture, *c.* AD 900–1200.

4–5   *Chacmool* and pillars in the form of feathered serpents, Chichen Itza. The Toltecs who emigrated from Tula under Quetzalcoatl's leadership about AD 1000 founded, a new home for themselves at Chichen Itza in the middle of the Maya country. The ancient Maya site 'at the spring of the Itza' was rebuilt and enlarged in Toltec style. Here we are struck, not only by the typical Toltec *chacmool* figures, but more especially by the pillars in the form of feathered serpents. Maya architecture did not make use of pillars until influenced by the Toltecs. Chichen-Itza, Yucatan. Postclassic period, Maya-Toltec culture, *c.* 900–1200.

6   Reconstruction of the 'earliest Mexican', based upon the skeleton discovered by Helmuth de Terra at Tepexpan, Valley of Mexico. The C-14 dating puts his age at about 11,000 years. (See p. 16 and note.)
Museo Nacional de Antropología, Mexico D.F.

7   Portrait of Hernando Cortés. Drawing from the *Trachtenbuch* of the Augsburg medallist Christoph Weiditz. This is the only authentic portrait of Cortés, and shows the conqueror of Mexico with his coat of arms. In the summer of 1529 Weiditz was travelling in Spain where he met Cortés. The caption reads: 'Don Ferdinando Cordesyus 1529 in the 42nd year of his age this man won the whole of the Indies for his Imperial Majesty Carolus the Fifth.'

Germanisches Nationalmuseum, Nuremberg.

8   Mixtec peasant with wooden plough near Apoala, La Mixteca Alta, north-west Oaxaca. More than 70,000 Mixtecs still live on the plateau, 8,000 feet above sea level. They lead a poverty-stricken and isolated life, and only place-names such as Tilantongo and Chalcatongo still recall the mighty dynasties whose history the pictographs trace back to the year 692.

9   Twelve-year-old Mixtec boy carrying his younger brother to market in Chalcatongo by means of a shoulder-cloth.

10   Mixtec couple at Chalcatongo market, La Mixteca Alta. In these highlands the weaving of straw hats is the only industry, and everyone has to weave perhaps one hat a day so as to exchange it with itinerant merchants for maize, since the local crop is insufficient for the population. The price of a straw hat is about a shilling.

Colour and monochrome plates

1   Standing female figure. Solid clay, unpainted.
Tlatilco, Valley of Mexico. Preclassic period, c. 1300–700 BC.
Height 4$^1/_2$ in.
Private collection, Munich.

2   Figure of an acrobat in the form of a vessel. Clay, reddish paint. There are only four known examples of this form, all from Tlatilco (Valley of Mexico). Preclassic period, c. 1300–700 BC
Height 15$^3/_4$ in.
Private collection, Los Angeles, Calif.

3   Standing two-faced female figure. Solid clay, unpainted. Tlatilco, Valley of Mexico. Preclassic period.
c. 1300–700 BC.
Height 3$^1/_2$ in.
Dr Kurt Stavenhagen collection, Mexico D.F.

4   Two-headed female figure. Solid clay, traces of former red and yellow paint. Tlatilco, Valley of Mexico. Preclassic period, c. 1300–700 BC.
Height 3$^3/_4$ in.
Dr Kurt Stavenhagen collection, Mexico D.F.

5   Seated female figure. Clay, traces of yellowish paint on red. Tlatilco (?), Valley of Mexico. Preclassic period, c. 1300–700 BC.
Height 7$^1/_4$ in.
Stendahl collection, Los Angeles, Calif.

6   Seated female figure. Solid clay, unpainted. Tlatilco, Valley of Mexico. Preclassic period, c. 1300–700 BC.
Height 3$^1/_2$ in.
Dr Kurt Stavenhagen collection, Mexico D.F.

7   Vessel in the form of an owl. Blackish-grey clay. Tlatilco, Valley of Mexico. Preclassic period, c. 1300–700 BC.
Height 6$^1/_4$ in.
Private collection, Mexico D.F.

8   Vessel in the form of a bird. Blackish-green clay. Provenance unknown, Tlatilco style. Preclassic period, c. 1300–700 BC.
Height 7$^1/_4$ in.
André Emmerich Gallery, New York.

9   Partial view of the pyramid of Cuicuilco, the oldest temple platform in the Mesoamerican area. Originally

Body stamp, rabbit. Teotihuacan

the structure was crowned with a small temple of non-durable material. Cuicuilco lies at the perimeter of the present capital. Preclassic period, begun *c.* 700 BC.

10   Fragment of female figure. Solid clay, remains of former red paint on lustrous off-white. Malinalco, State of Mexico. Preclassic period, *c.* 800–400 BC.
Height $3^1/_8$ in.
Private collection, Munich.

11   Standing female figure wearing a turban. Solid clay, unpainted. Aguascalientes, Oaxaca. This figure, found in the Zapotec region, bears a stylistic resemblance to the archaic figures of Cholula and Puebla. Preclassic period, *c.* 700–300 BC.
Height $3^3/_4$ in.
Museo Preistorico Etnografico Luigi Pigorini, Rome.

12   Two statuettes of 'dancing girls' with ornamental headdress and leg ornaments. Clay, traces of former red. yellow and white paint. Tlatilco, Valley of Mexico. Preclassic period, *c.* 1300–700 BC.
Height $6^1/_2$ in., $6^1/_8$ in.
Private collection, Mexico D.F.

13   Fragment of a figure. Solid clay, with remains of former polychrome painting. State of Morelos. Preclassic period, *c.* 800–400 BC.
Height $5^1/_2$ in.
Private collection, Mexico D.F.

14   Miniature mask, probably a small version of a shaman's wooden dancing mask. Clay. Tlatilco, Valley of Mexico. Preclassic period, *c.* 1300–700 BC.
Width $4^3/_4$ in.
Private collection, Mexico D.F.

15   Vessel in the form of a fat man squatting on his heels. He wears a helmet in the form of a duck's head. Black lustrous clay. Tlatilco, Valley of Mexico. Preclassic period, *c.* 1300–700 BC.
Height $9^1/_2$ in.
Private collection, Mexico D.F.

16   Large hollow figure of a baby. Mouth, eyes and shape of head are typical of the so-called 'baby-face' of the Olmecs, and indicate the influence of the La Venta culture. Whitish clay. Tlatilco, Valley of Mexico. Preclassic period, *c.* 900–700 BC.
Height $14^1/_2$ in.
Franz Feuchtwanger collection, Mexico D.F.

17   Small carved head, with 'Olmecoid' facial traits. The sculpture depicts very clearly the skull formation

of the living model. Jadeite. Tenango del Valle, State of Mexico. Preclassic period, La Venta culture, c. 600–200 BC.
Height 8³/₄ in.
Museo Nacional de Antropología, Mexico D.F.

18 Standing figure. Jade. The head displays the skull formation characteristic of the La Venta culture. Ocozocoautla, Chiapas. La Venta culture, c. 500 BC – AD 200.
Height 3 in.
Museo Regional, Tuxtl6 Gutiérrez, Chiapas.

19 Colossal head ('Head no. 1') with the typical helmet-like headdress. Basalt. The monument has a circumference of about 20 ft. and weighs over 20 tons. The nearest basalt quarry was about sixty miles away. La Venta, Tabasco. La Venta culture, c. 500 BC – AD 200.
Height c. 8 ft.
Park Museum, Villa Hermosa, Tabasco.

20 Fragment of figure. Dark green polished stone, with remains of red (vermilion) paint. Provenance unknown. La Venta culture, c. 500 BC – AD 200.
Height 3¹/₂ in.
Brooklyn Museum, New York.

21 Fragment of figure. Hard baked clay. The head is of the so-called Olmecoid type. Found in the south-east of Morelos State. Preclassic period, c. 600–200 BC.
Height 3³/₄ in.
Museo Nacional de Antropología, Mexico D.F.

22 Mask with wide open eyes and mouth. Greenstone. Perhaps worn as a pectoral or as an ornamental buckle for a belt. Like other early Mexican masks, this would originally have had eyes inlaid with some other material. Southern Gulf coast. La Venta culture, c. 600 BC – AD 200.
Height 5¹/₂ in.
Museo Nacional de Antropología, Mexico D.F.

23 Cylindrical stone with relief of a 'messenger'. The arrival of the 'messenger' or 'merchant' is indicated by the footprint on the left. The person in this relief differs both physically and in dress from the so-called Olmecoid type. He is wearing only a loin-cloth, sandals, a bead necklace and an elaborate headdress. In his left hand he bears a standard. Three glyphs to the right of the figure, including what is clearly a bird's head, give the name and probably the origin of the person depicted. La Venta, Tabasco. La Venta culture, c. 500 BC – AD 200.
Height c. 43 in.
Park Museum, Villa Hermosa, Tabasco.

24 Relief on one side of 'Altar B', also called 'Quintuple Altar', (cf. pl. 34), showing two helmeted priests or warriors with child-gods or heirs of a reigning dynasty. Scholars differ as to what these infantile, stunted figures are meant to symbolize; they are found in countless productions of the La Venta culture. It has yet to be decided whether these represent divine or daemonic beings, or whether they are the offspring of a dynasty suffering from thyroid disease. This 'altar', like all the other La Venta monuments, is now in the park museum of Villa Hermosa, the capital of Tabasco State. La Venta, Tabasco. La Venta culture, c. 500 BC – AD 200.
Height 42 in.
Park Museum, Villa Hermosa, Tabasco.

25 'Altar'. The warriors depicted in the relief might almost have been carved by the same artist as those of 'Altar B' at La Venta (pl. 24). This sculpture was discovered in a coffee plantation not far from Tazumal in northern El Salvador. La Venta culture, c. 500 BC – AD 200.
Height 4 ft 11 in., height of figures c. 2 ft 11 in.
Near Tazumal, El Salvador.

26 Figure of a kneeling man. Grey, speckled stone. Found in Honduras, it is indicative of the wide dissemination of the Olmec or La Venta culture. State of Cortés, Honduras. La Venta style, c. 500 BC – AD 200.
Height 3¹/₂ in.
Middle American Research Institute, New Orleans, La.

27 Fragment of a plaque which probably once served as a pectoral ornament. Jade. The dwarfish figure with knees drawn up has a jaguar's muzzle in lieu of a mouth. Olinala, Guerrero. La Venta culture, *c.* 500 BC – AD 200.
Height $4^3/_4$ in.
Museo Nacional de Antropología, Mexico D.F.

28 Ceremonial axe with a highly stylized human figure combined with jaguar characteristics. Dark green jade. La Mixteca Alta, Oaxaca. La Venta culture, *c.* 500 BC – AD 200.
Height $8^1/_4$ in.
Museo Nacional de Antropología, Mexico D.F.

29 Mask. Blackish stone. Probably worn as a pectoral or ornamental belt buckle. Southern Vera Cruz. La Venta culture, *c.* 500 BC – AD 200.
Height $3^1/_8$ in.
Robert J. Sainsbury collection, London.

30 Figure of a standing man holding a child. Dark green jade, highly polished. The child's features in the region of the mouth are like those of a jaguar. This type is called 'were-jaguar' by archaeologists. Provenance unknown, but this sculpture may be regarded as a pure example of the La Venta culture.
Height *c.* $8^1/_4$ in.
Brooklyn Museum, New York, on loan from Mr and Mrs A. B. Martin (Guennol collection).

31 Seated figure of a corpulent dwarf or child with outstretched arms. Haematite. Here, too, the child's wide open mouth takes on the features of a jaguar. Provenance unknown. La Venta culture, *c.* 500 BC – AD 200.
Height $4^1/_2$ in.
The Wadsworth Atheneum, Hartford, Conn.

32–33 Figure of kneeling man with crossed arms. Grey stone with traces of brown pigment. The flattened head and simple dress (loin-cloth) would suggest that he is a member of the lower classes. Its compactness is reminiscent of Ernst Barlach's work. Provenance unknown. La Venta culture, *c.* 500 BC – AD 200.
Height 9 in.
Private collection, Mexico D.F.

34 Front view of 'Altar B' (cf. *pl. 24*), with an almost free-standing figure of a priest sitting in a niche that is typical of the La Venta culture. This figure holds a child in its arms. It could represent a sacrificial offering to a vegetation deity. La Venta, Tabasco. La Venta culture, *c.* 500 BC – AD 200.
Height 42 in.
Park Museum, Villa Hermosa, Tabasco.

35 *Monumento triunfal.* Basalt. A seated, sculpturally modelled priestly figure in a niche. Above him, in bas-

relief, a highly stylized jaguar's muzzle. On either side, also in relief, are figures of women. La Venta, Tabasco. La Venta culture, *c.* 500 BC – AD 200.
Height 5 ft. 3 in.
Park Museum, Villa Hermosa, Tabasco.

36　Colossal head. Basalt. The helmet-like headgear would seem to indicate that this is a warrior. As with other colossal Olmec sculptures, it is far (45 miles) from the nearest quarry. San Lorenzo, Vera Cruz. La Venta culture, *c.* 300 BC – AD 200.
Height 8 ft. 6 in.
Museo Regional, Jalapa, Vera Cruz.

37　Dwarfish figure performing a sacrifice. Basalt. La Venta, Tabasco. La Venta culture, *c.* 500 BC – AD 200.
Height *c.* 29 in.
Park Museum, Villa Hermosa, Tabasco.

38　Prone figure of man. Basalt. The head is fully worked, while the back part of the body is still embedded in the rectangular block and is only indicated in outline. La Venta culture, *c.* 500 BC – AD 200.
Height of head *c.* 31 in., length 58 in.
Market-place, Tuxtla Santiago, Vera Cruz.

39　Standing female figure. Clay, painted with geometric motifs characteristic of the Chupicuaro style. The decoration may have been inspired by brightly-coloured textiles, which have not survived because of Mexico's unfavourable climatic conditions. Chupicuaro, Michoacan. Preclassic period, *c.* 800 BC – AD 200.
Height 13³/₄ in.
Private collection, Los Angeles, Calif.

40　Relief showing a helmeted priest or warrior with a votive offering; curved over him is a fire serpent. Basalt. La Venta, Tabasco. La Venta culture, *c.* 500 BC – AD 200.
Height 37 in.
Museo Nacional de Antropología, Mexico D.F.

41　Seated figure of hunchbacked musician with outspread arms. Clay, reddish brown pigment. In one hand he holds a percussion instrument (shell) and in the other a striker (bone). Provenance unknown. North-west coast culture, Colima style, *c.* AD 300–1000.
Height 12³/₄ in.
Southwest Museum, Los Angeles, Calif.

42　Mother and child. Solid clay, unpigmented. Provenance unknown. North-west coast culture, Colima style, *c.* 200 BC – AD 600.
Height 7¹/₈ in.
Stendahl collection, Los Angeles, Calif.

43　Crouching figure incorporating receptacle for burnt offerings; this figure probably represents the 'old god' of fire. Volcanic stone. Provenance unknown. North-west coast culture, Colima style, *c.* AD 300–1000.
Height 12¹/₂ in.
Dr Kurt Stavenhagen collection, Mexico D.F.

44　Seated couple. Solid clay, red pigment. The woman holds a small child in her arms. Provenance unknown. Preclassic period of the north-west coast, Colima style, *c.* 200 BC – AD 400 (accurate information is not yet available for this region).
Height 6¹/₂ in. and 6⁵/₈ in.
Private collection, Munich.

45　Ithyphallic figure of a seated man. Reddish painted clay. Figures of this kind are exceedingly rare in ancient Mexican art. Some are known in Tlatilco, where they were presumably intended as fertility symbols. The phallic sculptures of the north-west coast, which were created many centuries later, were more probably caricatures, for it can hardly be supposed that exaggerated representations such as this were the expression of any coherent religious idea. But this must remain a supposition until the wealth of material from that region has been examined by scholars. Provenance unknown. North-west coast culture, Colima style, *c.* AD 300–1000.
Height 8 in.

282

Dr Kurt Stavenhagen collection, Mexico D.F.

46   Vessel in the form of a pregnant woman. Blackish-green clay. Provenance unknown. North-west coast culture, Nayarit style, *c*. AD 300–1000.

Height 8 in.

Dr Kurt Stavenhagen collection, Mexico D.F.

47   Seated female figure. Reddish painted clay. Provenance unknown. North-west coast culture, Colima style, *c*. AD 300–1000.

Height *c*. 24 in.

Galerie Welz, Salzburg.

48   Figure of a warrior armed with a club, protected by a helmet, a breastplate and a belt. Ochre coloured clay. Provenance unknown. North-west coast culture, Nayarit style, *c*. AD 300–1000.

Height $17^1/_4$ in.

Private collection, Munich.

49   Standing female figure, wearing a loincloth and, round her neck, an amulet. Solid clay, unpigmented. She has three bracelets on either arm. North west coast culture, Colima style, *c*. AD 300–1000.

Height $7^3/_4$ in.

Private collection, Munich.

50   Seated female figure, wearing a loin-cloth, and, round her neck, an amulet in the form of an animal's head. Solid clay, unpigmented. Provenance unknown. North-west coast culture, Colima style, *c*. AD 300–1000.

Height $5^3/_4$ in.

Private collection, Munich.

51   Figures of dancers with bird and animal masks; one figure is holding a gourd rattle, while the other wears long, wing-like objects on her upper arms to represent a bird. Solid, clay, unpigmented. North-west coast culture, Colima style, *c*. AD 300–1000.

Height 7 in. and $6^1/_4$ in.

Stendahl Collection, Los Angeles, Calif.

52   Figure of a drummer. Solid clay, red and white pigment. North-west coast culture, Colima style, *c*. AD 300–1000.

Height $3^1/_2$ in.

Private collection, USA.

53   Figure of a dancer holding a rattle in one hand. Ochre coloured solid clay, with remains of reddish pigment. Provenance unknown. North-west coast culture, Colima style, *c*. AD 300–1000.

Height $7^1/_8$ in.

Stendahl collection, Los Angeles, Calif.

54 Incense burner in the form of a daemon with human features. Clay. On the front is a male figure, while a female figure on the back holds up the bowl on her neck. North-west coast culture, Colima style, c. AD 300–1000.
Height c. 15 in.
Galerie Welz, Salzburg.

55 Vessel in the form of a seated man. Clay, whitish pigment. The highly stylized raised hand serves for a spout. The shoulders and upper arms have raised tattooing. Provenance unknown. North-west coast culture, Colima style, c. AD 500–1000.
Height 14^1/$_2$ in.
Dr Kurt Stavenhagen collection, Mexico D.F.

56 Figure of a kneeling woman, her hands held close to the body. Clay, black pigment on red ground. Near Ixtlan del Rio, Nayarit. North-west coast culture, Nayarit style, c. AD 300–1000.
Height 14^1/$_2$ in.
Stendahl collection, Los Angeles, Calif.

57 Standing female figure, her hands held close to the body. Polychrome painted clay. Near Ixtlan del Rio, Nayarit. North-west coast culture, Nayarit style, c. AD 300–1000.
Height 18^1/$_4$ in.
Stendahl collection, Los Angeles, USA.

58 Figure of a ball player. Clay, red and black pigment on whitish ground. With both hands, he holds the rubber ball on his left shoulder. Barrancas region, Jalisco. North-west coast culture, Jalisco style, c. AD 300–1000.
Height 17^1/$_4$ in.
Stendahl collection, Los Angeles, Calif.

59 Figure of a ball player with disc-shaped back shield. Clay. The shield probably symbolizes the sun. He holds the rubber ball in his raised hand. Provenance unknown. North-west coast culture, Colima style, c. AD 300–1000.
Height 11 in.
Stendahl collection, Los Angeles, Calif.

60 Group of people eating round a sunshade. Solid, polychrome painted clay. Ixtlan del Rio region, Nayarit. North-west coast culture, Nayarit style, c. AD 300–1000.
Height 4 in. and 8 in., length 8 in.
Stendahl collection, Los Angeles, Calif.

61 Figure of a warrior with circular shield and spear-thrower. Coarse solid clay. Provenance unknown. North-west coast culture, Colima style, c. AD 300–1000.
Height 10^1/$_4$ in.
Dr Kurt Stavenhagen collection, Mexico D.F.

62 Seated figure of an orator. Yellowish clay, red and blackish pigment. This sculpture derives its forcefulness from the impressionistic approach and not from absolute naturalism. Barrancas region, Jalisco. North-west coast culture, Jalisco style, c. AD 300–1000.
Height 17^1/$_4$ in.
Stendahl collection, Los Angeles, Calif.

63 Figure of a hunchbacked child. Clay, reddish brown pigment. Provenance unknown. North-west coast culture, Colima style, c. AD 500–1000.
Height 11^3/$_4$ in.
Stendahl collection, Los Angeles, Calif.

64 Seated figure with bone rattle. Reddish clay. The patterns on the clothing are painted in off-white, brown and black. Provenance unknown. North-west coast culture, Nayarit style, c. AD 300–1000.
Height 13^3/$_4$ in.
Galerie Welz, Salzburg.

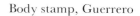
Body stamp, Guerrero

65 Seated figure of a girl wearing a skirt. Clay, reddish-brown pigment. Provenance unknown. North-west coast culture, Colima style, *c.* AD 600–1000.
Height 8¹/₂ in.
Dr Kurt Stavenhagen Collection, Mexico D.F.

66 Seated figure of a girl wearing a skirt. Clay, red and blackish pigment. Provenance unknown. North-west coast culture, Colima style, *c.* AD 600–1000.
Height 11¹/₂ in.
Dr Kurt Stavenhagen collection, Mexico D.F.

67 Vessel in the form of a resting man. Clay. The figure has been shaped into a vessel to obviate cracking of the clay in firing. (This work bears a striking resemblance to Maillol's 1902 sculpture *Night.*) Provenance unknown. North-west coast culture, Colima style, *c.* AD 600–1000.
Height 7 in.
Dr Kurt Stavenhagen collection, Mexico D.F.

68 Mother and child. Clay, reddish grey-black and whitish paint. Provenance unknown. North-west coast culture, Jalisco style, *c.* AD 300–1000.
Height 16 in.
Dr Kurt Stavenhagen collection, Mexico D.F.

69 Figure of a seated woman, holding a pot in both hands, with ornamental tattooing on the breasts. Clay, whitish ground with reddish and dark-grey pigment. Lake Chapala region, Nayarit. North-west coast culture, Jalisco style, *c.* AD 300–1000.
Height 14¹/₄ in.
Stendahl collection, Los Angeles, Calif.

70 Female figure making a gesture of repudiation. Clay, reddish ground, whitish, blackish and yellow pigment. On her left shoulder she carries a pot. As in most Nayarit style pottery, this one has a polychrome painted pattern on the loin-cloth. Near Ixtlan del Rio, Nayarit. North-west coast culture, Nayarit style, *c.* AD 300–1000.
Height 12¹/₂ in.
Galerie Welz, Salzburg.

71 Figure of rotund musician with pointed hat and ear decorations, seated behind a drum, holding a flute in his right hand. Reddish clay, off-white and black pigment. Provenance unknown. North-west coast culture, Nayarit style, *c.* AD 300–1000.
Height 13¹/₄ in.
Dr Kurt Stavenhagen collection, Mexico D.F.

72 Pair of vessels in the form of a man and woman. Clay, white and reddish pigment. Provenance unknown. North-west coast culture, Nayarit style, *c.* AD 300–1000.

Height 11¹/₂ in. and 13 in.

Dr Ernst Hauswedel collection, Hamburg.

73   Figure of seated couple. Reddish clay, traces of whitish and black pigment. Provenance unknown. North-west coast culture, Nayarit style, *c.* AD 300–1000.

Height 10 in.

Dr Kurt Stavenhagen collection, Mexico D.F.

74   Vessel in the form of a dog scratching itself. Clay, reddish pigment. Provence unknown. North-west coast culture, Colima style, *c.* AD 300–1000.

Height 11³/₄ in.

Stendahl collection, Los Angeles, Calif.

75   Vessel in the form of a dog wearing a human mask. Clay, reddish-brown pigment. Provenance unknown. North-west coast culture, Colima style. *c.* AD 300–1000.

Height 7³/₄ in., length 14¹/₂ in.

Museo Nacional de Antropología, Mexico D.F.

76   Vessel in the form of a sleeping dog. Clay, reddish pigment. Provenance unknown. North-west coast culture, Colima style, *c.* AD 300–1000.

Length 7³/₄ in.

Dr Kurt Stavenhagen collection, Mexico D.F.

77   Vessel in the form of a dog lying on its back. Clay, reddish-brown pigment. Provenance unknown. North-west coast culture, Colima style, *c.* AD 300–1000.

Height 10¹/₂ in.

Museo Nacional de Antropología, Mexico D.F.

78   Vessel in the form of a kneeling, naked woman. Clay, white pigment on red. Provenance unknown. North-west coast culture, Colima style, *c.* AD 300–1000.

Height 9³/₄ in.

Museo Nacional de Antropología, Mexico D.F.

79   Double figure of man and woman. Clay, white pigment on reddish ground. The patterns are painted on to the clothing. The woman is carrying a small bowl, and the man is holding an unidentified object, perhaps a tobacco pipe, in his hand. Provenance unknown. North-west coast culture, Nayarit style, *c.* AD 300–1000.

Height 14¹/₂ in.

Galerie Welz, Salzburg.

80   Pyramid of the Sun, Teotihuacan. Classic period, Teotihuacan II culture, *c.* AD 100–400.

Height 213 ft, length of longest side 730 ft.

81   Pyramid of the Moon, Teotihuacan. Seen from the Pyramid of the Sun, with which it is presumably roughly contemporary. Classic period, Teotihuacan II culture, *c.* AD 100–400.

Height *c.* 147 ft.

82   Detail of west façade, Temple of Quetzalcoatl, Teotihuacan. Note the serpents' heads in high relief, alternating with fertility symbols and stylized masks of the rain god. Classic period, Teotihuacan culture, *c.* AD 400–800.

83   Figure of the fire god Xiuhtecuhtli or Huehueteotl, with the fire bowl on his head. Hard pumice stone. Near Texcoco, Valley of Mexico. Classic period, Teotihuacan II culture, *c.* AD 200–500.

Height 16³/₄ in., diameter of bowl 16³/₄ in.

Stendahl collection, Los Angeles, Calif.

84   Seated figure, probably depicting the fire god. Solid clay, buff paint. Provenance unknown (Valley of Mexico). Classic period, Teotihuacan culture, *c.* AD 200–800.

Height 6 in.

Museo Nacional de Antropología, Mexico D.F.

85   Mural painting in a ceremonial building: a priest in ceremonial robes is walking with a sacrificial offering. Fresco, red, light blue, green-yellow and green painting on dark red ground. Tepantitla, Teotihuacan. Classic period, Teotihuacan III culture, *c.* AD 600–800.

Body stamp. Vera Cruz

86   Standing figure, highly stylized. Dark green and light green stone, abraded. Eyes and mouth were formerly inlaid with other materials. Provenance unknown. Classic period, Teotihuacan culture, c. AD 500–800.
Height 9 in.
Museum für Völkerkunde, Vienna.

87   Fragment of a head, made with a mould and then modelled by hand. Clay, unpainted. Santiago Ahuizotla. Valley of Mexico. Classic period, Teotihuacan culture, c. AD 500–800.
Height $2^1/_2$ in.
Private collection, Munich.

88   Standing figure. Green stone. Teotihuacan. Classic period, Teotihuacan culture, c. AD 400–800.
Height $4^3/_4$ in.
Private collection, Munich.

89   Standing figure, highly stylized. Dark to light green stone, abraded, eyes and mouth formerly inlaid with other material. Provenance unknown. Classic period, Teotihuacan culture, c. AD 500–800.
Height 8 in.
Museum für Völkerkunde, Vienna.

90–92   Three masks, probably worn as pectorals by high dignitaries. Stone, eyes and mouth formerly inlaid with obsidian and shells. It is a strange fact of archaeological research that as yet not one of these typical Teotihuacan masks has been found *in situ*. Classic period, Teotihuacan culture. c. AD 400–800.
Height (90) $7^1/_8$ in., (91) 5 in., (92) $6^1/_4$ in.
Museum für Völkerkunde, Vienna.

93   Mask. Hard volcanic stone, the mother-of-pearl and obsidian eyes recently restored. The Olmec type is easily discernible in the mouth. Origin probably Guerrero. Classic period, Teotihuacan culture, c. AD 200–500.
Height $8^1/_4$ in.
CDO collection, Zurich.

94   Seated and standing figures. Solid clay, traces of whitish pigment. Valley of Mexico. Preclassic period, Teotihuacan culture.
Height $2^1/_8$ in., $3^3/_4$ in.
Stendahl collection, Los Angeles, Calif.

95   Figures of dancers. Solid clay. The head is formed in a mould while the highly simplified body is freely modelled. Teotihuacan. Classic period, Teotihuacan culture. c. AD 400–800.
Height $3^1/_4$ in., $4^7/_8$ in.
Private collection, Buenos Aires.

Body stamp. Vera Cruz

96   Tripod vessel. Clay, coated in greenish plaster, cloisonné decoration. The partly cut out and partly abraded decoration shows four stylized eagles. Below them is a frieze with gods' heads in relief, these having been impressed on the soft clay with moulds before firing. Valley of Mexico. Classic period, Teotihuacan culture, *c.* AD 500–800.

Height $7^1/_4$ in., diameter $8^1/_2$ in.

Brooklyn Museum, New York.

97   Tripod vessel with lid, the handle in the form of a bird. Clay, coated in plaster, cloisonné decoration. The highly stylized decoration is cut away and rubbed out and abraded. Xolalpan, San Francisco Mazapan, Valley of Mexico. Late Classic period, Teotihuacan IV culture, *c.* AD 600–800.

Height with lid 8 in.

Etnografiska Museet, Stockholm.

98   Mother and child. Solid clay, traces of pigment. Produced by mould and worked by hand before firing. Teotihuacan. Classic period, Teotihuacan culture, *c.* AD 500–800.

Height $4^3/_4$ in.

Dr Kurt Stavenhagen collection, Mexico D.F.

99   Mural painting: a priest in jaguar costume on his way to the temple. Fresco. Tetitla, Teotihuacan. Classic period, Teotihuacan culture, *c.* AD 600–800.

Height of figure *c.* 27 in.

100   Mural painting: the rain god, in ceremonial robes, lets fall upon the earth symbols of precious gifts. Tetitla, Teotihuacan. Classic period, Teotihuacan culture, *c.* AD 600–800.

Height of fresco *c.* 3 ft 11 in.

101   Polychrome vessel. Clay, coated with plaster, cloisonné decoration. The decoration shows the rain god in the style of the Tetitla frescoes, Teotihuacan. Valley of Mexico. Classic period, Teotihuacan culture, *c.* AD 400–700.

Height $3^1/_2$ in., diameter $4^7/_8$ in.

Brooklyn Museum, New York.

102   Battleaxe in the form of a stylized human figure. Dark green stone. The compactness of this sculpture is reminiscent of the works of modern sculptors. Mescala region, Guerrero. Mescala style, no precise date (probably between the first and eighth centuries).

Height $8^1/_4$ in.

Dr Kurt Stavenhagen collection, Mexico D.F.

103   Ceremonial axe in the form of a seated figure, grey-green stone. Mescala region, Guerrero. Mescala style, no precise date (probably between the first and eighth centuries).

Height 5$^1/_2$ in.

J. C. Leff collection, Uniontown, Pa.

104   Mask. Green stone with mosaic inlay of turquoise and pounded shells; the necklace is made of pieces of pink shell. Guerrero? Classic period, Teotihuacan culture, *c.* AD 500–800.

Height 8$^3/_4$ in.

Museo Nacional de Antropología, Mexico D.F.

105   Polychrome figure of the rain god in a feathered robe. Clay, black, white and yellow pigment. Valley of Mexico. Classic period, Teotihuacan culture, *c.* AD 500–800.

Height *c.* 5$^1/_2$ in.

Museo Nacional de Antropología, Mexico D.F.

106   Left half of page 37 of the *Codex Vindobonensis Mexicanus 1*. It shows the genesis of the Mixtec noble houses from a tree in Apoala (La Mixteca Alta). To left and right of the mythical tree, with obsidian knives in their hands, stand Seven Eagle and Seven Rain. The other figures are also accompanied by their calendar name glyphs (cf. *pl. 109*). La Mixteca Alta. Mixtec culture, fourteenth century.

Dimensions of detail shown, 7$^1/_8$ in × 8$^3/_4$ in.

Österreichische Nationalbibliothek, Vienna.

107   Vessel in the form of a head with marked 'Olmecoid' features, for burning sacrificial offerings. Light coloured clay. The snarl is characteristic of Olmec jaguar symbolism. Valley of Oaxaca. Preclassic period, Monte Alban I culture, *c.* 500–200 BC.

Height 6$^3/_4$ in.

Private collection, Munich.

108   Drinking vessel with incised jaguar's head. Blackish clay. Valley of Oaxaca. Preclassic period, Monte Alban I culture, *c.* 500–200 BC.

Height: 6$^3/_4$ in.

Museo Frissell de Arte Zapoteca, Mitla, Oaxaca.

109   Standing figure with hands pressed against chest. Grey stone. Valley of Oaxaca. Preclassic period, Monte Alban I culture, *c.* 500–200 BC.

Height 11$^3/_4$ in.

Museo Frissell de Arte Zapoteca, Mitla, Oaxaca.

110   *Danzante.* Low relief on flattened stone slab. These monuments bear the earliest Monte Alban inscriptions, archaic glyphs which cannot as yet be deciphered. Monte Alban. Preclassic period, Monte Alban I culture, *c.* 500–200 BC.

Height 47 in.

111   Court of the *Danzantes.* When one of the earliest temple structures was excavated, numerous stones with flattened surfaces were discovered, upon which were carved the grotesque simian figures known as *Danzantes.* In the background, 'Monticulo M'. Monte Alban. Preclassic and Classic period, Monte Alban culture, the temple *c.* AD 100–800.

112   Urn depicting a musician playing a percussion instrument made from a tortoise-shell. Light coloured clay. San Pedro Martin, Oaxaca. Classic period, Monte Alban III culture, *c.* AD 500–800.

Height 17$^1/_4$ in.

H. Leigh Collection, Mitla, Oaxaca.

113   Fragment of an altar: four chiefs, portrayed in relief, are received by a priest or prince. Low relief on stone slab. Above the figures are name and place hieroglyphs. Monte Alban. Classic period, Monte Alban IV culture, *c.* AD 700–900.

Length 6 ft 3 in.

114   Stela depicting a speaking priest with Zapotec calendar and place hieroglyphs. Low relief on stone slab. No one has succeeded in deciphering the Zapotec inscriptions. Monte Alban, near southern platform. Classic period, Monte Alban III culture, *c.* AD 500–800.

Height 5 ft 2 in.

115   Urn depicting a seated male figure. Light coloured clay. The incised lines probably indicate body paint-

ing. San Lorenzo Albarradas, Oaxaca. Classic period, Monte Alban III culture. *c.* AD 500–800.
Height 18$^1/_4$ in.
Museo Nacional de Antropología, Mexico D.F.
116   Urn depicting a richly dressed figure, a bird's head motif and glyphs discernible in the headdress. Grey-brown clay. Provenance unknown, probably Valley of Oaxaca. Classic period, Monte Alban III culture. *c.* AD 500–800.
Height 15$^1/_4$ in.
Museum für Völkerkunde, Vienna.
117   Urn depicting a seated man with turban-like head-dress and jade bead necklace. Light coloured clay. Provenance unknown, probably Valley of Oaxaca. Classic period, Monte Alban III culture, *c.* AD 500–800.
Height 10$^1/_4$ in.
Museum für Völkerkunde, Vienna.
118   Urn depicting the Zapotec rain god Cocijo, the counterpart of Tlaloc, recognizable by his forked tongue. Grey clay. Provenance unknown, probably Valley of Oaxaca. Classic period, Monte Alban II culture, *c.* AD 200–500.
Height 9 in.
Museum für Völkerkunde, Vienna.
119   Urn depicting an unknown deity. Clay. These Zapotec 'funerary urns', the backs of which are cylinder-shaped vessels, did not serve to hold the ashes of the dead, but were used as grave offerings, containing food and drink to accompany the dead. Provenance unknown, probably Valley of Oaxaca. Classic period, Monte Alban III culture, *c.* AD 500–800.
Height 15$^1/_4$ in.
H. Leigh collection, Mitla, Oaxaca.
120   Fragment of head. Light coloured clay. Ejutla, Oaxaca. Classic period, Monte Alban III culture, *c.* AD 500–800.
Height 10$^1/_2$ in.
H. Leigh collection, Mitla, Oaxaca.
121   Fragment of head. Solid clay. Oaxaca. Classic period, Monte Alban III culture, *c.* AD 500–800.
Height 4$^1/_4$ in.
H. Leigh collection Mitla, Oaxaca.
122   North façade of Building of the Columns, Mitla. Walls of adobe decorated with geometric stone inlays. This is considered to be the best-preserved pre-Columbian structure in Mexico; the site continued to be inhabited until the arrival of the Spaniards. Mitla, Oaxaca. Postclassic period, Monte Alban V culture, 1200–1522.
123   Interior of Building of the Columns, Mitla. The monolithic pillars are an achievement of the Postclassic period, and are of Toltec inspiration. Postclassic period, Monte Alban V culture, *c.* 1200–1522.
124   Interior of Palace II, Mitla. The walls are like the outside façades, decorated with geometric motifs in a wide variety of step frets and zig-zags. The roof was constructed of perishable material (rushes, wood etc.). Postclassic period, Monte Alban V culture, *c.* 1200–1522.
125   Building of the Columns, Mitla. This site shows elements of both Zapotec and Mixtec styles, but its history is unknown, although it was inhabited until the arrival of the Spaniards. Mitla, Oaxaca. Postclassic period, Monte Alban V culture, *c.* 1200–1522.
126   Monte Alban, the sacred mountain of the Zapotecs, as the visitor sees it today. The first traces of building activity are discernible between the sixth and fourth centuries BC. The site continued to be enlarged up till the eleventh century, and underwent considerable change at the hands of the Zapotecs. Between the eleventh and thirteenth centuries it served as a burial place for high Mixtec dignitaries.
127   Ornamental pendant carved with the figure of a seated man with his knees drawn up, and surrounded by volute-shaped designs. Jade. Silacayoapan, Oaxaca. Postclassic period, Mixtec culture (?), *c.* 692–1522.
Height 4$^1/_4$ in.
Museum für Völkerkunde, Vienna.
128   Ornamental pendant. Gold, cast by the 'lost wax' method. From top to bottom the individual sections

represent: two ball players, the disc of the sun, a butterfly and the symbolic mask of the earth deity. Tomb 7, Monte Alban. Postclassic period, Mixtec culture, *c.* 1200–1450.

Height 8¹/₄ in.

Museo Regional de Oaxaca.

129   Comb with carved figure. Bone. Besides more than thirty similar bone carvings, Tomb 7 also contained gold ornaments and also valuable pottery. Tomb 7, Monte Alban. Postclassic period, Mixtec culture, *c.* 1200 –1450.

Museo Regional de Oaxaca.

130   Flute with incised representation of a religious ceremonial. Bone. Mitla region. Postclassic period, Mixtec culture, *c.* 1200–1450.

Length 6 in.

Museo Frissell de Arte Zapoteca, Mitla, Oaxaca.

131   Carving depicting warrior armed with a spear-thrower. Bone. Tomb 7, Monte Alban. Postclassic period, Mixtec culture, *c.* 1200–1450.

Museo Regional de Oaxaca.

132   Carving depicting two kneeling warriors. Jaguar bone. Tomb 7, Monte Alban. Postclassic period, Mixtec culture, *c.* 1200–1450.

Museo Regional de Oaxaca.

133   Pectoral with mask of death god Mictlantecuhtli. Gold, cast by the 'lost wax' method. Tomb 7, Monte Alban. Postclassic period, Mixtec culture, *c.* 1200–1450.

Museo Regional de Oaxaca.

134   Mask of god of spring, Xipe Totec. Gold, cast by the 'lost wax' method. Tomb 7, Monte Alban. Postclassic period, Mixtec culture, *c.* 1200–1450.

Museo Regional de Oaxaca.

135   Bead necklace. Gold, turquoise and shell. Tomb 7, Monte Alban. Postclassic period, Mixtec culture, *c.* 1200–1450.

Museo Regional de Oaxaca.

136   *Teponaztli*, gong consisting of a hollowed-out tree trunk left open at one end with an H-shaped incision forming two tongues to give different notes when struck. The relief contains mythical scenes in the style of the pictographic manuscripts. Provenance unknown. Postclassic period, Mixtec culture, *c.* 1200–1450.

Length 12³/₄ in.

Museo Nacional de Antropología, Mexico D.F.

137   *Teponaztli* with a young man in fine dress. Wood, inlaid with pyrites and mother-of-pearl. Tlaxcala. Post-

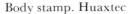
Body stamp. Huaxtec

classic period, Mixteca-Puebla culture, fifteenth century.

Length 2 in., height 5 in.

Museo Nacional de Antropología, Mexico D.F.

138–142 Rings and ornamental pendants. Gold, cast by the 'lost wax' method. The pendant in the form of a round shield is inlaid with turquoise (diameter $3^1/_4$ in., found Nochistlan, Oaxaca). Oaxaca. Postclassic period, Mixtec culture, c. 1200–1540.

Museo Nacional de Antropologia, Mexico D.F.

143 Left half of page 47 of *Codex Vindobonensis Mexicanus 1*. This Mixtec Codex was presumably brought to Europe by Cortés. There are many obstacles to the interpretation of these pictographs – the only original historical sources in pre-Hispanic America – and we can do little more than compare them with similarities in other sources derived from oral tradition soon after the Conquest, or with other related pictographs.

The *Codex Vindobonensis* contains a series of sacred pictures covering more than fifty-two pages. Originally the backs of the pages were blank. The picture sequence, painted on deerskin, tells of primeval times, the genesis of the gods and that of the Mixtec nobility (cf. *pl. 106*). It contains information on ritual, and a genealogy of the Mixtec rulers between 720 and 1350.

On the illustrated side, a mythical subject is depicted. After the collapse of a previous world, Quetzalcoatl, Nine Wind, raises the fallen heavens out of the water (figure at the top). This happens near the mountain of the rain god (Tlaloc, at the centre). Below an earth monster threatens the figure seated in the water. La Mixteca Alta, probably Tilantongo region. Postclassic period, Mixtec culture, fourteenth century.

Size of detail $8^5/_8$ in. $\times$ $5^5/_8$ in.

Österreichische Nationalbibliothek, Vienna.

144 Small figure of the god Xolotl in a dog mask. Dark brown hard wood, painted and inlaid with gold, silver, turquoise, malachite, white sea-snails and red shell. Xolotl ('beast') is Quetzalcoatl's infernal or nocturnal 'double'. The elaborate workmanship suggests that this is a ritual object. Postclassic period, Mixtec culture, c. 1200–1520.

Height $3^1/_2$ in.

Museum für Völkerkunde, Vienna.

145 Polychrome stirrup-spouted vessel in the form of a monkey. Clay. Provenance unknown. Postclassic period, Mixteca-Puebla culture, c. 1300–1522.

Height $5^1/_2$ in.

Museo Nacional de Antropología, Mexico D.F.

146 Polychrome tripod vessel. Clay, painted in the style of the Mixtec pictographs. In the decoration round the neck the glyph *atl* (water) is discernible. The bowl depicts a mythical scene. Quetzalcoatl in the mask of the wind god, and his fellow creator god Tonacatecuhtli ('lord of our subsistence'), form the centre of the scene.

Before them there is a temple or ceremonial building in some way related to the gods, and rendered in extremely stylized form. Nochistlan, Oaxaca. Postclassic period, Mixtec culture, *c.* 1200–1450.

Height 7$^1/_8$ in.

Museo Nacional de Antropología, Mexico D.F.

147   Seated female figure. Clay, polychrome. Tenenezpan, Vera Cruz. Northern Gulf coast. Postclassic period, Huaxtec culture (Panuco V), 1000–1250.

Height 7$^5/_8$ in.

Museo Regional de Jalapa, Vera Cruz.

148   Pyramid of the Niches, El Tajin. Presumably the 365 niches were used to house cult objects, probably figures of the patron gods of the days of the year. El Tajin, Vera Cruz. Central Gulf coast culture (El Tajin), *c.* tenth century.

149   *Palma* in the form of a sacrificial victim with his chest torn open. Andesite. Since the figure is wearing only a loin-cloth, it may be supposed that he is a captive. Coatepec, Vera Cruz. Central Gulf coast culture (El Tajin), *c.* 500–1200.

Height 22 in.

Museo Nacional de Antropología, Mexico D.F.

150   *Palma* in the form of a fish's head. Grey volcanic stone. Provenance unknown. Central Gulf coast culture (El Tajin), *c.* 500–1200.

Height 12 in.

Galerie Welz, Salzburg.

151   *Palma* showing a split face, half alive, half dead. Provenance unknown. Central Gulf coast culture (El Tajin), *c.* 500–1200.

Height 15$^3/_4$ in.

Dr Kurt Stavenhagen collection, Mexico D.F.

152   By way of comparison, a sculpture similar to that in *pl. 140*. Buff clay. Oaxaca. Classic period, Monte Alban culture. *c.* 800–1200.

Height 11$^3/_4$ in.

Museo Nacional de Antropología, Mexico D.F.

153   Fragment of *yugo*. Grey-green speckled stone. It has a human face in relief. Provenance unknown. Central Gulf coast culture (El Tajin), *c.* 500–1200.

Height 4 in.

Museo Nacional de Antropología, Mexico D.F. (Formerly in the Miguel Covarrubias collection.)

154   Prone human figure. Yellow-brown stone. Provenance unknown. Central Gulf coast culture (El Tajin), *c.* 500–1200.

Length 16$^1/_4$ in., height 6$^1/_2$ in.

Cleveland Museum of Art, Cleveland, Ohio.

155–156   Side and front views of a *yugo*. Grey-green stone, rich relief carving. The *yugo* or yoke is probably a symbolic reconstruction of the leather hip belt worn by ball players. On the front, below a jaguar's muzzle, is a human face seen from the front. A similar representation is found at either end. Provenance unknown. Central Gulf coast culture (El Tajin), *c.* 500–1200.

Length 16$^1/_8$ in., height 7$^1/_8$ in., width 13$^3/_4$ in.

The Minneapolis Institute of Arts, Minneapolis, Minn.

157   *Hacha* with a human figure surrounded by ornamentation typical of the El Tajin style. Grey-green stone. Provenance unknown. Central Gulf coast culture (El Tajin), *c.* 500–1200.

Height 9 in.

Museo Nacional de Antropología, Mexico D.F.

158   Standing, smiling figure of the *cabezas sonrientes* ('laughing heads') type. Yellow-brown clay, mould-made. The model's teeth had been artificially deformed. Tierra Blanca, Vera Cruz. Central Gulf coast culture (El Tajin), *c.* 1000–1500.

Height 14$^3/_4$ in.

Stendahl collection, Los Angeles, Calif.

159   Fragment of head, light coloured clay, hand modelled. Provenance unknown. Central Gulf coast culture (El Tajin), *c.* 1000–1500.

Height *c.* 5 in.

Stendahl collection, Los Angeles, Calif.

160   Standing human figure wearing a loin-cloth, *cabezas sonrientes* type. Buff clay, mould-made. The pottery bears a similarity to that of the Maya culture. Central Gulf coast culture (El Tajin), *c.* 1000–1500.

Height 15 in.

Stendahl collection, Los Angeles, Calif.

161   *Hacha* representing human head. Dark green stone. The cheeks are hollow and the tongue somewhat protruding; this may represent a dead man. Buff clay, mould-made. Central Gulf coast culture (El Tajin), *c.* 1000–1500.

Height $7^1/_4$ in.

Museum für Völkerkunde, Vienna.

162   *Hacha* representing human head. Grey stone. Tesecheacan, Vera Cruz. Central Gulf coast culture (El Tajin), *c.* 500–1200.

Height $7^1/_2$ in.

Middle American Research Institute, New Orleans, La.

163   Human head with elaborate head ornament, fragment of figure. Yellowish rough clay, eyes and part of the head ornament painted in bitumen. The expression is intensified by the fact that the eyes are worked in relief. Las Remojadas, Vera Cruz. Central Gulf coast culture (Remojadas), *c.* 400–800.

Height $13^1/_4$ in.

Stendahl collection, Los Angeles, Calif.

164   Human head, fragment of figure. Brown clay. Ignacio de la Llave region, Vera Cruz. Central Gulf coast culture (El Tajin), *c.* 700–1300.

Height $10^1/_4$ in.

Museo Regional de Jalapa, Vera Cruz.

165   Seated female figure with crossed legs, prominent necklace, rattles attached to upper arms, and short skirt. Reddish-brown clay, nipples and mouth painted with black bitumen, black scorch marks. Provenance unknown. Central Gulf coast culture (El Tajin), *c.* 700–1300.

Height $18^3/_4$ in., width $12^3/_4$ in.

J. C. Leff collection, Uniontown, Pa.

166–175   Ten clay fragments, representing animals, gods and chiefs. Light ochre-coloured clay. All the figures come from a grave. They could be the banner insignia of various orders of warriors, deriving perhaps from very ancient totemistic ideas. Central Vera Cruz. Central Gulf coast culture (El Tajin).

Height between 2 in. and 6 in.

Alan Sawyer collection, Washington, D.C.

176–177   Two reliefs on the southern ball court, El Tajin. The upper depicts the consecration of a ball player, and the lower, the sacrifice of the loser in this ritual game. El Tajin, Vera Cruz. Central Gulf coast culture (El Tajin), *c.* 600–1000.

178   Standing figure with outspread arms. Clay. The figure wears a skirt, belt, arm tassels and necklace. Provenance unknown. Central Gulf coast culture (El Tajin), *c.* 800–1200.

Height $18^3/_4$ in.

Dr Kurt Stavenhagen collection, Mexico D.F.

179–180   Front and back views of a standing figure. Stone. According to Herbert Spinden this represents the apotheosis of Quetzalcoatl. San Vincente Tancuayalab, San Luis Potosi. Northern Gulf coast, Huaxtec culture, *c.* 1200–1450.

Height 5 ft.

Brooklyn Museum, New York.

181   Pendant with partly carved and partly incised mythological scenes, probably representing the deities

Body stamp. Tenochtitlan

Mixcoatl and Tlazolteotl. Shell. Vera Cruz. Central Gulf coast, Huaxtec culture (Panuco V), *c.* 1000–1250. Height 5 in.

Middle American Research Institute, New Orleans, La.

182   Figure of a man with the face of a jaguar, grasping a serpent. Neither the provenance nor the symbolic content of this representation are known. Central Gulf coast, Huaxtec culture, *c.* 700–1200.

Height 20³/₄ in.

Museum für Völkerkunde, Vienna.

183   Vessel in the form of a stylized temple. Clay, polychrome. At the centre there is a human face representing an unknown god. Azcapotzalco, Valley of Mexico. Postclassic period, *c.* 1200–1400.

Height 23³/₄ in.

Museo Nacional de Antropología, Mexico D.F.

184   Cylinder-shaped vase depicting stylized priests or warriors. Clay, *sgraffito* decoration. Provenance unknown. Central Gulf coast, Huaxtec culture, *c.* 600–1400.

Height 15 in.

Middle American Research Institute, New Orleans, La.

185   *Chacmool.* Stone. The made-up Maya name *chacmool*, given to the characteristic Toltec recumbent figure averting its gaze from the bowl in its lap, means virtually nothing in itself, but has now become traditional in archaeology. It is not known what deity the figure represents. Tula, Hidalgo. Postclassic period, Toltec culture, 900–1158.

Height 2 ft 7 in.

186   Atlantean figure on Pyramid B, Tula. This figure, and the four others like it, possibly represent Quetzalcoatl as the morning star carrying the sun disc on his back. The four pillars behind the atlanteans (one is shown) carry reliefs which represent warriors, a new theme in Mesoamerican art. Tula, Hidalgo. Postclassic period, Toltec culture, 900–1168.

Height 15 ft.

187   Frieze representing fire serpents and seated priests on Great Temple, Xochicalco. The style is reminiscent of some Maya art. Xochicalco, Morelos. Postclassic period, Toltec culture (?), *c.* 800–1200.

188   Frieze representing fire serpents and warriors with spear-throwers on Temple of Quetzalcoatl, Tula. Adobe, traces of yellow, red and blue pigment. Tula, Hidalgo. Postclassic period, Toltec culture, 900–1168. Height 25 in.

189   Frieze representing serpents and dead warriors on Temple of Quetzalcoatl, Tula. Adobe, traces of yellow, red and blue pigment. This is the *coatepantli* ('serpent wall') encircling the temple precinct. Tula, Hidalgo. Postclassic period, Toltec culture, 900–1168.

Body stamp. Tenochtitlan

Length of figures 47 in.

190   Detail of frieze shown in *pl. 187.*

191   Cylinder-shaped drinking vessel showing priests officiating. Clay, low relief. Provenance unknown. Postclassic period, Toltec culture, *c.* 900–1300.

Height 10 in.

Museum für Völkerkunde, Vienna.

192   Drinking vessel showing two priest-kings. Brown clay. Postclassic period, Toltec culture, *c.* 900–1300. Height $5^1/_2$ in.

Museum für Völkerkunde, Vienna.

193   Figure of Xochipilli, god of the dance and music. Andesite. His skin is decorated with symbols of the sun and of flowers, and his face is hidden by a mask. Tamanalco, Valley of Mexico. Postclassic period, Aztec culture, 1350–1421.

Height with base 39 in.

Museo Nacional de Antropología, Mexico D.F.

194   Circular shield with step-and-fret and concentric circle design. Wooden laths bound with cords, leather rim, mosaic of pieces of feather. Such feather mosaic work was inspired on the one hand by the mature Mixtec culture, and on the other by that of the Gulf coast. Provenance unknown. Postclassic period, Aztec culture, *c.* 1480–1521.

Diameter 29 in.

Württembergisches Landesmuseum, Stuttgart.

195   The Calendar Stone. Basalt, weighing 24 tons. At the centre is the sun, surrounded by glyphs of the four previous suns or eras, the 'wind sun' the 'fire sun', the 'rain sun' and the 'water sun'. Round these symbols there is a circle with the twenty day signs of the Mexican calendar. Outside these, there is a further decorative circle of stylized sunray signs indicating the years. The whole is enclosed by two fire serpents *(xiuhcoa),* symbolizing space and time. Between the bodies of the serpents is the year sign 13 Reed, which corresponds with 1479, the year, presumably, in which this tremendous monument was consecrated. This stone was found under the Zocalo, the main square of Mexico City. The raw material for it had been brought over the lake from the mainland. After the Conquest, the Spaniards threw the ancient idols into the canals. For centuries they were concealed by mud and slime. Only with the modernization of the old city centre were some monuments brought to light. Countless others still lie buried. Tenochtitlan (Mexico City). Postclassic period, Aztec culture, 1479 (?).

Diameter 11 ft 3 in.

Museo Nacional de Antropología, Mexico D.F.

196   Circular sacrificial stone with skull relief. Tenochtitlan (Mexico City). Postclassic period, Aztec culture, 1450–1521.

Height $7^1/_8$ in., Diameter $15^1/_2$ in.

Museo Nacional de Antropología, Mexico D.F.

197   Figure of Coatlicue, goddess of earth and death. Volcanic stone. Valley of Mexico. Postclassic period, Aztec culture, 1350–1521.

Height $12^3/_8$ in.

Museo Nacional de Antropología, Mexico D.F.

198   *Chacmool*. Stone. On the underside is a relief of a mythical scene with the rain god Tlaloc at its centre. Valley of Mexico. Postclassic period, Toltec culture, *c.* 900–1200.

Length 40 in., height 29 in.

Museo Nacional de Antropología, Mexico D.F.

199 and 201   Model of the Temple of the Sun, Tenochtitlan. Basalt. This object, sometimes known as the *Teocalli de la guerra sagrada*, has the 'war' glyph ('water and fire') on the sides, a calendar stone (cf. *pl. 195*) on the top, and on the back *(pl. 201)* a relief of an eagle with a snake in its beak. According to the prophecy of the gods, the Aztecs were to settle where they saw this omen. This image has become the arms of the present republic of the United States of Mexico. Tenochtitlan (Mexico City). Postclassic period, Aztec culture, *c.* 1450–1521.

Height 36 in., width 34 in.

Museo Nacional de Antropología, Mexico D.F.

200   Pyramid, Tepanzolco. There are no very useful historical sources on the subject of this site near Cuernavaca. The name signifies approximately 'deserted temple'. Tepanzolco was the city of the Nahuatl tribe of the Tlahuica. In the reign of Acamapichtli (1375–1395), the Tlahuica lost their independence and became tributary to the Aztecs. Tepanzolco, Morelos. Postclassic period, Aztec culture, 1350–1521.

201   See *pl. 199*.

202   Round pyramid of the wind god Quetzalcoatl-Ehecatl. This site in the Toluca valley was settled by the Nahuatl tribe of the Matlatzinca. It was not until the reign of Axayacatl (1496–1481) that Calixtlahuaca lost its independence to the Aztecs. Structure 3, Calixtlahuaca. Postclassic period, Aztec culture, late fifteenth century.

203   Detail of the pyramid of Tenayuca. This structure, six miles from the centre of the present capital, was rebuilt and enlarged at least five times. Its present form probably dates back to 1502. A frieze of serpents fashioned out of rubble runs round the base on three of its sides,the fourth side being left free for flights of steps. Tenayuca, Mexico D.F. Postclassic period, Aztec culture, 1502.

204   Head of eagle in Temple I, Malinalco. Sculptured eagles and jaguars formed seats for high dignitaries inside this structure hewn out of the rock. Malinalco was built in 1501 on the orders of the ruler Ahuizotl.

Malinalco, State of Mexico. Postclassic period, Aztec culture, *c.* 1501.

205   Seated figure of the god Xipe Totec. Stone, red pigment. The god is wearing, on top of his own, the skin of a flayed human victim. Valley of Mexico. Postclassic period, Aztec culture, *c.* 1450–1521.

Height $15^3/_4$ in.

Museum für Völkerkunde, Basle (Lukas Vischer collection).

206   Detail of unfinished sculpture of a seated man. Volcanic stone. The face has been fully and beautifully finished. Provenance unknown. Postclassic period, Aztec culture, *c.* 1450–1521.

Total height 18 in.

Former Staatliches Museum für Völkerkunde, Berlin.

207   Figure of Coatlicue, goddess of earth and death. Basalt, formerly inlaid with turquoise and mother-of-pearl. The goddess, 'she with the serpent skirt', is shown here as an old woman with a skull for a head. Instead of hands and feet there are feline paws. Cozcatlan, Puebla. Postclassic period, Aztec culture, *c.* 1450–1521.

Height 3 ft 10 in.

Museo Nacional de Antropología, Mexico D.F.

208   Figure of a squatting man. Volcanic stone. Dressed in a loin-cloth, he is a plebeian. Provenance unknown. Postclassic period, Aztec culture, *c.* 1450–1521.

Height 13 in.

Museo Nacional de Antropología, Mexico D.F.

209   Figure of the god Ixtlilton ('little black face'). Volcanic stone. The god wears nothing but a loin-cloth. The fine work on the shoulders shows the anonymous sculptor's power of expression. Every detail of this piece has been seen and expressed with great sensibility. Valley of Mexico. Postclassic period, Aztec culture, *c.* 1450–1521.

Height 17^1/$_2$ in.

Museum für Völkerkunde, Basle (Lukas Vischer collection).

210   Male head. Volcanic stone, eyes and teeth of reddish and whitish shell inlay, the pupils of polished discs of pyrite. One of the few examples where the original incrustation has survived. Tenochtitlan (Mexico City). Postclassic period, Aztec culture, *c.* 1450–1521.

Height 7^1/$_4$ in.

Museo Nacional de Antropología, Mexico D.F.

211   Figure of the earth goddess Tlazolteotl giving birth to the maize god. Green speckled aplite. Provenance unknown. Postclassic period. Aztec culture, *c.* 1450–1521.

Height 8^1/$_4$ in.

Robert Woods Bliss collection, Dumbarton Oaks.

212   Tripod dish. Clay, black, reddish and brown pigment on ochre-coloured ground. The geometric motifs are typical of Aztec pottery. Valley of Mexico. Postclassic period, Aztec culture (Aztec IV), *c.* 1501–1521.

Diameter 6^1/$_2$ in.

Museum für Völkerkunde, Vienna.

213   *Quauhxicalli* in the form of a jaguar. Basalt. This object (the word *quauhxicalli* means 'eagle vessel') is a container for sacrificial blood. The relief inside the basin depicts death gods. Tenochtitlan (Mexico City). Postclassic period, Aztec culture, *c.* 1480–1521.

Length 7 ft 4 in., height 3 ft 11 in., width 3 ft.

Museo Nacional de Antropología, Mexico D.F.

214   Mask. Obsidian, eyes and mouth originally incrusted with different coloured material. Valley of Mexico. Postclassic period, Aztec culture, *c.* 1470–1521.

Height 7^1/$_8$ in.

Museo Nacional de Antropología, Mexico D.F.

215   Page from the *Codex Borbonicus* showing Tezcatlipoca as Chalchiuhtotolin ('precious turkey'), the god who drives the stars into the dusk. He guards a precious vase of pulque. Behind the star of darkness (Pole Star) there is Piltzintecuhtli (the planet Mercury) as a young priest who is sacrificing his blood and gold. A rainbow serpent, symbol of sin and incertitude, surrounds him

Above are depicted the offerings to Tezcatlipoca: the beheaded quails, sacrificed at dawn; beneath them the banners and ribbons of slain warriors lying in a dish; beside these, in another dish, the hearts of sacrificed warriors. A rabbit, symbolizing cowardice, and a bowl with sprouting corn plants (or narcotic mushrooms?), are also among the offerings. Below Tezcatlipoca, from left to right, the deity's gifts are ranged: a bowl of gold, and thorns for self-mortification set out on a stone. Success in war is expressed by a burning temple, with diagonally above it the fruits of the earth in a white bowl, under which is a pulque vessel full of water. Underneath, in square frames, are four of the thirteen day birds of omen and four gods of the underworld (or 'lords of the night').

The picture manuscript was probably painted in Tenochtitlan shortly before the Conquest. A note in Spanish reads: 'Those who were born here (i.e. on this day) were destined to be poor.' The 'Book of the [260] Days' *(tonalamatl)* is concerned with the art of soothsaying, and with ritual ceremonies for the gods who had assumed the patronage of various days and periods. Both good and bad days were foretold, and in this way the fortunes of new-born children were forecast. If the day of birth was inauspicious, the ceremony of name-giving was postponed. Since 1826 this manuscript has been in the Library of the Chambre des Députés, Paris. Postclassic period, Aztec culture, *c.* 1490–1521.

Bibliothèque de la Chambre des Députés, Palais Bourbon, Paris.

Bibliography

Alt-Aztekische Gesänge, translated from the ms. in the Biblioteca Nacional with a commentary by Leonhard Schultze Jena. Edited after his death by Gerdt Kutscher. *Quellenwerke zur alten Geschichte Amerikas*, Stuttgart 1957.

Anton, Ferdinand: *Alt-Peru und seine Kunst*, Leipzig 1962. *Mexiko, Indianerkunst aus vorkolumbischer Zeit*, Munich 1961. *Altamerikanische Schriftbilder*, catalogue of exhibition at Baden-Baden 1963. *Die Kunst der Schrift* (UNESCO) 'Bilderschriften im mexikanischen Raum'. Hamburg and Baden-Baden 1964.

Bernal, Ignacio: *Tenochtitlan en una Isla*, Mexico 1959. *Mexico: Prehispanic paintings* (preface by Jacques Soustelle), New York 1958. *Ancient Mexico in Colour*, London and New York 1968.

Burland, Cottie A.: *Art and Life in ancient Mexico*. Oxford 1948. *The Selden Roll, an Ancient Mexican Picture Manuscript*, Berlin 1955.

Bushnell, G. H. S.: see Digby, Adrian.

Caso, Alfonso: *El Pueblo del Sol*, Mexico 1953; English translation *People of the Sun*, Oklahoma 1958. *Calendario y Escritura de las antiguas Culturas de Monte Albán*, Mexico 1947. *Calendario y Escritura en Xochicalco*, Mexico 1962. *Urnas de Oaxaca*, in collaboration with Ignacio Bernal, Mexico 1952.

Castillo, Bernal Díaz del: *Historia verdadera de la Conquista de la Nueva España*, Mexico City 1955; English translation, *The Conquest of New Spain*, Harmondsworth 1963.

Codex Bodley 2858, commentary by Alfonso Caso, Mexico 1960.

Codex Vindobonensis Mexicanus 1, Akademische Druck- u. Verlagsanstalt, Graz 1963.

Covarrubias, Miguel: *Indian Art of Mexico and Central America*, New York 1957. *Mexico South*, New York 1947, London 1948.

Dahlgren de Jordán, Barbro: *La Mixteca, su cultura e historia prehispánicas*, Mexico 1954.

Die Geschichte der Königreiche von Colhuacan und Mexico. Text with translation by Walter Lehmann. *Quellenwerke zur alten Geschichte Amerikas*, Stuttgart and Berlin 1938.

Digby, Adrian, and Bushnell, Geoffrey H. S.: *Ancient American Pottery*, London 1955.

Disselhoff, H. D.: *Geschichte der altamerikanischen Kulturen*, Munich 1953. *Ancient America* (with Sigvald Linné), London and New York 1961.

Drucker, Philip: *La Venta, Tabasco: A study of Olmec ceramics and art*, Smithsonian Institution, Bureau of American Ethnology, Washington 1952. In collaboration with Robert F. Heizer and Robert J. Squier: *Excavations at La Venta, Tabasco, 1955*. Smithsonian Institution, Bureau of American Ethnology, Washington 1959.

Enciso, Jorge: *Design Motifs of Ancient Mexico*. Mexico 1947, New York 1953.

Esplendor de México Antiguo, 2 vols. collected by Carmen Cook de Leonard, Mexico 1959.

Feuchtwanger, Franz (photographs by Irmgard Groth-Kimball): *Art of Ancient Mexico*, London and New York 1954.

Garibay K., Angel María: *Historia de la Literatura Nahuatl*, Mexico 1953.

Historia Tolteca-Chichimeca, translated and anotated by Karl Theodor Preuss and Ernst Mengin, Baessler Archiv, Berlin 1937/38.

Katz, Friedrich: *Die sozialökonomischen Verhältnisse bei den Azteken im 15. und 16. Jahrhundert*. Ethnographisch-Archäologische Forschungen, Berlin 1956.

Keleman, Pál: *Medieval American Art*, New York 1956.

Krickeberg, Walter: *Märchen der Azteken und Inka-Peruaner, Maya und Muisca*, Jena 1928. *Altmexikanische Kulturen*, Berlin 1949. 'Mesoamerica', in *Pre-Columbian American Religions*, London and New York 1968.

Kutscher, Gerdt: *Präkolumbische Kunst aus Mexiko und Mittelamerika*, Exhibition catalogue, Munich 1958.

Lehmann, Walter: *Altmexikanische Kunstgeschichte*, Berlin n.d.

Lenz, Hans: *El Papel Indígena Mexicana*, Mexico 1948.

Leonard, Carmen Cook de: see *Esplendor del México Antiguo*.

Lienzo de Tlaxcala, annotated and edited by Alfredo Chavero, Mexico City 1892.

Linné, Sigvald: *Archaeological Researches at Teotihuacan, Mexico*, The Ethnographical Museum of Sweden, Stockholm 1934. *Zapotecan Antiquities*, The Ethnographical Museum of Sweden, Stockholm 1938. *Treasures of Mexican Art*, Stockholm 1956. See also Disselhoff, H. D.

Lothrop, S. K.: *Pre-Columbian Art (Robert Woods Bliss Collection)*, New York 1957.

Nowotny, Karl A.: *Erläuterungen zum Codex Vindobonensis (Vorderseite)*. Archiv für Völkerkunde, Vienna 1948. *Codex Becker I; Codex Becker II; Die Bilderfolge des Codex Vindobonensis u. verwandter Handschriften*, Archiv für Völkerkunde, Vienna 1957. *Mexikanische Kostbarkeiten aus Kunstkammern der Renaissance*. Vienna 1960. *Tlacuilolli; die mexikanischen Bilderschriften, Stil und Inhalt*, Berlin 1961.

Nicholson, Irene: *Firefly in the Night: A Study of Ancient Mexican Poetry and Symbolism*, London 1959.

Peterson, Frederick: *Ancient Mexico*, London 1959.

Piña Chan, Román: *Las Culturas Preclásicas de la Cuenca de México*, Mexico 1955. *Tlatilco a través de su Cerámica*, I and II, Mexico 1958. *Mesoamérica*, Mexico 1960.

Portilla, Miguel León: *Los Antiguos Mexicanos, a través de sus Crónicas y Cantares*, Mexico 1961. *Aztec Thought and Culture*, University of Oklahoma Press 1963.

Robertson, Donald: *Mexican Manuscript Painting of the Early Colonial Period*, Yale University Press, New Haven 1959.

Sahagún, Bernardino de: *Historia General de las Cosas de Nueva España*. 4 vols, ed. Angel María Garibay K. Mexico 1956. *Florentine Codex*, 12 vols. Aztec text with English translation. Translated and edited by Arthur J. C. Anderson and Charles E. Dibble. The School of American Research and The University of Utah, Santa Fe, New Mexico 1950–65.

Saville, Marshall H.: *Tizoc, Great Lord of the Aztecs 1481–1486*, Museum of the American Indian, Heye Foundation, New York 1929.

Schlenther, Ursula: 'Über die Auflösung der Theokratien im präkolumbischen Amerika', *Ethnographisch-Archäologische Zeitschrift*, Berlin 1961.

Body stamp, armadillo.
Vera Cruz

Séjourné, Laurette: *Pensamiento y Religión en el México Antiguo*, Mexico City and Buenos Aires 1957. *Un Palacio en la Cudad de los Dioses (Teotihuacán)*, Mexico 1959. *Burning Water*, London 1957.

Seler, Eduard: *Gesammelte Abhandlungen zur amerikanischen Sprach- und Altertumskunde*, vols I–V, Berlin 1903–23. New edn, Graz 1960-2.

Soustelle, Jacques: *The Daily Life of the Aztecs on the eve of the Spanish Conquest*, London 1961, 1964.

Spratling, William: *More Human than Divine*, Mexico 1960.

Stirling, M. W.: *Stone Monuments of Southern Mexico,* Smithsonian Institution, Bureau of American Ethnology, Washington 1943.

Tezozómoc, Hernando Alvarado: *Crónica Mexicana,* selection by Marie Mariscal, Mexico 1943.

Toscano, Salvador: *Arte Precolombino de México*, 2 vols, Mexico 1952.

Trimborn. Hermann: *Das alte Amerika (Grosse Kulturen der Frühzeit)*, Stuttgart 1959.

Vaillant, George C.: *Artists and Craftsmen in Ancient Central America*, The American Museum of Natural History, New York 1944. *Aztecs of Mexico*, revised edn., New York 1962, Harmondsworth 1965.

Wauchope, Robert: *Implications of Radiocarbon Dates from Middle and South America*, Middle American Research Institute, Tulane University, New Orleans 1954.

Westheim, Paul: *Arte Antiguo de México*, Mexico and Buenos Aires 1950. *Ideas fundamentales del Arte prehispánico en México*, Mexico and Buenos Aires 1957. *La Cerámica del México Antiguo*, Mexico 1962. *The Sculpture of Ancient Mexico/La Escultura del México Antiguo*, Garden City, NY 1963.

Body stamp, fantastic birds. Guerrero

Chronology

	Central Highlands	Oaxaca	Southern Gulf coast	Central Gulf coast	Northern Gulf coast	North-west Mexico
1500 BC	El Arbolillo Tlatilco Zacatenco Cuicuilco Tlapacoya	Monte Negro I (Mixtecs) Monte Alban I (La Venta influences)	La Venta culture La Venta Tres Zapotes	Remojadas culture	Pavén Huaxtec culture Panuco I	Chupicuaro
600						Colima Jalisco Nayarit
	Ticoman					
200	Teotihuacan I				Panuco II	
200	Teotihuacan II Teotihuacan III Teotihuacan IV	Monte Alban II (Zapotecs) Tilantongo (Mixtecs) Monte Alban III A Monte Alban III B Monte Alban IV	Cerro de las Mesas	Tajin culture	Panuco III Panuco IV	
600						
900	Toltecs of Tula 856–1168					
1200		Monte Alban V (Mixtecs)		Totonacs	Panuco V	Toltec influences
1400	Chichimec culture Aztecs	Mixteca-Puebla culture Aztecs		Aztecs	Panuco VI Aztecs	Tarascans
1521	Beginning of Spanish Colonial Rule					

303

Index

Italic figures refer to the plates

Roller stamp, stylized feathered serpent. Tenochtitlan

Acknowledgments

I would like to thank the following for their professional assistance: Gertrude Duby, Jane Powell, Ignacio Bernal, Frans Blom, Cottie A. Burland, Alfonso Caso, Eusebio Dávalos, Jorge G. Lacroix, Sigvald Linné, Robert Wauchope, Karl A. Nowotny and Alan R. Sawyer. I am indebted to the kindness and trust shown me by the private collectors. Frau Carmen Oechsle and Herr Franz Feuchtwanger, Messrs Howard Leigh, J.C. Leff, Robert J. Sainsbury, Alan Sawyer, and most especially Dr. Kurt Stavenhagen. For their ready cooperation in processing the photographs, I should like to thank the Haus der Kunst in Munich and its director, Peter Alois Ade, as also the following galleries: André Emmerich, New York, Ernst Hauswedel, Hamburg, Stendahl, Los Angeles and Welz, Salzburg. My thanks are also due to many museums and institutes: the Brooklyn Museum and Museum of Natural History in New York; the museums of the University of Pennsylvania in Philadelphia and of Tulane University in New Orleans; the Museo Preistorico Etnografico Luigi Pigorini, Rome; the Cleveland Museum of Art; the Minneapolis Institute of Art; the Württembergisches Landesmuseum, Stuttgart; the Wadsworth Atheneum, Hartford, Conn.; the Rietberg-Museum, Zurich; the Southwest Museum, Los Angeles; the Museo Frissell, Mitla, Oaxaca; the Entografiska Museet, Stockholm; the former Staatliches Museum für Völkerkunde, Berlin, and the Museen für Völkerkunde in Basle and Vienna. Special thanks are due to the Museo Nacional of the United States of Mexico, Mexico D.F., and the regional museums of Chiapas in Tuxtla Gutiérrez, Oaxaca in Oaxaca, Tabasco in Villa Hermosa, and Vera Cruz in Jalapa.

We owe a debt to the Instituto Nacional de Antropología e Historia for the selfless devotion of its staff in working to preserve the ancient sites from further decay, and for their efforts in opening up at least the most important of the ruins to the general public. Last but not least, I would mention three friends, Milton Bellovin, Rolf Hasenclever and Stan Smith, whose financial assistance helped me to undertake the long journey which has resulted in this book.

FERDINAND ANTON